Model-based System and Architecture
Engineering with the Arcadia Method

To Elisabeth. The essential thing is you.

Implementation of Model Based System Engineering Set

coordinated by
Pascal Roques

Model-based System and Architecture Engineering with the Arcadia Method

Jean-Luc Voirin

ELSEVIER

First published 2018 in Great Britain and the United States by ISTE Press Ltd and Elsevier Ltd

ISTE Press Ltd
27-37 St George's Road
London SW19 4EU
UK

www.iste.co.uk

Elsevier Ltd
The Boulevard, Langford Lane
Kidlington, Oxford, OX5 1GB
UK

www.elsevier.com

Notices

Knowledge and best practice in this field are constantly changing. As new research and experience broaden our understanding, changes in research methods, professional practices, or medical treatment may become necessary.

Practitioners and researchers must always rely on their own experience and knowledge in evaluating and using any information, methods, compounds, or experiments described herein. In using such information or methods they should be mindful of their own safety and the safety of others, including parties for whom they have a professional responsibility.

To the fullest extent of the law, neither the Publisher nor the authors, contributors, or editors, assume any liability for any injury and/or damage to persons or property as a matter of products liability, negligence or otherwise, or from any use or operation of any methods, products, instructions, or ideas contained in the material herein.

For information on all our publications visit our website at http://store.elsevier.com/

British Library Cataloguing-in-Publication Data
A CIP record for this book is available from the British Library
Library of Congress Cataloging in Publication Data
A catalog record for this book is available from the Library of Congress
ISBN 978-1-78548-169-7

Printed and bound in the UK and US

Contents

Preface

Everything should be made as simple as possible, but not simpler.

Words attributed to Albert Einstein[1]

I shall not rest until this opaque island, impenetrable, the fertile ground for ungoverned ferment and mischievous turmoil, is transformed into an abstract, and transparent construction, intelligible to the bone!

Michel Tournier – Friday, or, The Other Island

Thank you Eric L. for this quote

Objectives of this book and foreword

The Arcadia (Architecture Analysis and Design Integrated Approach) method, dedicated to the mastering of engineering systems and the definition of architectures based on the use of models, is the fruit of a collective effort lasting for around a decade now, which is still ongoing.

If a single particularity had to be retained, it would probably be that the method has been conceived and validated, as part of a real operational context, by its users and beneficiaries, namely those involved in engineering, seeking above all to minimize difficulties in the engineering of current complex systems.

---

1 In a less pithy form, Einstein's original sentence would be: "It can scarcely be denied that the supreme goal of all theory is to make the irreducible basic elements as simple and as few as possible without having to surrender the adequate representation of a single datum of experience". See https://en.wikiquote.org/wiki/Albert_Einstein.

Far from being an end in itself, it is intended to provide answers to the major questions being raised in engineering:

– In what forms can the expression of customer needs be assumed or expected? Requirements, documents, models, or work in co-engineering...

– How can this need be analyzed, how can its consistency, its feasibility, be guaranteed?

***

– What steps must the construction of the solution undergo to be secured and optimized? How can the associated complexity be managed?

– How can the solution be described, in the various stages of its engineering? How can it safely evolve throughout the engineering lifecycle?

– What means can be used to perform the impact analysis, in terms of this solution, of the evolution of needs or of technical, industrial or architectural constraints?

***

– How can different alternatives to potential solutions be analyzed and evaluated in order to choose the best compromise?

– How do different professions and specialties collaborate for this purpose?

– How do we justify the solution compared to the needs and expertise likely to impact its definition?

***

– How to build and justify an effective product policy? How can solutions compatible with these constraints be constructed?

– How can the different engineering levels be coordinated, how can the framework and what is expected from subcontractors be defined?

***

– How do we define an effective strategy of integration, verification and validation and control for its implementation?

– How can the integration, verification and validation be oriented in the event of hazards and regression risks?

This book is an attempt to provide answers to these fundamental questions of our engineering which can serve as references in deploying model-driven engineering in a given context.

It is primarily intended for engineering practitioners, for current users or those wishing to apply the method in practice. The reader will therefore find little justification for the choices that have been made because the length of the book imposed that the choice be made to prioritize support over implementation.

Subsequently, this book is not a treatise on model-driven engineering systems in general. In fact, there is little explicit reference to the state of the art in the field, although the Arcadia method has sometimes found some basis therein. The concepts involved are to be considered by themselves and not in reference to similar concepts in the literature, so that this reference be as self-sufficient as possible, with the least amount of prerequisite as possible for readers.

Organization of the book

The first part describes the fundamentals of the actual engineering approach, which form the core of the method:

– the motivations that led to its design, the history of its definition and its deployment, its scope of application;

– the main perspectives structuring the approach;

– the functional analysis procedure, central in the approach promoted by Arcadia;

– the detailed content of the development of each perspective: operational analysis, system needs analysis, logical architecture, physical architecture, solution building strategy.

The second part illustrates the use of the fundamentals of the method and models that it defines, through the implementation of key engineering activities:

– the integration of specialty engineering in the definition of the architecture;

– requirements engineering;

– the integration, verification and validation processes;

– the relationship between different engineering levels;

– system states and modes and supervision engineering;

– the contribution to product lines engineering.

The third part describes the language and concepts of the method, as well as the relationships between them, in detail, in a form resembling an encyclopedia:

– concepts used for the functional description;

– concepts formalizing the description of states and modes;

– concepts used for the structural description;

– relationships between functional description and structural description;

– concepts describing data exchanges and their relationships with previous ones;

– various complementary concepts, including those concerning the product line or the integration, verification and validation;

– the way of building global models aggregating these concepts.

Suggestions for quick reading

For a quick reading of the method, the eager reader may refer to Chapter 2.

For a detailed view of the method and its implementation, it is recommended that at least the chapters that follow be read, as they outline the functional analysis approach and prospects, preferably following the numerical order.

The second part is a good illustration for understanding the contribution that Arcadia provides to engineering.

When applying the method, the third part, which is a reference about the Arcadia language, gives the necessary elements. At that point, it might be wise to also refer to the examples of figures and tables that can be found throughout the first part, as an illustration of the use of these concepts.

Acknowledgments

The definition of Arcadia, its tools and deployment within the Thales Group have been (and still are) for me an exciting adventure, both on an intellectual and a professional level, but also – and perhaps above all – on the human level. I am able today to quantify the luck I have had in finding such a very supportive enterprise environment, as well as rarely available means, and above all a group of people remarkable for their skills, their creativity, their investment capacity, their desire to participate toward a collective project and their confidence, and just because they are passionate about their profession.

All of you with whom I have especially worked on Arcadia and its deployment, and to whom I wish to pay tribute here, belong to different organizations and areas (aerospace, land transport, civil avionics, air mission systems, naval systems, acoustics, optronics, air traffic control, surveillance and protection systems, communication systems, technical management, operations, methods and tools, etc.) and to a lot of countries where Thales is largely integrated (Germany, Australia, Canada, France, Netherlands and the United Kingdom, in particular). Despite that, I marvel every day at the fact that, under the sole common hierarchical responsibility of the Thales CEO, we have achieved such a collective project together. Of course, many other people, in Thales and elsewhere, and in many countries, give their energy and expertise to implement much more widely these works – they should be thanked for it. However, I was able to directly evaluate your human and professional qualities and I repeat that this is a great privilege.

Therefore, many thanks to Martin D., without whom nothing would have really been possible, who has kindly placed his trust in us and offered unwavering support as the inspiration and the necessary impetus for already 10 years. Thanks to Pascal F., who with Martin was able to see beyond clumsy premises a promising avenue, which he strongly supports even today, while preparing "the next two moves".

Thanks to Stéphane B., my accomplice in many places and circumstances, whose kindness, availability and capacity in so many areas still impress me so much.

I thank Eric L., my alter ego and my counterpart for the method, who knows how to give shape to my sometimes confusing ideas or reduce them to nothing. Thanks to Loïc P. and Yannick T., as well as Daniel E. and his team, who were able to implement our ideas in tools customized for end-users; to Frederick M., our thorn in the side, who brings us back to Earth from time to time for the benefit of those end-users.

Finally, thanks to each and every one of you for your unique contribution. I would like to quote here[2]:

Pierre-Marie P., Xavier L., Eric G., Jean-Luc W.; Véronique N.; Béatrice B., Anne D., Eric M., Tony S., Guillaume J., Philippe F., Alexandre G., Denis A., Sébastien D., Franck T., Gilles B., Philippe S., Matthieu P., Arnaud H.; Stéphanie C., Laetitia S., Frédéric F., Muriele P., David A., Stéphane V., Philippe L.; Michael S., Gunnar S., Frank M., Rodney I.; Laurens W., Peter H.; Marine M., Claire L., Florence S., Philippe B., Alain P., Laurent S.; Vincent I., Nicolas M., Jean-Baptiste C., François C.T., Marion M., Alain L., André L., Emmanuel R.;

---

2 Grouped and ordered by organization affiliation.

Joe S., David Mc.P., Allan E., Andy H.; Milos K., Dean K., Fabrice L., Gilles B.; Ismaël D., Olivier T., Olivier H., Michel R.; Gregory C., Arnaud B.

And I apologize to anyone I have not mentioned and that would merit it, including all our partners outside of Thales, part of this community that continues to grow today thanks to your openness and your dynamism.

***

All of the figures in this book are available to view in color at: www.iste.co.uk/voirin/arcadia.zip.

Jean-Luc VOIRIN
October 2017

PART 1

Foundations of the Method: General Approach and Major Prospects

1

Motivations, Background and Introduction to Arcadia

1.1. Context and challenges

Current complex systems are subject to numerous requirements or concurrent constraints, sometimes conflicting: functional requirements (service(s) expected by the end user), and non-functional requirements (ergonomics, security, safety of operation, mass, scalability, environments, interfaces, etc.), within a context of competition calling for still more responsiveness and adaptation, shorter design cycles and especially a very good understanding of aspirations and objectives of customers.

The initial definition and engineering stages of such systems are critical because they condition the ability of the retained architecture to satisfy customer needs, and the proper steps to take requirements into account within the subsystems or components emerging from this architecture. In order to control schedules and costs, it is essential that the adequacy of the solution with regard to needs and constraints can be verified, as early as during the design stage of the system; this enables the minimization of the risk of belatedly discovering solution limitations, and of more or less deeply calling into question the architecture during advanced development stages, or at the time of integration or validation of the system.

The complexity is further increased given the large number of key players involved in engineering: customers, end users, operational analysts, architects of different system levels, experts (performance, algorithmic, security, operation

---

safety, product line, mechanics, thermal, electronics and information systems, etc.), development (design office, software, hardware, etc.) and integration teams.

Another type of constraint is also increasingly becoming prominent in system and product development today which could be summed up in two words: variability and agility.

On the one hand, customer needs are diverse, continuously evolving, because they are themselves faced with a constantly evolving environment. On the other hand, to reduce costs, manufacturers strive to identify a maximum of genericity and communities to which a product policy can be applied, thus maximizing reuse.

In parallel, it is increasingly necessary for manufacturers to develop a capacity for agility, in order to reduce design cycles, to be able to define and assess more and more alternatives as quickly as possible, to quickly and safely respond to demands for development, or design or implementation problems.

Finally, the distribution of work between several organizations and companies (general contractors, contracting authorities, main subsystems suppliers) also reinforces the difficulty in federating and coordinating works and practices necessarily different because responding to different constraints, but under the obligation of contributing to a common solution.

It is therefore crucial to develop the capacity of a large team, multidisciplinary and distributed over several entities, for deploying collaborative engineering or an agile co-engineering approach, focused on the construction and validation of the system architecture, while at the same time best securing joint works and the consistency of works carried out individually by each participating entity in an optimal manner. This is the purpose of the Arcadia (Architecture Analysis and Design Integrated Approach) method presented in this book.

1.2. A bit of history: the creation of a method

1.2.1. *Evolution of engineering*

In the early 2000s, the company Thales[1] was facing a major transformation in its markets and its products in a number of areas, in which a shift was driving the

---

1 "Thales is a world leader in advanced technologies for aerospace, transport, defense and security markets. Counting 64,000 employees in 56 countries, Thales has achieved a turnover of 15 billion EUR in 2016. With more than 25,000 engineers and researchers, Thales helps its customers around the world to master ever more complex environments to make quick efficient decisions at every critical moment". (Thales communication)

company from the status of separate equipment supplier, integrated by third parties, to a role of provider of turnkey solutions and comprehensive systems: namely air traffic control systems, defense missions, satellite systems, communication infrastructures and networks, surveillance and security systems, critical information systems, etc.

This relatively new situation introduced transformations within engineering problems: engineering had to assume the transition from an expression of need mainly centered on technical performance, on the part of customers, to a capability-based expectation, in other words, the ability to provide operational capabilities with a guaranteed quality of service, without prejudice to the nature of the solution that could or should address it. Simultaneously, within the development of the solution, precisely, the problems that had to be solved were themselves undergoing a transformation: historically, they comprised a dominant technical characteristic related to engineering expertise, such as algorithmic processing, mechanical characteristics, resilience in facing environmental conditions, absolute performance, etc. Gradually, new challenges became more important: namely the global optimization of the solution rather than the juxtaposition of local optima, the adaptation to various and shifting operation contexts, product policies, the use of off-the-shelf products, the increasing impact of security and safety of operation, certification constraints, human factors, etc. Large-scale architectural features became major and even pre-eminent in certain areas.

1.2.2. 2001–2006: First experiments using a model-based approach

A first initiative to assist engineers [EXE 04, NOR 05] was launched in 2001 in the form of a research program in the field of software systems (named MDSysE for *Model-Driven SYStem Engineering*), in order to study the emerging field of modeling methods, standards and technologies. Although modeling has been already used in a limited manner in practice to document designs, the ability to drive engineering and to fully support the analysis and design of the architecture had yet to be validated. Methods, languages and solutions for tools were defined and experimented, relying on the state of the art at the time – languages and profiles such as the formalism of UML [UML 15], or the Rational Unified Process [KRU 98] as a modeling process, etc. This research activity has contributed to the construction of methodological and technological skills in modeling inside Thales' teams, and to the gathering of the first lessons learned from operational trials.

The results of the first operational deployments proved to be mixed: although perceived as useful, and likely to guide the thinking of engineering, this approach proved that it covered a too limited part of engineering activities, too shifted with regard to practices and business processes, too scarcely expressive at the functional level. In addition, the use of languages relying on UML was deemed complex, unnatural for system engineers and insufficiently expressive because concepts were missing which they needed to express their concerns and specificities.

1.2.3. *2006: From an engineering transformation plan toward a method*

At the same time but separately from this first initiative, and to satisfy prospective challenges of system engineering, a global analysis of existing practices of system engineering was launched by the general management, in order to collect feedback, ideas for improvements, to propose and experiment with changes in practices. All key players in engineering in various areas and products (operational analysts, requirement managers, architects, software/hardware developers, security/safety experts, logistics experts, integrators, etc.) were invited to describe not only the state of the art and possible difficulties in their practices, their expectations, but also to contribute to the definition of new practices. Still more significant was their commitment to experiment with the recommendations and practices that these works would generate, in their own large-scale operational context, in order to obtain a real evaluation of their effectiveness.

It soon appeared that most units in Thales shared the same type of engineering practices (despite areas with very different fields and domains of application) and were aware of the same gaps that had to be filled to meet these new market constraints. Still more notable, the new practices that they considered as being desirable were very similar in most cases, namely:

– deepening the analysis of customers' requirements for a clearer understanding of their expectations, objectives, capabilities, etc., and of how the solution satisfies these expectations;

– strengthening the quality of the definition of architectures and the place of architects, with a view to improve the effectiveness of engineering and system integration;

– strengthening the relationships between architects and engineering expertise (security, performance, interface management, etc.) for coherent and joint decision-making;

– increasing continuity and coherence between the different engineering levels (software, hardware, system, subsystems and mechanical processing);

– detecting architecture definition and design defects as soon as possible, during the design phase rather than in system integration phases;

– improving the efficiency of integration, verification and validation (IVV) by a functional strategy focused on capabilities, defined at the outset in the design phase;

– capitalizing the design definition and its results, including justifications, in order to improve reuse and product policies.

Based on best practices and expectations collected, recommendations were developed and then detailed. As a result, activities were defined, in addition to concepts used to represent the elements manipulated, and exchanged within engineering fields, as well as various analysis approaches, and development and control procedures for most of them. Pretty quickly, the generic and widely covering character of this aggregate appeared as a process that could transform it into a structured approach based on a formalized representation language, which constituted the premises of the Arcadia method.

1.2.4. *First deployments – new setbacks*

The first version of the method was rather a top-down, strongly structured – with strictly and logically ordered activities – relatively rigid implementation process. The first language elements obviously equally borrowed from architecture frameworks such as the NATO Architecture Framework [NAT 07], from the already mentioned UML language and its profile targeting system engineering, SysML [OBJ 15] as well as from the AADL architecture description language [FEI 06]. The approach was an important part of functional analysis, some of its aspects corresponding to external functional analysis approaches such as APTE [DEL 00].

The method was implemented in operational projects, through the successive use and evaluation of several commercial off-the-shelf modeling tools, in turn supporting these different languages, in the course of the experiments.

Unfortunately (or maybe fortunately), in this case again, feedback was unsatisfactory: the method certainly offered a broad coverage of engineering requirements, it was regarded as properly guiding and securing engineering; however, the effectiveness of its implementation was considered insufficient for several reasons:

– none of the modeling languages successively tested satisfied expectations, or provided support for mastering complexity. They suffered from the same type of issues as that of the first initiative, MDSysE, which resulted in a rejection from system engineers, and in the best of cases in pairing them with modeling experts;

– the approach was too rigid and its implementation cycle too theoretical, incompatible with lifecycles (bottom-up, middle-out, incremental, iterative, agile, etc.) encountered in real-life projects and products;

– supporting tools did not break the complexity wall and struggled in shifting to the scale of large-sized models, built and used simultaneously in different ways by several authors or users; the definition and especially the maintenance cost of a large model became prohibitive;

– these tools were considered to be too generic, not sufficiently guiding during the implementation of the method, often causing a "blank paper syndrome", which made the adoption of the approach difficult;

– finally, they left little room for taking into account the specific characteristics of each profession and mainly encouraged descriptive models (essentially destined for documentary usage) rather than prescriptive and analysis-supporting models.

1.2.5. Transition to an agile definition process of the method

It was then decided to base the development of the method and its tools on an "agile" approach, based on user requirements and on deployment tests in real conditions. New directions were implemented:

– start from the engineering practices and challenges of each engineering discipline, developing methodology elements that can address these challenges;

– define a language specific to the engineering field, inspired by the architecture descriptions encountered in engineering documentation;

– submit the method to new engineering challenges such as the integration of expert engineering, multi-level engineering and IVV concerns, in order to evaluate its possible contribution to these challenges;

– confront the method to different lifecycles and engineering practices, in order to define and verify its adaptability;

– ensure a generic nature to the method and the language, while allowing both to be customized and enhanced with the know-how depending on each field.

The application of principles promoting operational returns involved systematically testing the application of these method elements in a real operational context in units, within a period of a few months. To this end, a dedicated modeling tool was prototyped, constituting a full-scale experimentation platform for the usability of concepts and the feasibility of practices recommended by the method. This enabled a very short iterative definition, implementation, testing, deployment and validation or development, compatible with the deadlines for the iterations with operational users.

1.2.6. Global operational deployment and maturity

The following years were devoted to evaluating, improving and consolidating the method by comparing it to real-life engineering situations. The first training material was published at this time and most of the method stopped evolving at that date. During 2008, it became clear that, in many situations, the prototyping tool was considered by operational engineers as very beneficial. The decision was then made to capitalize on this prototype to apply the Arcadia domain-specific language and build a dedicated industrial engineering workshop, at the heart of which was a modeling tool dedicated to the implementation of Arcadia, named Capella[2] [POL 17a].

The method and improvement of the tool lasted approximately 2 years following the same agile principles, mainly supported by operational experiments in real contexts. The core of the method was found to be stable in 2009.

At the end of 2010, the method and tool were considered by management as constituting a major lever for a real transformation of engineering, which contributed with better quality and efficiency thereto; they had also reached the first level of maturity deemed sufficient to be deployed on a large scale, and Thales management took the decision for a deployment in initial major operational projects.

It should be noted that the first version of the global Model-based System Engineering (MBSE) solution (its basic capabilities, including the method and its supporting workbench) was at last finalized approximately 8 years after the beginning of the adventure [VOI 15b].

As the MBSE maturity of Thales engineers rapidly increases, the development of Arcadia and those of its supporting modeling tool Capella is still ongoing today. The milestone of a thousand engineers trained at Thales was exceeded at the end of 2015, and today most divisions and units deploy the approach and its workshop in operational projects in most of the countries where Thales is successfully established.

In 2015, a new step was completed, beyond Thales's borders, with the releasing into the public domain of the method elements and those of the Capella modeling tool, its code being released as open source by the Polarsys industrial working group within the Eclipse Foundation [POL 17b].

At the same time, the Clarity consortium [CLA 15], bringing together manufacturers, software publishers, service providers and academics, was put in place to ensure the promotion and dissemination of the method and the tool, which allowed its use by a growing community of industries, academics, organizations, etc.

---

2 The internal name of Capella at Thales is Melody Advance.

1.3. Scope of application of Arcadia

The scope of application of the method should be briefly defined since activities centered on the concepts of architecture or engineering are numerous.

Work on the definition of architecture and the scope of operation of the architect cover a continuum of key activities for the further definition of a solution: exploring and synthesizing stakeholders key expectations or requirements, as well as the major constraints influencing the framing of the solution; exploring the solution space by considering a set of alternatives to architectural concepts; and instructing associated trade-off studies.

These works have in common the search for an overall compromise in which a local decision can question this compromise. Design can be initiated when a local decision no longer influences the global level.

This architecture work covers various levels of abstraction, ranging from a very high-level vision and concerns (intention-based description), governing the emergence and the orientation of the major choices of architecture, to the *in-extenso* implementation of the fine architecture decisions, directly driving the design.

1.3.1. *The collaborative development of the architecture, not the exploration*

The Arcadia method centers its scope for action on engineering and architecture definition works and particularly on the second concern mentioned previously.

Arcadia endeavors to strengthen the collaboration between the major players of engineering, the customer, the end user and the solution architect being at the forefront, but also engineering experts, subsystem and implementation engineering, and integration teams. It thus defines which requirement the system solution will satisfy, its implementation conditions, its expected behavior and its internal organization. The method supports, in particular, designers up to the specification of hardware, software, mechanical components, etc., of the system or its subsystems, in their contribution to expected functionalities, their interfaces and interaction modes.

On the other hand, Arcadia considers that the problem and solution spaces are already sufficiently characterized to be able to compare functional and structural alternatives explicitly described, *in extenso*. Therefore, it does not cover the above-mentioned orientation activities.

***

Arcadia has been designed to be applied to the construction of a comprehensive solution to a requirement, which is not necessarily limited to a product or system, but also includes supporting means to its deployment, its implementation and its lifecycle (*enabling systems*), operators and contributors, etc., which will be considered as part of the "system" object of engineering. This term "system" is therefore to be taken in the broad sense, and may even sometimes apply to an organization less tangible than a system in the classic sense of the term. However, in the rest of the book, we have used the word "system" for convenience.

1.3.2. Cooperation with experts, but not their core profession

Being centered on architecture and engineering concerns in a broad sense, Arcadia does not also cover the core of so-called expertise engineering (security, operation safety, logistics, reliability, customer support, human factors, etc.), or the definition of algorithms or processing, for example. On the other hand, it empowers these engineering disciplines to express their constraints about the architecture, to influence the choices and compromises that will define it, and to base their own work on the description of the architecture, which is structuring for all these trades.

1.3.3. Definition and design of the architecture, not its development

The applicability of the method also ends when development itself begins: the geometric definition of parts or mechanical assemblies and the verification of their mechanical properties, for example, are excluded therefrom. Even if the simulation of the engineering model is sometimes possible, it is not one of the primary goals of Arcadia.

Similarly, it may contribute to the definition of an electronic processing-centric, high-performance computing architecture, or software components architecture, but it does not cover the detailed design of these software or electronic components. However, it can provide them with inputs, such as structural description or interface files, principle wiring diagrams, operation and test scenarios, etc.

1.3.4. Some very broad application scopes and areas

No method can claim universality and, beyond the activities that Arcadia includes or not, such as presented earlier, the question arises of the areas for use to which it is adapted. It seems that its possible scopes for application are broad: today, they equally concern aerospace equipment and systems, air traffic control, ground and space satellite systems, railway safety critical systems, systems for the surveillance of areas, the supervision of cities, for telecommunications and networks, defense mission systems, detection equipment such as radars or optronic devices, power generation systems and thermal machines, power plants from their supervision up to reactor or fuel maintenance components, the automotive sector, etc. Actually, any system submitted to functional or non-functional constraints that impact its architecture can be a candidate for using the method.

***

Furthermore, the potential for addressing complex areas, systems and engineering should not mislead one into believing that Arcadia is reserved for these high-complexity contexts, for large-sized systems, requiring numerous engineering teams with a lot of different players. The experiment shows that the method can be effectively applied in small developments, for bidding in calls for tender or even in student projects, as is currently the case in a number of engineering schools.

1.4. Arcadia presentation

Arcadia is thus a structured engineering method for defining and verifying the architecture of complex systems. It promotes collaborative work among all key players, often in large numbers, from the engineering (or definition) phase of the system and subsystems, until their IVV. It provides a means to perform as early as the definition phase the iterations that will allow the architecture to converge toward the adequacy of all identified requirements.

Arcadia emerged as a major support for engineering and its mastery, based on a formalization of the analysis of needs with operational, functional and non-functional characteristics (expected functions of the system, functional chains, etc.), then on the definition/justification of the architecture from this functional analysis. The general principles of Arcadia are briefly described in the following, before an in-depth presentation throughout the various chapters of this book.

***

One of the ambitions of the method is that all stakeholders in engineering should share (concerning previous common objectives) the same methodical approach, the same information, the same need and product description in the form of a set of shared models[3], described by a common language. Apart from this descriptive use, the purpose of these models is that they are also prescriptive for the development

---

3 The notion of model taken here is, in the broadest conceptual sense, of a simplified but formalized representation of an element for a given use. It should not be reduced to a computer implementation view of this concept.

and implementation of the system, as well as support for the analysis of the choice of architecture and the anticipated verification of its properties.

All information produced by engineering, describing requirement and solution, are grouped within a single model (or set of models) shared by the various actors involved. This model will be designated as an engineering model. Other models and bases of information also exist, of course, such as requirements, study and simulation models dedicated to various specialties (safety, security, performance, 3D digital representation, etc.), and everything else in engineering data (configuration management, campaigns and test results, defects database, etc.), however, the link between all these models and information, and the entry point for each stakeholder, should be this engineering model.

***

Co-engineering between the different engineering levels (system, subsystem, mechanical design, electronics, software, etc.) is supported by a framework allowing for joint model development, and the models of the different levels and trades are deducted/validated/linked between each other.

These models are part of the technical "contract" between engineering and their coherence is the guarantor of contract satisfaction, all the more in that they also enable the subsystem verification and validation strategy.

***

Co-engineering with specialty engineering (security, operation safety, human factors, performance, cost, mass, scalability, environment, interfaces, logistics, etc.) is supported by a multi-perspective approach.

Each set of constraints associated with one of these specialties is formalized in a dedicated "perspective", which first characterizes the expectations of the system as seen from this specialty ("requirements", feared events, expected performance or behavior, etc.). Each candidate solution architecture is then subject to the verification of "standards" concerning the perspective. These standards for the verification of the architecture are established so as to be able to verify at the earliest the proposed architecture, during the definition/design phase, through the analysis of the models that describe it. The benefit is to be able to make the best compromise integrating all these constraints emerge more quickly, but also to justify the choices that lead to it and its adequacy to requirements.

***

IVV activities take advantage of modeling, first by defining their strategy from the functional capabilities that the model defines and from their links with the architecture of the components to be integrated; then test campaigns, and their impact on system components, are defined on the basis of the functional chains and use case scenarios defined in the model. Finally, defaults analysis and localization, testing optimization, in particular for non-regressions, are also greatly facilitated by the use of models.

GENERAL COMMENT.– *This book is dedicated to the Arcadia method itself and not to its application modes within a modeling centric engineering environment. The practices presented here are without prejudice to their possible mechanization or automation by a construction and analysis tool for models and engineering data. However, a very large majority of these practices may benefit from supporting tools, which can control their complexity, as shown by the numerous operational deployments implemented to date.*

Main Perspectives Structuring the Modeling Approach

2.1. From the need to the solution

The different perspectives that structure the implementation of Arcadia at a given engineering level (as well as associated models) are detailed in the following chapters. There are five of them and the role of each one is briefly described here.

2.1.1. *Operational analysis (or OA)*

"What system users must achieve".

This perspective analyses the issue of operational users, by identifying actors that have to interact with the system, their goals, activities, constraints and the interaction conditions between them.

2.1.2. *System needs analysis (or SA)*

"What the system must achieve for users".

This perspective builds an external functional analysis, which is constructed based on the operational analysis and textual input requirements, and outlined with respect to them, to identify in response functions or system services necessary to its users, under the constraint of non-functional properties requested.

All the figures in this book are available to view in color at: www.iste.co.uk/voirin/arcadia.zip.

2.1.3. Logical architecture (or LA)

"How the system will work to meet expectations".

In response to the need expressed by the two previous perspectives, it enables the first major choices of solution design, first via an internal functional analysis of the system: it describes the functions to be performed and assembled in order to implement the service functions identified in the previous phase.

It continues with the identification of the operational components implementing these solution functions, integrating the non-functional constraints that we chose to be addressed at this level.

2.1.4. Physical architecture (or PA)

"How the system will be built".

This perspective has the same objective as the logical architecture, except that it defines the finalized architecture of the system, as it should be completed and integrated.

It adds the functions required by the implementation and technical choices, and reveals the behavioral components that perform these functions. These behavioral components are then implemented using host implementation components that offer them the necessary material resource.

2.1.5. Product building strategy (or BS)

"What is expected of each component, and the conditions of its integration into the system".

This perspective deduces, from the physical architecture, conditions that each component must comply with to satisfy architecture design constraints and choices, achieved in the previous phases. It also defines the integration, verification and validation strategy of the system as a whole.

2.2. Overview of the main concepts

Figure 2.1 presents the – simplified – overview of the main views, perspectives and relationships guiding engineering and modeling. Different views coexist within each perspective:

– functional view (activities, in orange, and functions, in green);

– behavioral structural view (behavioral components, in blue);

– implementation structural view (host physical components, yellow rectangles);

– representation of exchanged elements (data, gray circles);

– analytical viewpoints and specialty (viewpoints, in gray).

These different views (detailed further in the book) are connected to each other in each perspective through allocation (of functions on behavioral components, for example) and deployment links (of behavioral components on host resources, for instance). Moreover, between two perspectives, the elements of each one are connected to each other through traceability and justification connections, used in particular for the impact analysis in the event of changes in models, needs, technical solutions, etc.

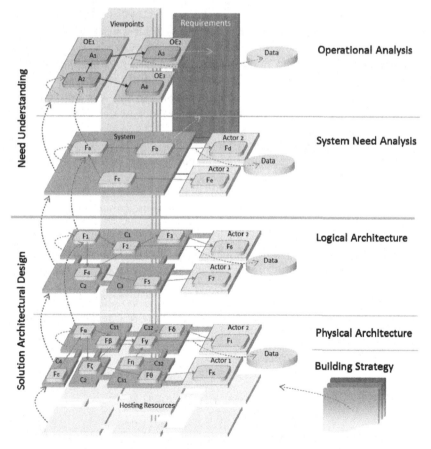

Figure 2.1. *Main views and perspectives structuring the Arcadia approach*

2.3. An illustrative example: traffic regulation in the vicinity of a level crossing

The different principles of action, concepts and activities of the method are illustrated throughout this book by using an example of practical application. The purpose of this example is of course solely to help understand the concepts presented. There are certainly gaps in it, shortfalls and even errors in understanding the field, the need and the design choices made; *the reader is thus required to show a level of indulgence over the lack of realism or even of relevance of this example, and to not make hurried judgments about its significance, but to focus only on the illustrative nature of the process and underlying concepts.*

The subject is that of the rail and road traffic regulation in the vicinity of a level crossing located near a train station in built-up areas. It was chosen because it enables the illustration of applications of the method, both in subsystems with a prevailing control or computing aspect and mechanical subsystems, for example.

The chosen level of engineering is that of control system of rail and road traffic near the level crossing, as a whole. The level of detail of the subsystems retained here is thus rather coarse-grained, but obviously should not be taken as a recommendation for stopping conditions, for example, as it targets above all educational considerations.

Another example, borrowed from the automotive sector, is illustrated in Chapter 15 ("Contribution to Product Line Engineering").

EXAMPLE.– *Further in the book, the illustrations based on examples are highlighted.*

The model from which the illustrations are extracted has been designed using the modeling tool Capella, available at the Capella website [POL 17a]. This model will also be made available on this site.

A book on the same topic describes in detail the use of Capella to build models according to Arcadia [ROQ 18].

3

Adaptation to Project Context and Life Cycle

The presentation of the approach proposed by Arcadia, as it is discussed previously, may give the impression that the method can be applied in a sequential manner, in a "top-down" fashion from one perspective to the next. In effect, it is a logical disposition for the various activities implemented in the application of the method to be presented: it proposes an intellectually satisfying order, a thinking progression logically ordered by the dependencies between engineering data produced and required by each activity. Therefore, it is maintained throughout this book for pedagogical reasons.

Nonetheless, this presentation is purely theoretical, and often not applicable in its strict order, within the context of an operational project. In most cases, industrial or technical constraints result in a cycle entwining several approaches, which have to deviate from the theoretical top-down approach.

This fact, observed since the first experiments of the method, has meant that Arcadia and its language (as well as the functionalities of the method supporting tools) has had to be adapted rather deeply to be compatible with these different lifecycles, which often overlap and intertwine. Some examples are given, for the language in Chapter 4 (section 4.3), and for non-top-down lifecycles in Chapter 15 (section 15.4.3); however, the method has been subjected to many other use cases encountered in operational situations.

This chapter quickly presents a few adaptations or constraints that may be imposed by the context of each project. The activities described in the rest of the book must be considered in this perspective of potential multiple cycles.

All the figures in this book are available to view in color at: www.iste.co.uk/voirin/arcadia.zip.

3.1. Iterative or incremental approach

It is infrequent that analysis or an architecture definition can be performed only once, in a linear fashion. Most of the time, reflection will be gradually constructed, including increasingly more detailed reflection states (iterative approach), and/or a gradual extension of concepts to be considered, starting with the most important and critical, then expanding to the full required perimeter (incremental approach). Flashbacks and feedback from previous works and results, or conversely anticipations of the following activities, are common and inevitable. A few sources of iterations in the course of engineering include the following:

– the conceptual high-level vision of the architecture is often established and verified in the first step, before moving on to the detailed design of the solution. This is the case of the exploration phases of the space of need and of the solution prior to the use of Arcadia. It is also the case between logical and physical architecture, for example;

– in the absence of an operational analysis provided by clients, it is often necessary to start with an analysis of the requirements defined by them, and thus a first version of the analysis of the system needs, before attempting to generalize these needs into an *a posteriori* operational analysis that will seek to abstract itself from focusing on the system;

– during the analysis of system needs, in order to verify the feasibility of a requirement, it may be necessary to carry out an initial projection over a reduced section of the logical architecture, or even of the physical one. In the event of feasibility failing, the analysis of the system or operational needs might have to be reviewed;

– similarly, the consolidation of the logical architecture can justify the definition and the analysis of the premises of a limited physical architecture, to verify a scaling of performance, for example;

– the physical architecture may need to be adapted to the constraints of reuse of existing components, or be reviewed in the light of the limitations imposed by a technology, for example;

– the difficulties encountered during integration, verification and validation can cause that part of the architecture definition to be called into question (nevertheless, Arcadia strives to maintain it to a minimum).

This sequence of iterations produces different intermediate versions of engineering constituent elements (models, requirements, justification files, etc.), through a process of continuous refinement, in which the level of detail of each element increases at each iteration, along with its stability.

3.2. Scheduling activities

It can be seen that the different engineering activities proposed by the method can or must often be executed in parallel, in anticipation, in an iterative or progressive manner, etc. Similarly, depending on the context and especially on the input data available, they may have to be initiated without having all their inputs available, or interrupted to consolidate them, without necessarily following the logical order of their mutual dependence.

Nevertheless, as far as possible, each planned activity in the method should be performed at least once (except adjustment), and its technical results (produced engineering elements) must be verified against relevant design rules, in order to ensure that the task has contributed with real added value.

3.3. Top-down or bottom-up approach

The natural approach when starting from scratch for a new product, such as described in the following chapters, is said to be top-down, because it follows the different perspectives in their order of presentation, as successive stages where each one benefits from the products of the previous.

However, in most cases, engineering does not start with a white paper sheet, but must take into account constraints such as an existing system of which part or the whole must be reused, commercial components whose definition and capabilities are imposed and ought to be included or a product policy to be maintained requiring that changes be minimized and the reuse of existing components be maximized.

This leads to constraining and often reconsidering the top-down definition, as a more bottom-up or ascending approach (starting from the constraints of the solution), the two having to be reconciled. An illustration thereof is given in Chapter 15 (section 15.4.3), in which the analyses of needs for a new given customer and the ideal logical architecture desired to respond thereto (developed in a conventional top-down manner) are confronted with the physical architecture constituting of existing components that must respond to this need (for its part, built in a bottom-up fashion based on the assembly and reuse of existing elements). In general, the initial development of a new product often has a definition and development cycle clearly differentiated from that of changes in the product.

The possibility that both approaches, top-down and bottom-up, meet at some point also applies at the intersection of system and subsystem: although in most cases, it is system engineering that defines the inputs of each subsystem engineering, it is also common that the expected outcome of the system definition has to be confronted with the constraints of subsystem engineering and its existing potential.

However, in all presented cases, it is essential that the top-down approach not be sacrificed, otherwise the adaptation to operational requirements, the control of performance and global properties expected from the architecture may be seriously compromised.

3.4. Progressive and focused architecture construction

Rather than exhaustively and uniformly modeling the problem and the solution, it is often a good idea to start with part of it only, judiciously chosen. The temptation to model what we know must then be fought back, because it is probably in the parts that were not finely analyzed that the potential difficulty will hide.

Consequently, focus will be first, for example, on what is new with regard to the customer context to existing products; the aspect that has main operational importance to the customer, or that constitutes a differentiator for the company; sections where the most significant risks have been identified, where the level of control is the lowest, etc.

This focused and progressive construction of the architecture and associated models is clearly outlined in the development cycle: for example, in many cases, engineering and therefore modeling should be launched during the offer phase, or before in the event of a proactive product policy, to define enterprise reference architectures. It will focus, for example, either on the adequacy of reusing existing elements, or on new problems to be addressed and will consequently have modeling at its core. A first coarse-grained version of the architecture should be drafted at this level, to support cost estimates in particular. Once the development is notified, engineering will depart from this original architecture to complete it at a fine-grained level of detail this time, to verify assumptions and to finalize the definition of the product.

***

Anyway, it is recommended that, when the definition is completed, coverage of the system perimeter by the models be as complete as possible, even if its entire content is not so finely detailed, such that global impact evaluations can be performed without any risk of neglecting unexpected behavior from the system parts that would not have been modeled.

In particular, it is important to model not only the elements of the system that need to be developed under the company's responsibility, but also subsets thereof, or external actors with which the system components interact. Even if engineering had no latitude in defining these elements external to its scope of action, it is nonetheless responsible for the overall functioning of the system, including its interactions with them, which justifies that they should be included in the modeling.

3.5. Activity adjustment and adaptation to a particular area

The logic behind the method that each activity contributes to product and model development or to their justification gives each one a purpose, all the more in that they share for the most part interdependencies with other activities, which justifies the consideration of them globally. However, the application of the method should not be monolithic but adapted to each application area, depending on its context and its constraints.

The most important factor in the implementation of Arcadia is of course that all engineering questions and expectations be properly addressed, and that the contribution of the method to their solution recorded. Based on this initial analysis of the peculiarities of the engineering context, an adjustment has to be made.

The first adjustment lever is the scope and the level of detail that each activity endorses, as mentioned earlier, and this level of detail depends on the objectives of engineering and of the model. It is often preferable to address most of the activities prescribed by the method, by acting on their level of detail rather than by arbitrarily removing some of them.

***

If this first adjustment turns to be insufficient to meet the constraints inherent to the field under consideration, then it may be preferable to seek to optimize the number of activities carried out: although all activities prove to be useful, they are not necessarily possible or do not have any priority in a given context.

For example, in the context of the limited evolution of an existing product, operational analysis is not necessarily justified, or may be reduced to design scenarios for the new required features. The rest of the model, while covering the totality of the preferential product, could be detailed only for sections affected by changes and those added on that occasion.

For a really simple system, the logical architecture can be omitted, or be limited to a very high level view, as a first level of synthesis of the physical architecture.

However, in order not to lose the benefits of the comprehensive approach proposed by Arcadia, any adjustments should be carefully analyzed in their consequences and justified, particularly when subjected to the constraints and priorities of engineering.

***

Apart from this general work of adjustment, every application area of the method should adopt and apply the method adapting it to its own constraints and know-how, products and projects. For instance, this adaptation often involves:

– the definition of an engineering process, and more specifically of a modeling strategy and its adjustment rules, adapted to the specific area;

– the definition and capitalization of a reference architecture for every product, with appropriate architectural styles;

– the formalization of appropriate viewpoints adapted to the area, product and architecture;

– the formulation of specialized engineering rules specific to the field in question, which will govern the verification of the architecture.

4

General Approach to Functional Analysis

4.1. The role of functional analysis in Arcadia

Functional analysis constitutes the major support for the understanding and the expression of need in Arcadia, as well as for the definition of the expected behavior of each system component during the design stage.

It also expresses a large part of the associated performance and non-functional constraints, which are expressed by characterizing the elements of the analysis, through analysis rules and properties specific to every viewpoint being considered.

The solution architecture will also be defined and justified with respect to the functional analysis, by means of grouping or segregating functions required, for example, under constraints of the multiple viewpoints that have to be considered by the architect.

Different functional analyses are established in each of the main perspectives that the method proposes (in the operational analysis, in the system requirements analysis, in the logical or physical architecture definition, in the definition of production contracts); each functional analysis satisfies the specific objectives of the perspective, however all are built according to the same general principles, outlined hereafter. More information and details about the concepts used are provided in Part 3 (Language Encyclopedia and Glossary of Concepts of Arcadia), in particular in Chapter 17.

All the figures in this book are available to view in color at: www.iste.co.uk/voirin/arcadia.zip.

4.2. General principles of functional analysis in Arcadia

4.2.1. *Functions and exchanges*

A function is an action, an operation or a service performed by one of the key players (actors), the system or one of its components, contributing to its behavior. This behavior is defined by a set of partial "functional views" involving these functions, these functional views being correlated and consistent with each other.

Each function is first defined by its name (most often and in this case, by a verbal form describing what is expected from this function), what it is able to provide or produce (its "outputs") and what has to be supplied thereto to operate (its "inputs"). It can also be refined into subfunctions or child functions, which detail and clarify its content.

EXAMPLE.– *Thus, the traffic regulation system at the level crossing should chiefly provide functions responsible for detecting and monitoring road and rail traffic and report back to trains and vehicles the prohibition or authorization to access the crossing. A function "supervise the departure procedure" will generate the authorizations or prohibitions for crossing the level crossing, and to this end will need to have access to train timetables, as well as to information about the state of road and rail traffic at any moment.*

The outputs produced by a function are likely to be necessary to other functions, and its inputs may originate from the outputs of one or several other functions, and so on. These "producer to consumer" relationships between functions, called functional exchanges, thus gradually constitute a graph of functional dependencies or graph of data streams (commonly called "dataflow"), which constitute the first of the functional views under consideration.

EXAMPLE.– *The functions responsible for reporting to trains and vehicles the prohibition or authorization to cross the crossing will receive from "supervise the departure procedure" the associated permissions or prohibitions, successively, during the execution of the procedure. "Supervise the departure procedure" must also determine whether there are vehicles on the track, and verify that vehicles properly stop (function in blue in Figure 4.1).*

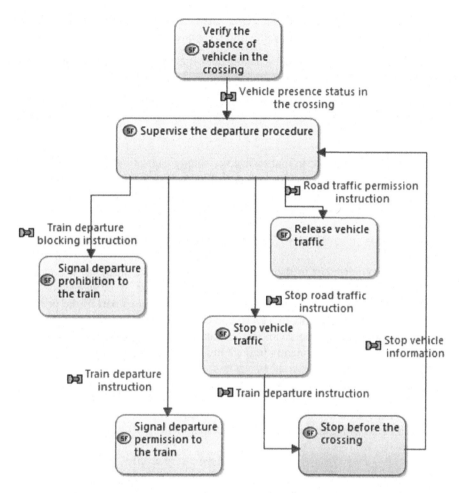

Figure 4.1. *Functions executed during a train departure (partials)*

From now on, it is important to note that functional exchanges assume explicit exchanges, whose nature is expressed through their name, between producer and consumer functions. By default, they provide no sequence, precedence, chronology, etc., semantics between these functions. Such semantics could be added as needed, but it should preserve the orientation of dependence of exchange between functions, and prohibit any precedence relationship non-materialized by an explicit exchange.

Functional exchanges reflect functional dependencies between functions only. To verify the validity of a dataflow, the following questions should be addressed:

– Considering any functional exchange, does it actually channel exchange items (data, flow, materials, etc.)?

– Does every function correctly receive all exchange elements (exchange items) required for its execution? Is it legitimate that it provides requested exchange elements?

We will see further that to materialize the supply capacity and input needs in a function, the method utilizes the concept of ports attached to the function and connecting it to the exchanges.

4.2.2. Missions, capabilities, functional chains and scenarios

The system contributes to the execution of one or more missions, and each of these missions requires a number of capabilities in order to be achieved. Each capability is described by a sequence of functions, which uses part of the previous functional dependencies graph, in a given context. This second functional view, thus contextual with regard to the conditions of implementation of a capability, can be formalized in various ways, mainly through multiple functional chains and scenarios that define the capability.

A functional chain describes a "path", which is a subset of the graph of functional dependencies, thus comprising functions and functional exchanges connecting them, taking part in obtaining the capability.

EXAMPLE.– *Therefore, the functional chain "stop traffic" particularly brings into play functions and exchanges highlighted in blue in Figure 4.2. The blue frame indicates a departure and/or arrival function.*

A scenario adds a chronological dimension to the functional chain, and more particularly focuses on the temporal positioning of the activity of functions and their exchanges. It can be described, for example, by a relative placement of these exchanges on a single time axis, or by precedence links between function activities (and activations). These links are purely contextual to the implementation of the capacity, and should by no means be confused with functional exchanges. A scenario can, in particular, be defined between functions, or between the system/its components and external actors.

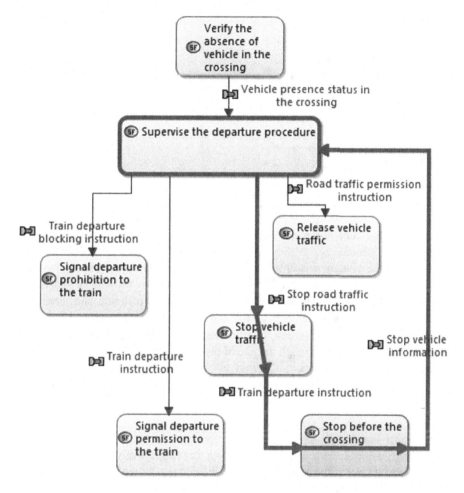

Figure 4.2. *Stop road traffic functional chain (partial)*

EXAMPLE.– *Furthermore, the chronology of exchanges between the previously defined functions can be more specifically described in the context of the capacity being considered, based on the scenario shown in Figure 4.3, especially the moment when the train is allowed to start, for instance.*

Functions participating in the scenario are displayed at the top of the figure; the time axis is vertical; the activity of each function is illustrated by vertical green bars, whereas horizontal arrows reflect communication between two functions by means of a functional exchange.

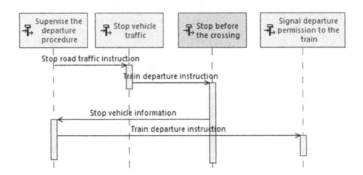

Figure 4.3. *Traffic stop scenario (partial)*

Missions and capabilities are essential elements for the comprehension of the model and its structuring, as they describe the major expectations and operating conditions of the system, as well as the implementation conditions of functions and exchanges comprising the dataflow. They particularly provide a basis for documentary structuring (requirements, for example), for planning and measuring the progress of modeling, but also, as we will see (Chapter 12, section 12.1.2), for the definition of the integration, verification and validation strategy, and for measuring their progress, through the use of the functional chains and scenarios (for this topic, see Figure 23.2).

4.2.3. States and modes

The third functional view concerns the concept of modes and states. A mode (respectively, a state) characterizes a chosen context (respectively, incurred) in which can be found an actor, the system or one of its component, and as such defines its behavior in this context.

This behavior is most often defined by the functions (and possibly by the exchanges, or even components) available or not in the mode or the state under consideration.

Each possible transition between two modes or between two states is potentially triggered by a functional exchange.

A scenario can reference a mode or state to indicate at any given time the transition and the start of this mode or state.

States and modes associated with an element are generally defined by a state machine (respectively, mode machine), which describes them and possible transitions between them, as well as the conditions of these transitions.

EXAMPLE.– *The main expected operating modes of the system are train departures, train arrivals and the movement of road vehicles in the absence of circulating trains. The three modes are (and should be) mutually exclusive. Transitions to shift from one to the other are triggered by the announcements of train departures and arrivals, and in their absence the authorization for road vehicles to pass.*

In Figure 4.4, modes are in gray and arrows represent transitions by which the trigger condition of the transition is enabled.

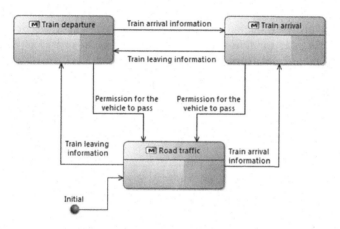

Figure 4.4. *Main system modes*

4.2.4. *Data model*

The fourth structuring functional view of the functional analysis is the data model that describes the content of functional exchanges. Each exchange enables one exchange item (in the broad sense of the term, including complex information including fluids or pairs of forces, for example), which can be described as a set of data, each with its structure, composition, relationship with other data, etc.

EXAMPLE.– *A hydraulic fluid may be itself described by its nature or its composition, its viscosity index, the extreme temperatures that it has to endure, the standards that must be satisfied, etc. When in use, as it travels between two sections of the system, it will also be possible to characterize its pressure and its temperature at this point.*

Train schedules will be described as a list mentioning for each case their number, their destination, the time of departure or arrival, the expected platform, etc.

4.2.5. Non-functional characterization and analysis viewpoints

In order to take into consideration non-functional constraints that the solution must abide by and their impact on its design, functional analysis is improved by additional concepts, for each analysis viewpoint being considered (see Chapter 10). It may concern new concepts (e.g. a feared event), or characterization elements of previous concepts (such as a criticality level associated with a function or data).

4.2.6. Summary

Functional analysis is at the core of architecture modeling: it describes behaviors expected by the user, and those chosen for the solution. It is based on four types of views correlated to each other:

– functional dependency graph (called dataflow);

– missions, capabilities, functional chains and contextual scenarios;

– modes and states governing function availability and system capabilities;

– data model describing the content of exchanges between functions.

4.3. Functional analysis construction approach

There are many ways to approach and build functional analysis, based on the inherent context of each project and organization; some commonly encountered in projects are mentioned here, without being restrictive however. Subsequently, none is necessarily better than another. On the other hand, these different construction approaches require that the method, the language and supporting tools be adapted to this diversity, which has led to several developments in Arcadia and in its language in particular.

Unless operational restrictions are expressly mentioned, all these steps can be applied in all cases where functional analysis is required, whether the object is a need or solution description. Despite the fact that they are often illustrated by an application to the system, they can also be used for one of its component or an external actor.

4.3.1. Top-down hierarchical approach

The conventional top-down hierarchical approach such as promoted by structured analysis [ROS 77] and its derivatives, expresses the required functionality in the form of a limited number of first-level functions and then determines necessary exchanges between these functions. This high-level synthetic vision is then refined, on a function basis, through the definition of subfunctions (or child functions) for each identified function; this is achieved recursively, thus creating a hierarchical function decomposition. This conventional approach is often used to build a specification starting with a blank sheet of paper, without any preliminary requirement.

EXAMPLE.– *The approach applied to the example of traffic regulation at the level crossing could first identify first-level functions such as "control vehicle traffic" and "manage train traffic". Control vehicle traffic would consist of verifying the absence of vehicles on the level, prevent their crossing or release it, which would constitute the subfunctions. Manage train traffic could be separated into the implementation of departure and arrival procedures for a train, etc., as shown in Figure 4.5. The links reflect a parent function/child subfunction relationship.*

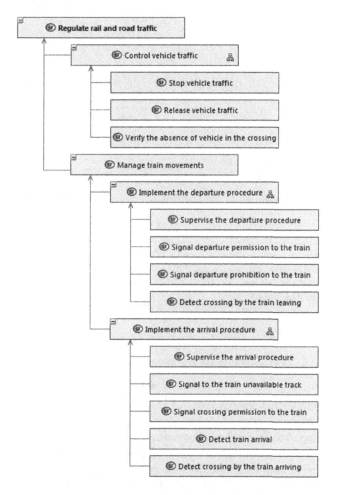

Figure 4.5. *Traffic regulation functional decomposition*

This hierarchical decomposition can also be applied to functional exchanges: exchanges between parent functions can be maintained during functional refinement; exchanges between children functions can be freely defined, but they ought to be compatible (in nature and content) with previous ones, and thus will be connected through traceability links with the exchanges of parent functions.

(In Figure 4.6 and more generally, when an element [function, component, etc.] is represented inside another one, this depicts a composition or kinship relationship.)

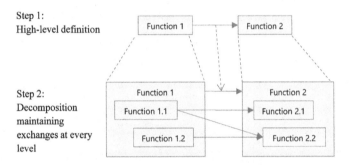

Figure 4.6. *Conventional top-down functional decomposition approach*

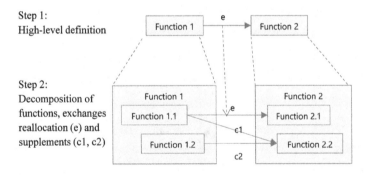

Figure 4.7. *Functional decomposition/reallocation process in Arcadia*

Another approach, making use of exchange reallocation, is nevertheless advocated by Arcadia, in view of minimizing modeling efforts, coherence controls between exchange levels and the maintenance cost of the model (and also in order to adapt to other analysis construction cycles, as discussed further in the text). It simply consists of moving each exchange from the parent function to the child function that must take it into account, such that when the analysis is complete, only terminal or leaf functions (not decomposed) are connected by exchanges.

Nonetheless, this assumes two synthesis capacities that the method is capable of and that the supporting tools of the method have to provide: to be able to represent exchanges between child functions when parent functions only are being visualized, as if they were directly allocated to them, and to synthesize several elementary exchanges into a synthetic representation (category) visually grouping them, in order to reduce the representation complexity, and possibly keep track of the first exchanges achieved between parent functions. These principles are described in more detail in Chapter 17 (section 17.5).

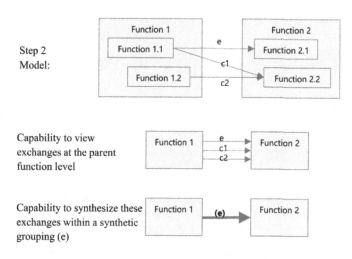

Figure 4.8. *Automatic synthesis in Arcadia*

A significant advantage of the reallocation-based approach is its simplicity in managing collaborative functional analysis, distributed between several authors (see Figure 4.9): each of them is assigned the refinement of a top-level function, for example; for this author, the other first-level functions are considered to be "black boxes" whose content (i.e. their subfunctions during the edition process) is unknown to the author.

During the refinement of this high-level function whose responsibility belongs to the author, the latter will create her own subfunctions and exchanges between them, internal to the high-level function; she will also move each exchange placed in the parent function into the child function, which will have to take it into account. However, she is also likely to require new data from other high-level black-box functions, and it may be the author's responsibility to provide them with data. In this case, the author will create new exchanges for these subfunctions, destined to or originating from the other black-box functions, the only ones that she has knowledge of.

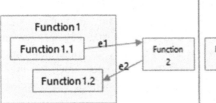
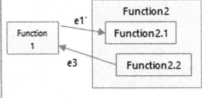

2nd A1 must then take into account exchanges in Function 1, originating from the requests of author A2: e1', e3

2nd A2 must take into account requests from author A1: e1, e2

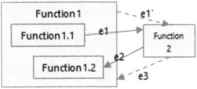
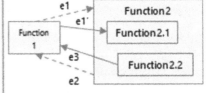

3rd A1 examines e3, considers in agreement with A2 that e3 is necessary, and moves it onto sub-function 1.2

3rd A2 examines e1, considers that it is identical to e1' and in agreement with A1 replaces e1' by e1; he/she also moves e2 onto Function 2.2

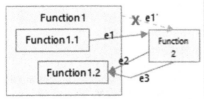
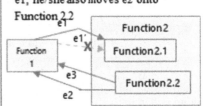

Final consolidated model:

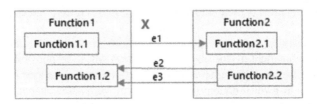

Figure 4.9. *Joint modeling between two authors*

Subsequently, each author responsible for a top-level function will find on top of this latter the exchanges placed by other authors, and that he or she will have to take into account. Two cases can occur:

– in the case that he or she had not yet processed this interaction with the other high-level function, he or she will then simply be able to move the end of the exchange toward that of its subfunctions that is its legitimate origin or destination;

– if he or she has already created an exchange taking into account this interaction, then in addition he or she will have to delete his or her own exchange to replace it with that originating from the other author. Naturally, this has to be done in consultation with the other author, to verify that intentions and needs are consistent on each side.

Once this procedure has allocated all exchanges to leaf functions, consistency between authors is guaranteed.

4.3.2. Functional grouping bottom-up approach

The functional grouping bottom-up approach first defines the set of elementary functions (leaf functions) and their exchanges, then builds synthetic views "hiding the content of the boxes", in other words, by *a posteriori* grouping these leaf functions inside parent functions (eventually over several hierarchical levels).

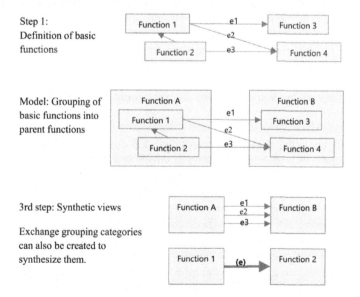

Figure 4.10. *Bottom-up functional construction*

This approach is often implemented when the functional analysis is built from a corpus of requirements describing the need. Each textual requirement is "translated" into functions and exchanges, linking them to those already created (which brings forward links between requirements); in this manner, a set of elementary functions connected by functional exchanges is gradually developed, which constitutes a first functional formalization of need.

EXAMPLE.– *A requirement such as "the system should prevent the train from leaving in case a vehicle is present on the track" will be translated by the creation of functions such as "verify the absence of vehicle in the crossing", "signal to the train that it cannot leave", "supervise the departure procedure" and exchanges between them (state of the presence of a vehicle in the crossing, blocking or train departure instructions). Another requirement such as "the system will prohibit road traffic during train departure time" will lead to the creation of "prevent vehicles from crossing", "authorize vehicle traffic", etc. (see Figure 4.1).*

Functional hierarchy is then also implemented in this case, by defining *a posteriori* parent functions grouping and synthesizing basic functions (leaves), and their exchanges.

Synthesis capacities mentioned in the top-down hierarchical approach can be used in the present case too, because they make it possible to *a posteriori* create these parent functions, to visualize the exchanges allocated to children in these parent functions and in turn to synthesize exchanges by grouping them so that they also have a role in the synthetic view. The modeling effort corresponding to the reconstruction of the hierarchical view is thus minimal, because it is limited, once the graph of the leaf functions is established, to defining the functional hierarchical tree, and possibly the categories for grouping exchanges to synthesize them. This facility is to be compared with a conventional approach in which exchanges have to be defined at every level in addition to the delegation links between decomposition levels.

It should be noted that the conventional top-down hierarchical approach is difficult to apply as such in this context in which leaf functions are assumed to be the starting point: as a matter of fact, the construction of the graph of functional dependencies thus developed is highly incremental. It is thus difficult to stabilize a definition for high-level functions very early; moreover, a hierarchical vision appears as opposing the need for maximum reuse of already defined leaf functions, often inside different parent functions. This reuse is nevertheless of paramount significance, both as a means to confront requirements to each other and to verify their overall coherence, but also to minimize the complexity of the model.

4.3.3. *Functional construction/allocation approach*

The functional construction/allocation approach is intended to define the functional content of a set of structural elements (system, components, operators or actors external to the system, etc.), from a set of activities or services to be collectively achieved. Most often, the concern is not refinement *per se*, but the creation of a solution by parts guided by a need expressed as a graph of functional dependencies.

The first case of exemplary usage of this approach is the definition of the system needs based on operational analysis (see Chapters 5 and 6): the main object consists of identifying, for each operational activity to which the system must contribute, the functions that the latter will have to perform and those that will be the responsibility of its operators or of other external actors. The same process will be employed for functional exchanges.

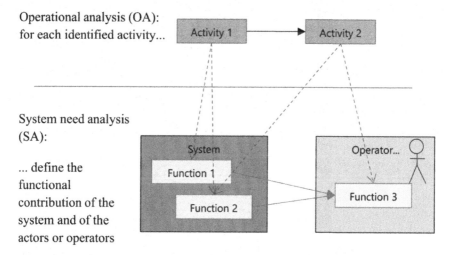

Figure 4.11. *Definition procedure of system needs based on operational analysis*

EXAMPLE.– *Thereby, the operational activity "analyze potential collision risks", allocated to a traffic control authority, will be taken into account in system needs by system functions such as "verify the absence of vehicle in the crossing", and operator functions such as "monitor instructions status".*

The function "supervise the departure procedure", which ensures the intelligence of decision-making, could be entrusted either to the system or to operators themselves, according to customer expectations – or even split between the two, thus creating two new functions; in Figure 4.11, this is the case of the operational activity named activity 2, which is taken into account by two functions, namely function 2 allocated to the system and function 3 allocated to the operators of the system.

The second typical use case concerns the definition of the behavior of system components based on functional needs, mainly in the logical and physical architecture, based on the previous perspective (see Chapters 7 and 8). For each function and exchange of this previous perspective, which constitutes a requirement to be satisfied, the main question is to identify functions and exchanges describing the contribution allocated to each system component, operator or external actor.

It should be recalled that, here again, what is in question is not functional refinement (in the sense of the previous hierarchical approach) between the two functional perspectives, but designing a solution behavior in response to a need.

EXAMPLE.– *In the logical architecture, three functions for detecting vehicles have been defined: "detect approaching vehicles", "detect vehicles stopping before the barrier" and "detect the length of the waiting line of vehicles". These three functions could be satisfied in the physical architecture either by three homologous functions allocated to multiple proximity detectors, or by a 3D detection function localizing elements in the environment (via a radar, for example). It can be seen that in the latter case, the relationship between functions of both perspectives is far from being a simple refinement.*

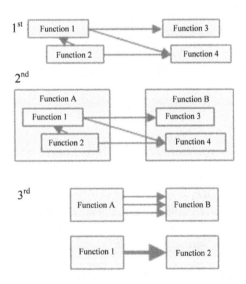

Figure 4.12. *Functional grouping based bottom-up approach*

These two cases here again lead to a graph of gradually built functional dependencies, therefore including basic functions. The definition of high-level parent functions synthesizing the set of these basic functions then appears to be following the same construction approach as the one mentioned previously in Chapter 4 (section 4.3.2).

4.3.4. Service functions and traversal functional chains based approach

This approach begins by identifying use cases of system users and external actors, and for each of them the required functional services, namely the main interactions of users and external actors with the system, to define the functional content expected therefrom and the associated external exchanges.

This conventional approach is often used to build a specification starting from a blank sheet of paper, without any preliminary requirement. The starting point may be to determine service functions "traversing" the system (based on the solicitation of an external actor, and destined to the same or another actor) to characterize the expectations therefrom. The beginning of the use case approach is also outlined in Chapter 4 (section 4.3.5).

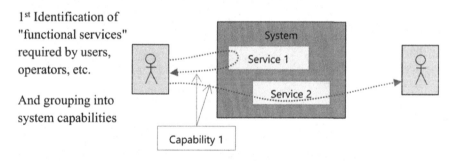

1st Identification of "functional services" required by users, operators, etc.

And grouping into system capabilities

Figure 4.13. *Initial service functions and use case based approach*

On the other hand, this is only a first step for Arcadia in functional analysis: first, the use cases identified are structured by system capabilities.

Then, once a function interacting with external elements is identified with associated exchanges, its links and synergies with other functions already defined in other services or "traversed" are searched for (pooling, service delegation, use of the outputs provided by others or by one of them, etc.). Eventually, this leads to the creation of new functions, to the decomposition of some of them and to establishing system-internal functional exchanges (but still in terms of need) between these functions. This allows both the enrichment and clarification of the need, but also the simplification of its expression (by pooling and through system-internal communications rather than paths totally independent from each other).

To preserve visibility and the orientation of services and traversals identified, a functional chain is built for each of them that identifies functions and exchanges contributing to it. It is recommended that analysis and resulting functional chains be structured by capabilities to which they contribute.

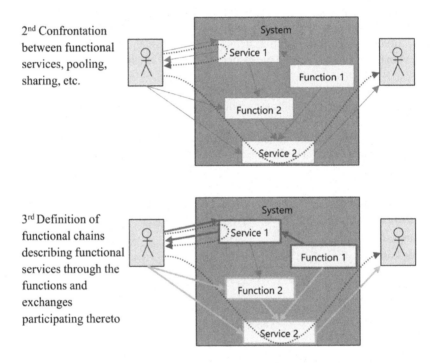

Figure 4.14. *Construction of functional chains by service*

As a result, a gradually built graph of functional dependencies is once again obtained, which will then benefit from the same construction and synthesis approach as that referred to in Chapter 4 (section 4.3.2).

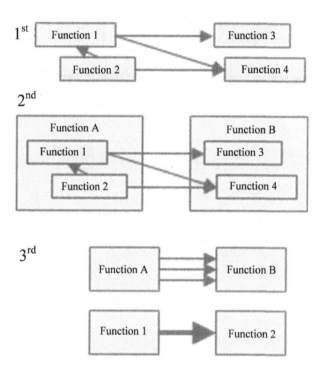

Figure 4.15. *Bottom-up functional grouping approach*

4.3.5. *Use case scenario based approach*

This approach identifies key system use cases and operating situations, by formalizing them in the form of time-ordered scenarios of interactions with users and other external actors. It is mainly used as part of a capability analysis process, associated or not with that based on service functions and functional chains, with which it shares the same usage-oriented philosophy. It is also recommended to structure the analysis and the scenarios developed by the capacities which they contribute to.

For each scenario, the next step consists of identifying the functional content involved in every interaction mentioned in the scenario. In other words, the question is to identify the source and destination functions of the interaction, thus constituting a functional exchange between these two functions.

The required functions of the system, but also of the operators or external actors existing in the scenario considered, are thus brought forward. In this case again, we should look forward to reusing and pooling functions and functional exchanges between two interactions, or two scenarios, and to completing the functional description based on missing functions and exchanges within each element of the scenario, to ensure the global expected behavior.

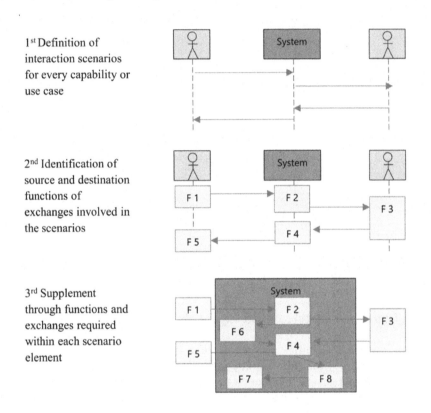

1st Definition of interaction scenarios for every capability or use case

2nd Identification of source and destination functions of exchanges involved in the scenarios

3rd Supplement through functions and exchanges required within each scenario element

Figure 4.16. *Construction of scenario-based functional analysis*

As a result, a gradually built graph of functional dependencies is still obtained, which will then benefit from the same construction and synthesis approach as that referred to in the bottom-up functional grouping based approach.

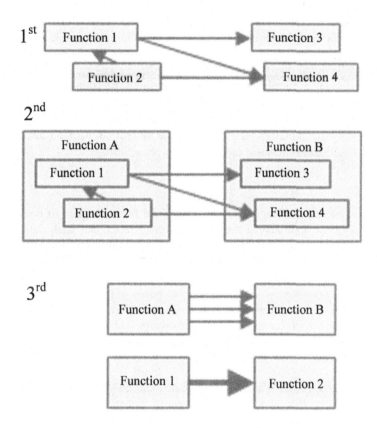

Figure 4.17. *Bottom-up functional grouping approach*

4.3.6. *The practical approach of functional analysis*

The steps and previous situations are in practice employed in operational projects, but very rarely in an exclusive manner. Most of the time, a pragmatic approach borrows from each approach, which best corresponds to its own context, even if it means mixing them.

Thus, even in the event that a hierarchical top-down approach is possible to start the functional analysis, it is very common to switch to a bottom-up approach when requirement changes are necessary, or to a building /allocation-based approach if the structural architecture needs to be reviewed. Similarly, the definition of testing and integration scenarios, or performance or safety engineering, leads to partially applying functional chains and scenario-based approaches. Finally, when a third-party component is reused, it is often through interface scenarios, the only ones initially available, that the functional view of its behavior and usage is built.

It should be noted that system states and modes, as well as the data model, are mostly developed in parallel with the other previous functional views. The data appear at the same time as functional exchanges that enable them. States and modes appear in the analysis by capabilities, in the scenarios that order them, and structure the availability of functions gradually as the definition of their usage inside capacities, functional chains and scenarios takes place.

***

The method and the language of Arcadia have been designed to not impose a particular order or approach in the construction of functional analysis in a given context, taking into account the various situations mentioned previously. Functional views constituting the underlying model can thus be developed in any random order, intertwined if needed, iteratively or incrementally, while ensuring a construction-based modeling consistency and correction, by means of the expected links between all concepts. *On the other hand, if possible, it is recommended that all of these views be built, because their crossing, the confrontation of their viewpoints and the coherence between them thus resulting contribute very significantly to the quality and to the robustness of the functional analysis thus constituted.*

NOTE.– *Subsequently, when the term "functional analysis" is mentioned, it will actually designate this analysis in its entirety (functions, exchanges, but also scenarios and functional chains, modes and states, data model) along with non-functional elements associated, unless otherwise stated.*

4.3.7. Summary

In the lifecycle of models, functional analyses can be built according to different procedures, most often simultaneously or sequentially applied, depending on the context and the modeling stage. The different views of a functional analysis, when a finalization step is completed, should be all described as much as possible, and properly connected to one another, to encourage the overall consistency and robustness of the model.

Operational Analysis

5.1. Principles

Operational analysis (referred to as OA in the following) is a means to capture what system users must achieve as part of their work or mission, and the associated conditions, regardless of any solution – and particularly of systems that they will be able to use for this purpose.

At first, its distinctive feature resides in the very general level of its character: goals, intentions, objectives, required capabilities, activities and interactions with other actors and the environment, situations and scenarios most often encountered, etc.

It is particularly useful when trying to best satisfy a customer need, without having an imposed system scope, or when looking for innovative ways to meet this customer need. It is thus valuable and highly recommended to formulate it in cooperation with one or more customers and potential end-users. It is also valuable for the construction of a multi-client product policy, as we will see.

One of the important particularities of this perspective, which may come as a surprise, is that OA *should not mention the system, so as not to bar itself from potentially interesting alternatives for achieving the satisfaction of customer needs*: it aims at understanding this need without any *a priori* assumptions about how the system will contribute thereto; this is to not restrict the scope of possibilities too quickly[1].

All the figures in this book are available to view in color at: www.iste.co.uk/voirin/arcadia.zip.

1 The choice of the scope and the role of the system will only be carried out during the analysis of system needs (or system needs analysis, referred to as SA, see the following),

EXAMPLE.– *Suppose that the customer need is to be able to hang a mirror on a wall. If this need is translated too quickly into "how to attach a dowel to the wall with a drill?", this prematurely excludes other possibilities (such as using glue, for example), and also criteria that would help guiding the process toward the right solution (such as the need or not to be able to disassemble the mirror at a later time).*

Arcadia thus suggests restricting the OA to what the customer needs to do: here the (operational) capability to have a means of fastening localized in a specific location, and not the different ways to achieve this fastening, which will be identified and evaluated in the further perspectives.

Revisiting the OA at each technological evolution can also allow new products, solutions or features to be proposed, thus making the customer offer more complete.

Following are the main activities to achieve during the OA:

– define missions and required operational capabilities;

– perform an analysis of the operational needs.

5.2. Define missions and required operational capabilities

The first step consists of determining future system and environment users' missions – or more generally their motivations, expectations, goals, objectives, intentions, etc., as well as the capabilities required to assume these missions.

Sometimes considered as being partial goals in view of the fulfillment of the mission, these capabilities represent "know-how" necessary for its successful completion, which must be possible in order to properly achieve it.

EXAMPLE.– *If the mission is to hang a mirror on a wall, required capabilities include being able to attach it, holding it in place for the time necessary to fix it, adjusting its position, eventually taking it down, etc.*

The main concerned actors and operational entities are to be considered from this moment onward.

EXAMPLE.– *In our level crossing example, the road and rail traffic regulatory authority, as well as trains and road vehicles will be identified (by separating train departure and arrival because they necessitate a different form of management).*

---

deciding – at this time only – what will be required of the system and what will be the responsibility of users and external systems.

Existing constraints on the execution of the mission must also be identified at all levels likely to impact it: actor skills, operating modes and responsibilities, rules and associated procedures, existing means and systems, regulatory constraints, temporal and programmatic aspects, etc.

EXAMPLE.– *The missions expected from the customer rail and road traffic regulating authority in the case of the level crossing, for example, will be:*

– to prevent any collision between train and road vehicles;

– to ensure fluidity in rail and road vehicle traffic.

The required capabilities will predominantly be:

– to acknowledge approaching trains (required for both missions);

– to acknowledge approaching road vehicles (required for both missions);

– to forbid the simultaneous access of vehicles and trains to the crossing (required for the first mission at least).

In the case of a crossing located near a train station and inside urban areas, as in our example, one of the constraints identified will be to block road traffic as little as possible. This can generate an additional required operational capability for the second·mission:

– temporarily prioritize road traffic.

Another constraint might be, for security reasons, that a road vehicle must not be able to drive forward through the crossing if passage is prohibited.

Quantitative and qualitative metrics should be defined to evaluate the conditions for success of the mission and necessary capacities to achieve it.

EXAMPLE.– *The following quantification should be respected: no train departure or arrival delays longer than 5 minutes.*

5.3. Perform operational needs analysis[2]

The goal is to capture the conditions for the completion of a mission previously identified, and those for the implementation of associated capabilities, mainly through the activities and interactions of the key players that contribute thereto.

---

2 The recommended approach is based on functional analysis as described in Chapter 4, which should be referred to.

The various situations that directly shape and influence the missions, nominal or non-nominal, and the worst cases likely to be met, should be formalized. The analysis and the comparison of situations and conditions of missions must constitute a permanent concern; in fact, they are likely to guide both the needs analysis, to develop it by revealing constraints likely to have a high impact, but also the opportunities for development of processes, the principles behind the implementation of the mission, etc.

EXAMPLE.– *Thus, a feared event can be the presence of a vehicle on the track during the passage of the train (which can be illustrated in a scenario, for example). A choice may then be made to request that a road vehicle be physically prevented from engaging on the track when its access is prohibited.*

However, note that this does not prevent the vehicle from unintentionally stopping on the track when passage is allowed, consequently this constraint will have to be integrated in one way or another. We will thus choose to add a procedure for delaying a train during departure.

In the case of a train arriving, however, the situation is different because the stoppage of the train must be widely anticipated, considering its inertia and the induced braking time. As it seems unrealistic that it is possible to physically remove the stationary vehicle before the train arrival in any situation, the means to stop this train before the crossing must thus be provided. This should be captured as a strong constraint on the arrival conditions of the train, and will necessarily impact the solution and, even further, a maximal approaching speed can be imposed on the train, for example, outside the strict limits of the system.

The actors, organizations and operational entities concerned are more accurately identified, as well as their required activities during the mission, their interactions and the information exchanged.

EXAMPLE.– *We will more precisely identify the regulating authority of the rail and road traffic (distinguishing if needed control and maintenance roles and responsibilities), trains (separating departure trains from arrival trains as they require a different form of management), road vehicles (but among these cars, heavy goods vehicles and motorcycles would only be distinguished if each one had its own expectations, such as a specific behavior or processing, which is not necessarily the case here; similarly, the vehicle and its driver will be considered as a single entity). The station is also likely to play a role in the departure of trains and rail traffic information, and will therefore also be added here; in this case again and under this common name, we will designate the body responsible for rail traffic, and not the building.*

Rather than defining a single vehicle, one could argue about a more general definition such as "road traffic", nevertheless it is important that the behavior related to a single vehicle be addressed as such (such as parking on the rail track, for example). Furthermore, several vehicles could also be defined, but this is justified only if a differential behavior calls for it, which is not the case at this level of detail.

The development approach for activities and their interactions is that of functional analysis, in which activities assume the role of functions.

EXAMPLE.– *Figures 5.1 and 5.2 show a high-level view of OA, presenting operational entities (in beige), activities allocated to each one of them (in orange) and the interactions required between these activities (enabled by the arrows), whose nature is described by their name.*

As a first step, an analysis based on the principles governing the most widespread passages results in merely suspending the vehicular traffic at every train departure or arrival notification.

When a train departs, the station triggers the train departure and stops road traffic; the latter is restored once the train has passed the level crossing. For its part, a train arriving will directly trigger the traffic to be stopped.

On the other hand, in terms of security, this procedure is unsatisfactory, because road traffic itself is not guarded, and there is no ability to delay the departure of a train in the event of a problem occurring in the crossing, for example. A review of the previous analysis is therefore necessary.

With regard to the authority, the main activities will then be to analyze the potential risks of collisions, to authorize or prohibit the arrivals and departures of trains, to delay them or eventually stop them and to authorize or forbid road traffic. Trains and vehicles arrive at the crossing and have to stop by order of the authority or cross it with its permission (interactions with the authority entity).

By the way, it is clearly visible that this description is independent of any system implementation and that there is no reference thereto: all procedures and activities mentioned here could ultimately be achieved simply by traffic wardens.

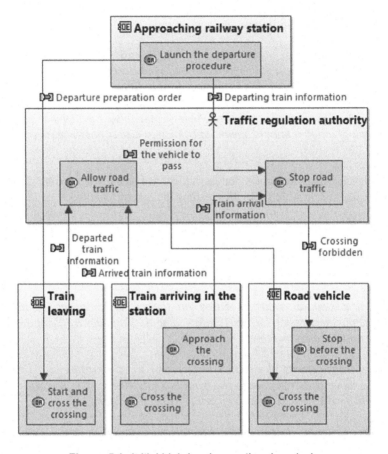

Figure 5.1. *Initial high-level operational analysis*

The following activities have been added to the initial analysis as a result of the analysis of risk situations mentioned previously:

– regarding the regulatory authority: delay the train departure, stop the train arriving, authorize the train arrival;

– regarding the leaving train: wait for the departure authorization;

– regarding the arriving train: stop before the crossing.

Notions such as different mission phases, operational contexts, situations encountered can also be captured by means of operational statuses or modes, and transition conditions allow shifting from one to the other.

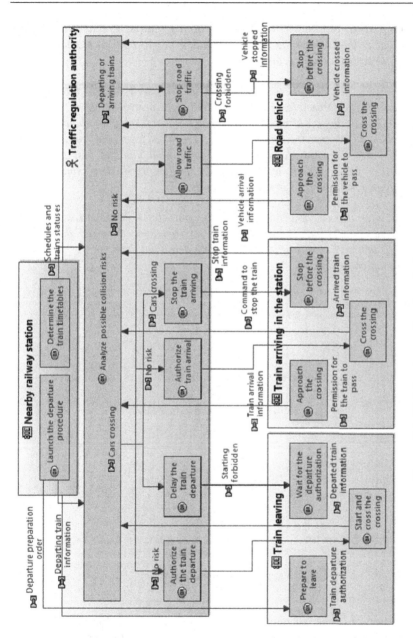

Figure 5.2. *High-level operational analysis*

EXAMPLE.– *It is reasonable to consider at least three operational modes exclusive to each other, which the regulatory authority will have to manage: train departure, train arrival and free road traffic.*

The transitions between these modes will be triggered by the interactions previously defined: for example, a shift from the train arrival mode to the train departure mode will be performed, on receiving the information about a train leaving (indicated on the transition arrow), received from the station. This transition, however, can only happen if the information that the first train has indeed arrived is received (provided by the train arriving itself). This condition, or guard, is indicated in Figure 5.3 in square brackets.

Moreover, it is also necessary to indicate the activities to be undertaken by the authority in each mode (not shown here); for example, for the train departure: authorize and interrupt road traffic, authorize or delay the departure of the train, analyze potential collision risks.

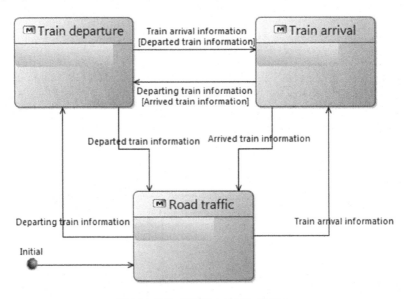

Figure 5.3. *Traffic control modes*

The different situations encountered during the mission are formalized in the form of scenarios that specify conditions for the implementation of the required capabilities and the contributions of each stakeholder (actors, activities, interactions, etc.), as well as operational processes that implement activities contributing to a capability or part of the mission.

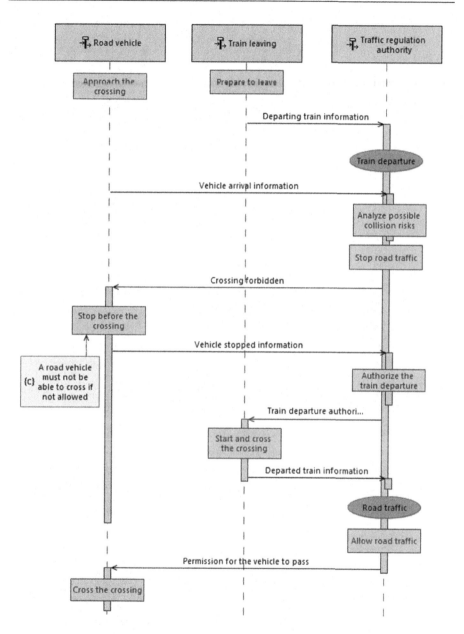

Figure 5.4. *Nominal train departure scenario*

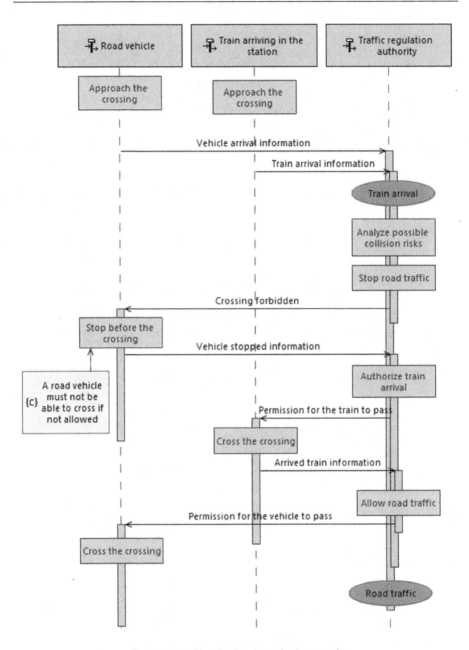

Figure 5.5. *Nominal train arrival scenario*

EXAMPLE.– *The capability "forbid the simultaneous access of vehicles and trains" will be illustrated by nominal train departure and arrival scenarios (Figures 5.4 and 5.5), and by operational processes such as the departure of a priority train or the free passage of vehicles (Figures 5.6 and 5.7). In scenario diagrams, operational entities are on top, operational activities in orange, arrows represent interactions and the vertical axis is the axis of time elapsing. Gray ovals express the mode or the current state of the entity. Requirements or constraints on elements are shown in yellow, indicated by a (c).*

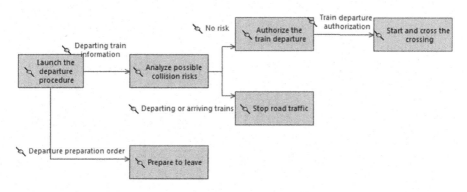

Figure 5.6. *Priority train departure operational process*

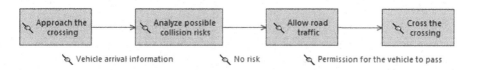

Figure 5.7. *Free vehicle crossing operational process*

EXAMPLE.– *These processes (Figures 5.6 and 5.7, also represented by colored paths Figure 5.8) are in fact projected over the previous operational entities, in which they illustrate the interactions and scenarios. The train departure thus involves unsurprisingly the regulatory authority, the departing train and road vehicles, illustrating the interactions between them required in this situation.*

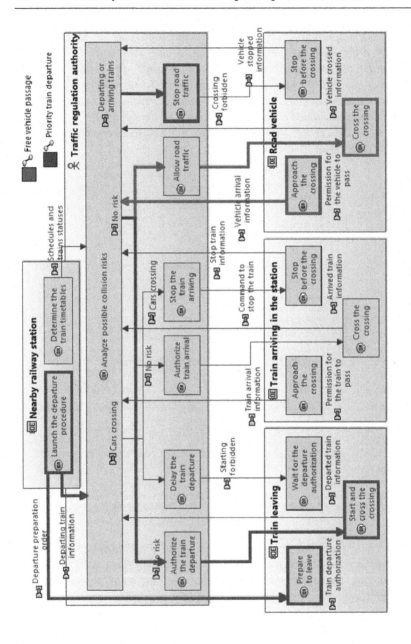

Figure 5.8. *Processes, entities and activities*

EXAMPLE.– *The capability "temporarily prioritize road traffic" will be illustrated by a scenario prior to the previous one (in Figure 5.9, the rectangle is a reference to the previous "nominal train departure" scenario, which will be executed as such after this first phase). A constraint (denoted by (c) in the figure) is however applied to the activity for delaying the train departure.*

It should be noted that taking this ability into account by means of delaying the train departure also satisfies the security constraint in case a vehicle unintentionally stops on the track.

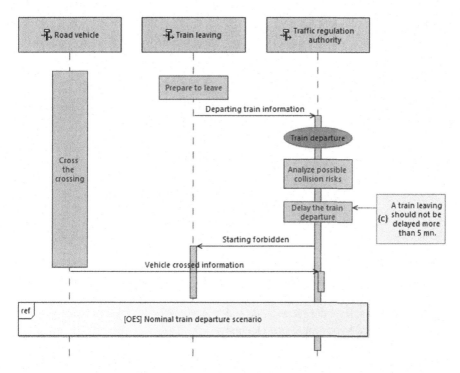

Figure 5.9. *Delayed train departure scenario*

EXAMPLE.– *The situation mentioned previously, of a train arriving while a vehicle is stopped on the track, is illustrated by the following scenario, with the constraints mentioned earlier.*

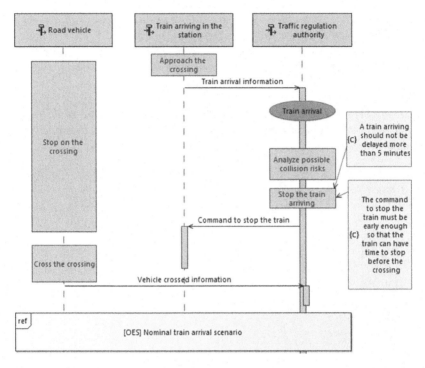

Figure 5.10. *Train arrival delayed by a vehicle on the track*

The first non-functional and performance constraints applying in the context of each mission should be identified at this stage, in addition to the elements to which they apply (an operational process restrained in time, human factors to comply with, feared events for safety and security, etc.). Similarly, the metrics previously defined should be allocated to prior analysis elements.

It is also recommended to define priorities, significance or criticality levels for collected OA elements, in order to guide subsequent choices and compromises.

All these elements will in particular constitute a valuable input for the system verification, validation and qualification phases, mainly in terms of the realism of system operating conditions.

Customer requirements may be used as input in the OA, on the same level as interviews and user situation simulations, or existing documents and systems available, etc. It is recommended that their traceability be ensured with the model elements defined in the OA, for justification purposes.

5.4. Summary

The OA perspective defines what the users of the system must accomplish: it analyzes the challenges of operational users, by identifying the actors that have to interact with the system, their goals, activities, constraints and the interaction conditions existing between them.

The main activities to be undertaken for the OA are the following:

– define missions and required operational capabilities;

– perform an analysis of the operational needs. Prior to the definition of the expectations of the system itself, the OA should not refer to this system, whose outline is not yet clearly identified at this stage.

5.5. Exercise

As a recreational illustration (and therefore not to be taken too seriously), imagine what could be the OA of a door.

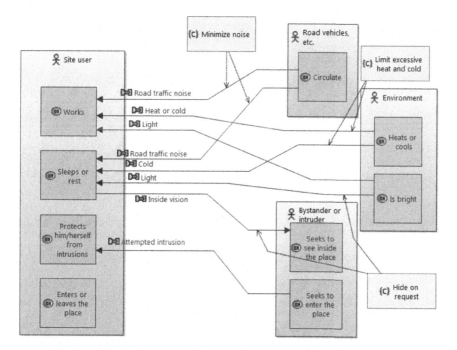

Figure 5.11. *Operational analysis of a door*

6

System Needs Analysis

6.1. Principles

The purpose of system needs analysis (referred to as SA further in the text) is to define the contribution expected of the system to users' needs, as they are described in the previous operational analysis (OA) and/or in the form of requirements expressed by the client.

This definition of expectations concerning the system is mainly formalized in the form of a functional needs analysis describing functions, or services, which the system must perform in different required scenarios and capabilities, and thus the role it must assume in users' activities. In effect, the SA delimits the functions required of the system, distinguishing them from those assumed by the users or external systems. It also brings forward the exchanges that the system will have to carry out with these, and acts as a support to the capture of the non-functional constraints to be taken into account.

It is essential to limit the functional analysis conducted in SA to the sole capture of the need, and only of need, excluding any implementation choice or details. This allows freedom of choice to be maintained during the subsequent development of the solution, and to maintaining the dialogue with customers by means of focusing them on their needs (in conjunction with the OA).

The main activities to be undertaken for the SA are the following:

– perform a capability trade-off analysis;

– perform a functional and a non-functional needs analysis;

– formalize and consolidate the expression of system needs.

6.2. Performing a capability compromise analysis

This analysis is intended to define the essential characteristics necessary for the fulfillment of each operational capability (the problem space), to uncover different alternative orientations likely to satisfy these required capabilities as well as the criteria for associated appreciation and choice (the solution space), and to compare these orientations to find the one(s) exhibiting the best compromise between the desirable characteristics. Similarly to the OA, it is preferable that it be established in cooperation with the customer and end-users (if not by themselves), and that at least it receives final approval from the client.

The first step consists of identifying deviations between the required operational capabilities and existing means, systems, resources, processes, practices, etc.

It is also an opportunity to show the major parameters able to support or hinder the effective implementation of each capability. These parameters may concern the functional contribution and the expected performance of the system, obviously, but much further: organization, doctrines, procedures and users' roles, human factors, skills and training, logistics footprint and deployment conditions, hosting facilities, etc. Quantitative and qualitative metrics should be defined to evaluate the satisfaction conditions for each of these parameters.

EXAMPLE.– *For instance, the analysis of existing systems could show that there are manual and automatic level crossings; for a manual crossing, a manual barrier mechanism triggered by operators can be devised, and for an automatic one, it can be completely autonomous or controlled by human agents who explicitly validate the interruption/authorization conditions of the traffic. A first choice thus has to be made.*

Assuming that operation supervised by operators is preferred, the analysis of the task of the traffic control authority described in the OA should indicate that here again several alternatives are possible: the operators can directly monitor the traffic through visual contact, and in this case, this monitoring requires no functionality or capacity from the system or any action upon it. Nonetheless, depending on available infrastructures, the location of the operators may not allow them to have a direct view of the level crossing; in this case, it may be necessary to provide them, through the system itself, with a visualization of the status of the crossing and the traffic.

Similarly, an analysis of human factors could result in choosing – depending on the availability and the workload of the operators, and on their qualification – either a simple visualization of the status of the traffic and of the instructions generated by the system, or support for the detection of emergency or dangerous situations, or adequate training and education. This naturally calls for additional system functionality, just as the logistics and the action level of maintenance operators, who may or may not require capabilities from the system for monitoring the correct functioning, for locating faults, for example.

Also assume that the customer asks for a safety requirement such as "a road vehicle should not be able to drive on the track if transiting is prohibited". Most often, barriers indicate transit prohibition for road vehicles, but they do not constitute a real obstacle to the crossing, capable of ensuring the physical blocking of vehicles, which seems compulsory to satisfy the requirement. On the other hand, this results in the need for an emergency opening device for the crossing protection device, should a vehicle be blocked on the track, and in potentially stopping the train arriving. These additional features should be taken into account in the functional analysis of this alternative.

Further expanding this alternative for security reasons, another issue that may arise relates to an imposed and controllable emergency stop for trains on departure as well as on arrival (e.g. by way of shutting the power down). This requires a new feature – and thus would incur additional costs – but enables certain situations to be secured, such as that where a road vehicle would be stopped and blocked on the track.

It can be seen here how capability analysis takes into account considerations much more general than the mere functional issues: namely, and in particular, the client organization, organizational operating principles, roles and responsibilities, nature and infrastructure capacity, safety, human factors and users' skills/training, logistics, acquisition and operation costs, but also the potential complexity and implementational risks.

Based on the OA and the required capabilities previously identified, the second step yields a number of alternative policy orientations capable of responding thereto. *The approach leading to the emergence of alternatives, although essential, falls however outside the scope of this book and will not be discussed here.*

EXAMPLE.– *In the example of hanging a mirror on the wall, alternatives to be considered will be power drill, hole and dowels, a self-drilling head and a hammer, or adhesive hooks, contact cement, double-sided adhesive, etc.*

For the control system of the traffic in the vicinity of the level crossing, a remote-controlled but manual solution may be retained, for example, which requires qualified and trained staff, but with a moderate acquisition cost; an all-automated but supervised operation for cost issues; and another uncontrolled one, which in order to maintain the safety level would impose the possibility of emergency stop in trains and prevent crossing.

Finally, these alternatives are evaluated against each of the parameters mentioned previously (let us recall those previously cited, for example the client organization, organizational operating principles, roles and responsibilities, infrastructure nature and capacity, safety, human factors and users' skills/training, logistics, acquisition and operating costs, potential complexity and implementation risks) in a parametric analysis, and the best compromise is sought after to find the directions to prioritize.

EXAMPLE.– *In case the capability of removing the mirror is imperative, a drill and a dowel, or an adhesive hook will be the preferred solutions depending on the weight of the mirror (another capability aspect).*

In the following text, we will preferentially consider, regarding the safety of the level crossing, the following compromise:

– the system is not controlled (it autonomously decides and applies control decisions);

– but the system is supervised (operators monitor the situation from a distance and are able to access an emergency stop);

– it includes automatic emergency stop in trains and transit prevention;

This choice prioritizes safety, but also the total cost of ownership by reducing requirements for supervisory staff, who is no longer in the critical loop of security.

NOTE.– *Only the most promising alternative(s) will be subjected to the functional analysis that follows, and it is normal that in each perspective, a certain number of them will be eliminated after evaluation and comparison. However, it is recommended to not be too hasty in eliminating an alternative, and to consider it as long as it does not present any prohibitive character compared to all of the assessment criteria.*

This observation applies to all perspectives mentioned in this book. The rest of the process will nevertheless be described for a single alternative, for reasons of simplicity.

However, it is advised that Chapter 23 (section 23.1) be referred to in addition to section 23.2 for some details about the predisposition of models to this support.

6.3. Performing a functional and non-functional needs analysis[1]

The intent is to formalize the functional needs allocated to the system, and to identify constraints, namely non-functional, to which it will have to respond through its use under operational conditions.

The development process is that of a functional analysis. Only a few specific concerns that have to be accounted for are mentioned here, without prejudging to their order of execution.

When an OA has been carried out, the natural approach first consists of defining the real actors, which the system should be interacting with. These may be key players defined in the OA, or new players, operators, external systems with which it will have to interact, etc.

EXAMPLE.– *In the case of the traffic regulation close to the crossing, previously defined operational entities and actors will globally remain unchanged (vehicles, departing or arriving trains), but the traffic control authority will be replaced by operators responsible for its implementation, and more specifically, the station will be replaced by its information system that delivers timetables and train movements.*

It should be noted that, implicitly, this actor named "station information system" also includes the operators of this information system (they are the ones, for example, who decide and launch a departure procedure, even if in our system they do it through the station information system).

The next step (or in parallel) will assess the operational capabilities to which the system will have to contribute, taking the preliminary capability trade-off analysis into account. Each of these system capabilities is linked by a justification link to each operational capability to which it contributes.

EXAMPLE.– *With regard to the operational capabilities defined previously, system capabilities could in particular be:*

– secure train departure, which could involve more basic capabilities such as managing and controlling train departure traffic, and managing and controlling road vehicle traffic;

– secure train arrival, which will also involve managing and controlling road vehicle traffic, and also managing and controlling the train arrival traffic;

– detect and secure a vehicle stopped on the track, which will itself make use of previous basic capabilities, etc.

---

1 The recommended approach is described in Chapter 4.

For each of these capabilities (that we will call "system capability"), the operational activities assigned to system users are analyzed, and for each activity, functions that will be the responsibility of system users (or operators) or of external actors are defined, and others that will be assigned to the system. The resulting interactions are defined by functional exchanges between these functions. The main data manipulated by the system and its users are also formalized at this point, and contribute in clarifying functional exchanges.

EXAMPLE.– *Thus, the operational activity "analyze possible collision risks" will result in three functions expected of the system – supervise the departure procedure, supervise the arrival procedure, verify the absence of vehicle onto the crossing – as well as additional functions destined to secure the control and to deliver information requested by operators (rather than the direct observation by these operators): in particular, detect the arrival of the train, detect crossing by the train leaving (or arriving).*

These functions are the result of the capability choices and compromises made earlier about the level of automation and security; this is the reason why they do not appear in the OA.

Similarly, for very general operational activities such as allow/delay the departure of the train, stop/allow road traffic, the functions expected of the system will be more specific: signal departure permission to the train/signal departure prohibition to the train, stop/release vehicle traffic.

They also specify what the system or external actors/operators are responsible for: for example, signaling the train departure could be performed by the conductor or the head of station, but it was decided that the system would implement it via the function: signal departure permission to the train.

The functions allocated to other actors remain in this case similar to operational activities, because the introduction of the system does not alter their general behavior.

Functional exchanges are added to characterize the expected inputs and outputs of every function. Figure 6.1 gives a preview of these functions and exchanges for the train departure procedure.

In Figure 6.1, the perimeter of the system is shown in mid-blue, external actors in light blue and the functions allocated to each one in green.

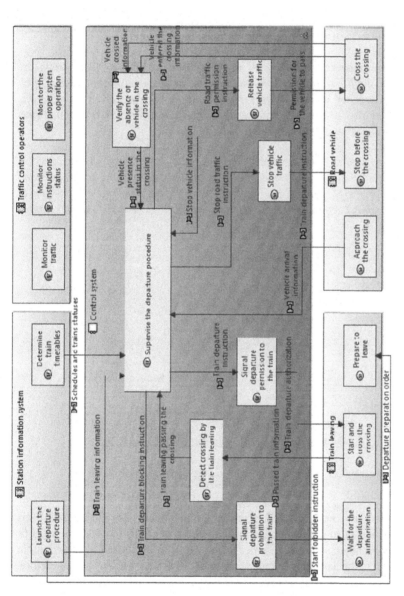

Figure 6.1. *Control and command of a train departure*

It is important to note that the emergence of the functions is not merely a simple refinement of operational activities: the object is a different analysis, in which, for example, several operational activities can result in the same system function, and system needs functions may appear without necessarily corresponding to an operational activity (self-tests or reconfigurations, for example).

EXAMPLE.– *Supervision functions are required of the system, such as: summarize the traffic status, collect instructions/system operational status, stop trains in an emergency or shut down the power supply in case of emergency; this need is not identified in the OA, because they are designed to address constraints and security policies chosen during the capability analysis.*

It should be noted that the function "shut down the power supply in emergency", responds and contributes to both operational activities "delay train departure" and "stop the train arriving". Finally, also note that one of these functions – stop trains in an emergency – has been added to the operators' actor, because the action requires his intervention.

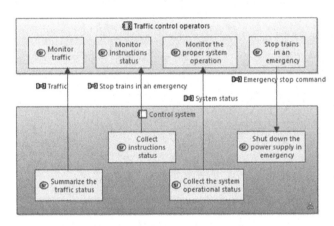

Figure 6.2. *Traffic and system monitoring needs functions*

Recall that only needs-related considerations should be included in this perspective dedicated to the expression of the system needs as required by users or clients, excluding any choice of design or refinements not requested by the client, in order to preserve the largest flexibility possible of design further on. Therefore, certain choices delegated to the provider are not addressed here, but will have to be considered in the perspectives dedicated to the solution.

EXAMPLE.– *For example, the client imposes no special procedures in monitoring functions (operating mode, data source, etc.); therefore, they are not connected to information sources at this stage of the analysis (which could be command functions issuing instructions, or detection functions separated from the previous ones, for instance). The nature of the data exchanged in this context is also not specified for the same reasons.*

Similarly, if the client does not enforce any mechanism to signal instructions to trains and vehicles (traffic lights, obstacles, etc.), it is recommended to not mention them at this point, and thereby neither the more accurate nature of exchanges with external actors, trains and vehicles.

As described in Chapter 4 (section 4.2), several approaches are possible to develop this analysis. In a large number of cases, we will obtain a set of basic functions connected by exchanges. In order to constitute synthesis views, these functions will be grouped into higher level functions (parent functions), and the exchanges will be grouped by categories.

EXAMPLE.– *The functions previously developed are grouped into new parent functions according to the hierarchy described in Figure 4.5. This allows us to provide a simplified view of the system needs, such as the view shown in Figure 6.3.*

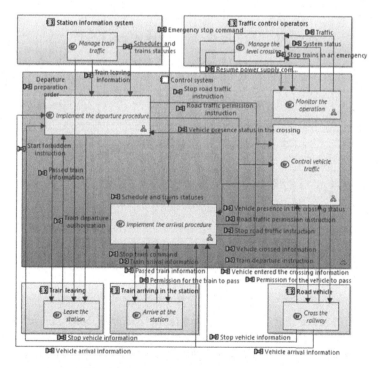

Figure 6.3. *Overview of system functions*

Similarly, exchanges are grouped into categories: for example, the category "road traffic management instructions" includes "road traffic stop/authorization instructions" and the category "vehicle status" includes "arrival/stop vehicle information exchanges", and "crossing/crossed vehicle information". This simplifies the previous figure, as shown in Figure 6.4, which only shows the exchange categories (thick arrows indicated by Cat).

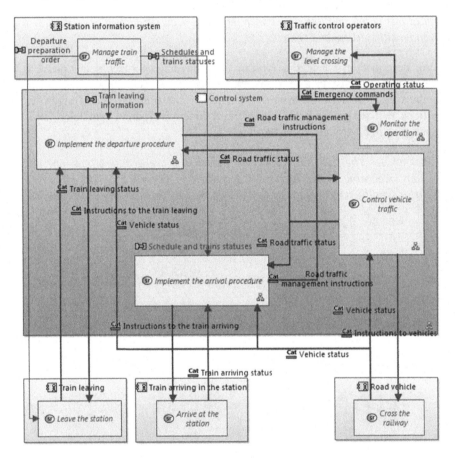

Figure 6.4. *Overview of system exchanges categories and functions*

To simplify even further, it is possible to combine both parent functions "implement the departure/arrival procedure" into a single "grandparent" function "manage train movements". A very high level view of the system needs is obtained, which also underlines the context of interactions with external stakeholders.

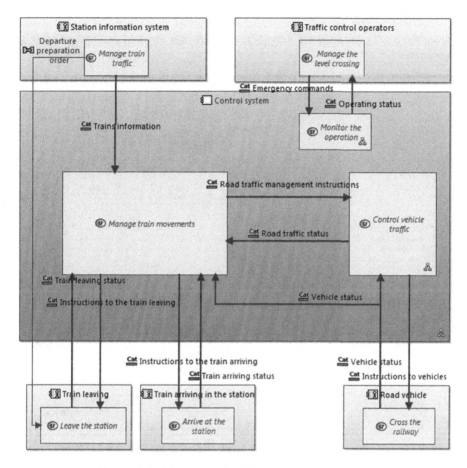

Figure 6.5. *System needs high-level contextual view*

Operational scenarios and processes defined in the OA are also included, to define scenarios between the system and its environment, as well as functional chains traversing the system. These scenarios and functional chains will define the content of the retained system capabilities, and enable a first level of verification and consolidation of the SA, especially to verify that functions and exchanges defined so far are sufficient and adapted to the scope of application of the system thus defined; this often leads to adding missing functional exchanges, to modifying or adding functions, etc.

EXAMPLE.– *The operational scenario presented in Figure 5.4 is expressed, during the SA, by the scenario hereafter, which brings forward the expected role of the system.*

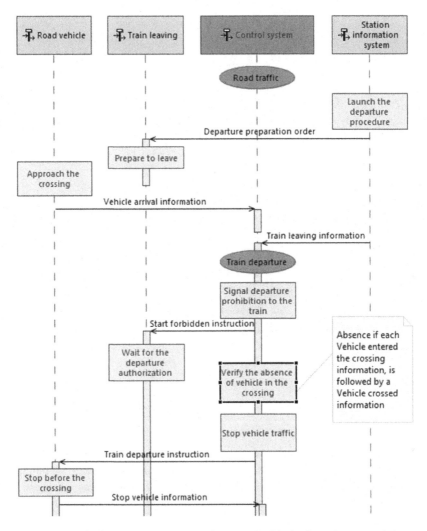

Figure 6.6. *System needs scenario – nominal train departure – part 1*

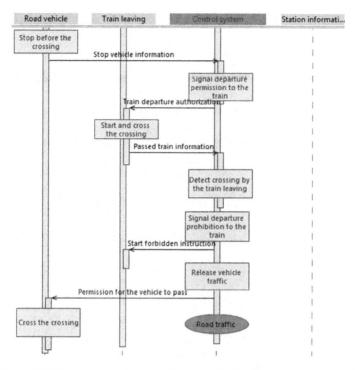

Figure 6.7. *System needs scenario – nominal train departure – part 2*

It is also sometimes helpful to detail the interactions between system functions over time, such as presented in the following scenario, in which lifelines (vertical) no longer represent the system and actors, as in the previous scenario, but functions.

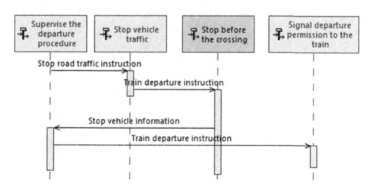

Figure 6.8. *Road traffic stop operational scenario (partial)*

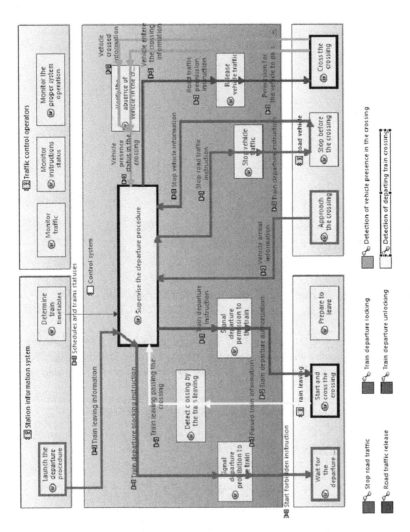

Figure 6.9. *Train departure functional chains*

The operational process described in Figure 5.6 is also traced within the context of system analysis (see Figure 6.9); it is simply divided here into several functional chains, which will also be used to define the testing and integration strategy. The colored paths are the functional chains; the functions inside a black border are those traversed by several functional chains.

The functional chain "stop road traffic" (Figure 6.10) is divided into vehicle actor (functions in blue) and system itself (green functions).

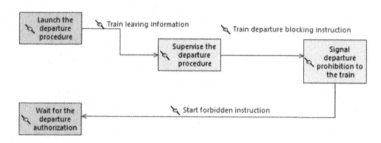

Figure 6.10. *Blocking departing train functional chain*

A global functional chain, covering the scope addressed by the priority train departure operational process can also be restored by way of assembling the previous chains. In Figure 6.11, elementary chains are assembled by links expressing which terminal function in one is the starting function of the other (the link has the name of this function).

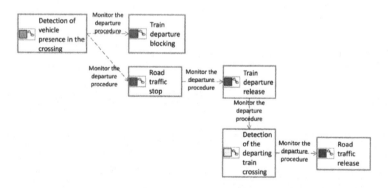

Figure 6.11. *Assembly-based train departure functional chain*

In Figure 6.12, the functional chain is described verbatim. It can be seen how the choices of functional allocation to the system have enriched it compared to the version that is described in the OA. The functions allocated to the system are in green; the actor functions in blue.

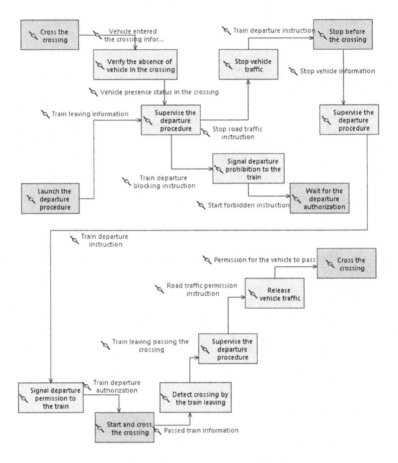

Figure 6.12. *Verbatim train departure functional chain*

The system states and modes planned or desired by the client are also formalized, with the functions whose availability they will govern, and events (functional exchanges in particular) that will be able to trigger the switch from one mode or state to another.

EXAMPLE.– *The modes described in the OA for the mission concerning the traffic in the vicinity of the level crossing remain unchanged in the SA, because they appear as prevailing regardless of the contribution expected from the system. However, they must be considered from its viewpoint. Therefore, it is necessary to add an emergency stop mode, which will be triggered by an emergency stop signal from the operators.*

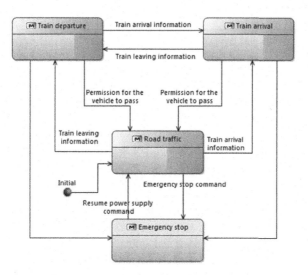

Figure 6.13. *Expected system modes*

Nonetheless, the review of the mode machine shows that it is also necessary to define a condition to exit this mode, which leads to adding two functions: Unlock the trains after an emergency stop, for the operators, and Re-establish the power supply to trains, for the system, as well as a Power supply restoring command functional exchange (Figure 6.14).

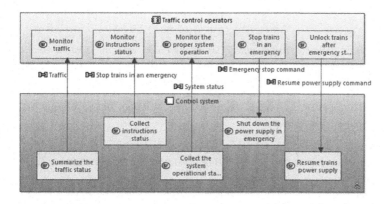

Figure 6.14. *Supplement to traffic and system monitoring, following the definition of the modes expected from the system*

In the event that actors or external systems are imposed by the client (or the state of the art) and exhibit a complex or critical level of interactions with the system, it is recommended to carry out minimal functional and non-functional analyses for these external systems or actors, and to compare them with the SA, to ensure the compatibility between the two.

At this point, an analysis of available interfaces is desirable, to verify that planned functionalities and interactions will be possible. It will be possible to define the main data exchanged, as well as actual exchanges and interfaces, and the nature of the physical links to be used (more details are given later in the book, and especially in perspectives of architecture, see Chapter 7, section 7.4). Some critical data, which can be complex or whose content needs to be discussed with the client, can be defined as early as in the SA. Otherwise, they will be at least included in the physical architecture.

EXAMPLE.– *Exchanged data and their structuring about the system for controlling the level crossing will be defined in the logical architecture below (refer thereto). For now, we will just describe them using the name of the functional exchanges that transmit them (schedules and train status; departing train information). An analysis of the information needed for the system functions making use of this information will be carried out in the logical or physical architecture depending on the case.*

We will here limit ourselves to identify actual means of communication between the control system and the information system of the station. According to the functional analysis, this interface should provide the system schedules and train statuses, in addition to the information about the train leaving.

Several additional model elements will be defined for this purpose (see Figure 6.15):

– a behavioral exchange (blue) is defined between the system and the actor (named train schedule service); it includes in particular the constraints and conditions of the transmission (e.g. an RSS stream over HTTP);

– this exchange will transmit the data (the exchange item) actually provided by the actor (train schedule update);

– a physical link (red), expressing the communication medium required to obtain this information, is created (representing, for example, a Wi-Fi network).

It may come as a surprise that this interface is addressed in detail as part of the needs analysis phase and not during the construction of the solution. In reality, the aim here is only to attempt to capture the constraints imposed on the system, and to verify at the earliest that the knowledge about the needs is compatible with these constraints. For example, the nature of connections and associated protocols is mentioned here, because customer requirements explicitly mention them, and it is important that their acceptability be verified at this early stage. However, note that it would be also possible and legitimate to prefer that these details be captured in the logical or physical architecture, even if this is done in anticipation from the need analysis phase.

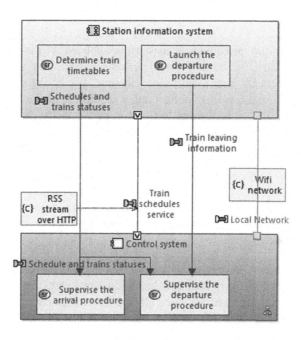

Figure 6.15. *Interface with the station information system*

Traceability and justification links are established during all this work, between elements of the SA and OA: for example, between activities and functions (system, operator) that support them, between operational processes and functional chains, between capacities and between scenarios of both.

When user or customer requirements are available, another way to address the needs functional analysis consists of implementing each functional requirement into a few functions and exchanges between them (often the verbs of the requirement), the manipulated data (the names) and actors or external systems. At each new requirement being considered, a search for functions, data and exchanges already defined is carried out, allowing at the same time to simplify the resulting model, but also and especially to highlight dependencies between requirements, and to verify their consistency and completeness.

As in the previous case, justification and traceability links are established between the model elements thus created and the requirements from which they originate.

Naturally, this approach is not exclusive to the one based on the OA, both can be achieved jointly and improve each other.

***

Non-functional and performance constraints applying to the system must be identified at this stage, in addition to the elements of functional analysis to which they apply (a functional chain constrained in time, the operator load caused by allocated functions, the level of confidentiality of data, safety and security feared events and the chains or exchanges likely to generate them, etc.). Similarly, the metrics previously defined should be allocated to prior analysis elements.

6.4. Formalizing and consolidating the expression of system needs

The good understanding and consolidation of system needs rely on the three dimensions mentioned earlier, which are the OA, requirements and the functional analysis of the system need.

It is through their comparison that consistency and completeness of the system need is assured: Are all activities and operational processes correctly taken into account in the functional analysis? Are all functional requirements (or even non-functional) correctly captured? Is there any incompatibility between them?

It may even be the case that the functional needs analysis results in modifying the OA (e.g. changing an operator role for a more secure behavior, or reviewing the distribution of roles should an opportunity for system automation emerge); or alternatively, that the functional analysis reveals an inconsistency or something missing in the requirements.

The constitution and updating of links between OA, functional analysis of the system needs and requirements, is consequently very important: on the one hand, they allow the system functional analysis to be justified, and its consistency to be verified with the two other dimensions, including in the event of changes in any of them. On the other hand, they constitute the basis for impact analyses that will make use of the model during design phases. For example, if a functional requirement is complex or difficult to achieve, the negotiation with the client will be easier when considering the operational issues of this requirement, and therefore when assessing its real scope and its criticality.

It is also recommended to define priorities, significance or criticality levels for the elements of the functional analysis of need as for the requirements, in order to guide choices and subsequent compromises through a value analysis. The links with the OA can also be useful in this context to evaluate the real operational contribution of such requirement, or of such function required of the system.

***

The previous work of consolidation of functional analysis is essential, because it formalizes and summarizes large part of system needs, and constitutes, as we will see, the pivot point of the shift to the solution and its justification.

In fact, in Arcadia, functional needs analysis replaces all the requirements that can be correctly represented in the model, because it is more formal, less ambiguous, likely to be automatically analyzed and to some extent verifiable by the construction approach described here.

Accordingly, customer or user requirements, when they form the main vector for expressing need, are preserved as such and linked to the model traceability links. System requirements, resulting from the analysis of client needs, are expressed by the model, except those that cannot be properly represented through this means (such as regulatory, environment requirements, etc.). Therefore, system requirements are not rewritten based on the model, to reformulate it in text form, as it would introduce new ambiguities, without added value but not without effort, and along with a risk of inconsistency, growing with changes in the need.

***

Regardless of how thorough the previous securing of needs has been, its feasibility however cannot be guaranteed so far. In order to analyze this feasibility in a proactive manner, we must be able to project the constituted needs onto a foreshadowing of what will be the possible architecture and analyze the projection conditions of the need according to the most significant risks.

This foreshadowing is achieved by following a similar approach to the one described in the next chapters for the construction of the solution, but specifically focusing on more complex or risky subsets, functionalities, performance, etc., and limited to the level of detail required to address the identified risks (the premises of a logical architecture are in most cases sufficient).

In cases where feasibility cannot be established, the requirements must be reconsidered and renegotiated, based for the associated impact analysis on the traceability links established in the model and with the requirements.

6.5. Summary

The SA perspective defines the expectations of the system, that is to say what the system has to perform for users: it builds an external functional analysis, based on the OA and input textual requirements, to identify in response functions, services and expected system behaviors, necessary to its users.

The SA is intended to exclusively capture the system needs, excluding any early solution design. The need is consolidated based on the triptych comprising textual requirements, the OA and the SA, which formalizes most requirements to which the solution design will have to respond.

The main activities to be undertaken in the SA are the following:

– perform a capability compromise analysis;

– perform a functional and a non-functional needs analysis;

– formalize and consolidate the expression of system needs.

6.6. Exercise

SA of the door is shown in Figure 6.16.

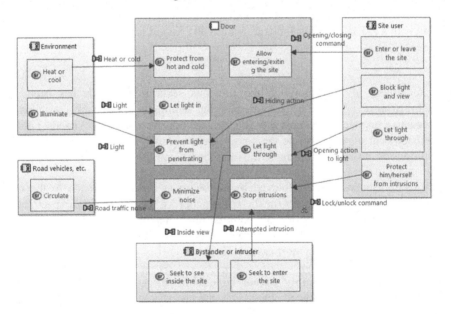

Figure 6.16. *SA of the door*

7

Definition of the Principle Architecture or Logical Architecture

7.1. Principles

The principle architecture, commonly called logical architecture (subsequently abbreviated as LA), implements the big decisions of the solution, in terms of principles of construction, and ways to fulfill the expectations of stakeholders; it is then formalized by means of a decomposition into abstract components, namely principles of behavior and interaction between one another, in response to the previous needs.

The definition of the LA (an activity often – and wrongly – designated "logical architecture" for convenience) consists mainly of a comparison between the needs expressed in previous perspectives, a functional analysis describing the system behavior chosen to satisfy requirements, and a structural analysis intended to identify the components that will constitute the system, taking the chosen constraints and structuring principles into account.

The LA is therefore a first general vision, moderately detailed, somehow an abstraction, of what the architecture of the system will be (described in detail in Chapter 8).

Its definition is deliberately maintained at a quite coarse-grained level of detail, just enough to be able to make major decisions for guiding the design, nothing more. Any design detail or accuracy that does not influence the construction or choice decisions of the LA is not justified and will be described later in the physical architecture.

All the figures in this book are available to view in color at: www.iste.co.uk/voirin/arcadia.zip.

This makes it possible to hide the complexity of the solution, in order to reason about a level of abstraction that can easily be understood and manipulated by the different actors to which it will be submitted; these can be, for example, needs analysts; marketing, business services and product line managers; specialty engineers, etc., who do not need to go into much detail to make a decision about the important choices that govern the design of the LA.

Other reasons justify the interest of a first solution architecture level: first, it is easier and less expensive to define several alternatives of potential solutions and compare them, without leaving this level of abstraction, which allows non-viable solutions to be eliminated at an early stage. It then offers the possibility to hide variabilities that are not of primary importance, considering that at this level of abstraction several variants may have a common description (which can also make the LA stable against changes in the implementation technology, for example). On the other hand, we will see that it constitutes a major reconciliation place when we reuse an existing one to satisfy a new need (Chapter 15, section 15.4.3).

***

The main activities to be undertaken for the definition of the logical principle architecture are as follows:

– to define the factors impacting the architecture and analysis viewpoints;

– to define the principles underlying the system behavior;

– to build component-based system structuring alternatives;

– to select the architecture alternative offering the best compromise.

7.2. Definition of the factors impacting the architecture and analysis viewpoints

Any properly designed architecture satisfies a number of expectations and constraints of various kinds, which constrain and influence or even direct its definition, and whose satisfaction should be verified as early as possible to minimize possible subsequent resumption costs.

These factors that constrain the architecture depend largely on each domain, and each profession. As examples we mention: delivered services and costs of course, expected performance, safety of operations, privacy, ease of maintenance, life duration, energy or logistical footprint, availability, product policy, scalability, but also more "aesthetic" considerations such as customer satisfaction.

EXAMPLE.– *In the case of the traffic control system, the first impact factor is obviously the safety of goods and people. An additional factor involves system operators, their training and their required skills, the scope of their responsibility and the role that must be assigned to them. We should also take into account factors such as environmental conditions, life duration, constraints on logistics and maintenance.*

For each factor previously identified, the associated constraints (especially non-functional and performance ones), which can be applied to the needs and the solution, must be expressed and quantified by metrics; each candidate architecture will be analyzed according to this viewpoint, to verify that good practice is correctly followed. This approach is described in more detail, although from the modeling perspective only, in Chapter 10.

EXAMPLE.– *In the case of the traffic control system, let us mention the required reliability rate and the system failure probability, the capability to be able to operate in the event of partial failure of certain subsystems; the maximal eligible number of operators; extreme temperature ranges, humidity, resistance to possible salt sprays; etc.*

***

In addition to the identification of the major "imposed" factors constraining the definition of the architecture, the major design decisions structuring it must also be defined and formalized. These decisions reflect know-how, the craft, in addition to the creativity of the engineering team, and will guide the emergence of different alternatives as well as their comparison.

These may concern styles of architectures (centralized or distributed, federated or integrated, for example), predefined "templates" or "patterns" applicable in several places in the architecture (safety barriers, majority vote or redundant critical parts, or still behaviors, mechanisms and conventional processes of the state of the art) and construction criteria (functional grouping or segregation) in particular.

EXAMPLE.– *A few principles that can govern the design of our system are as follows:*

– the safety management carried out by the system must be separated from the rest of the command control to minimize common modes among them;

– given the time required for a train to stop, it is imperative to physically prevent any vehicle intrusion on the track from the moment the train has exceeded the ultimate braking stopping point. This also makes it possible to simplify the security analysis and associated solutions (to avoid having to provide an emergency evacuation solution for a vehicle on the track, for example);

– road and rail facilities should be clearly separated, for reasons of standardization constraints (because many of them abide by separate standards and certification authorities);

– in a nominal situation, the system should work independently, without needing the intervention of operators, so as to minimize their number and workload, as well as their responsibility;

– in case of emergency, stopping the traffic and securing it can be automatically implemented by the system, to secure any human failings;

– however, only operators will be responsible for resuming power supply to trains and for traffic resumption, to limit safety constraints induced on the system and related legal constraints.

Imposed factors and design choices must be categorized by importance or priority, in order to be able to arbitrate between them when they result in antagonistic properties, or when certain constraints will have to be released to find an acceptable compromise.

It should be noted that the previous elements may also affect the behavior as well as the structuring of the solution.

7.3. Definition of the behavior principles of the system[1]

The objective is to formalize the principles of the desired behavior of the system, and to take into account the constraints, namely non-functional, to which it has the responsibility to respond during its operation under operational conditions.

The development approach is that of functional analysis. Only a few specific concerns that have to be accounted for are mentioned here, without prejudice to their order of execution.

A common mistake consists of considering the behavior of the solution as a simple refinement of the previous functional expression of need at a finer level of detail. The solution design is much more than that: it is a "creative" definition effort of a behavior that meets the need (and that does not refine it), detailing the processes and steps starting from the solicitations of the system, up to the provision of services, results or outputs, taking into account design decisions, mainly guided by the factors and constraints identified previously.

---

1 The recommended approach is described in Chapter 4.

In the majority of cases, designers do not start from scratch in this task: they have the expertise of mental or concrete schemes of existing partial solutions, of examples borrowed from previously designed systems or from the state of the art and very often also the behavior of existing components, which we have to reuse, even if it means that they have to be adapted.

The first task to be achieved is therefore, starting from each need item previously captured, to identify and formalize these different elements of partial behaviors likely to respond thereto. This is the time where traceability and justification links are initialized between the behavior thus created and the services defined in the system needs analysis (SA). This traceability can be carried out on every type of element of formalized model, functions, exchanges, functional chains, data, scenarios, states, modes, etc., and textual requirements. It is often convenient to start with the definition of the functions describing the basis of the desired behavior (but this is not compulsory).

EXAMPLE.– *Need functions (in the SA) such as "signal departure prohibition to the train" must be satisfied by functions at the LA level (in the LA) indicating the retained type of solution for the signaling, because this is a structuring choice, especially for safety studies; we will therefore create LA functions such as:*

– switch off (respectively, switch on) the signal of train departure, related to the SA function "signal departure prohibition (respectively, permission) to the train";

– switch off (respectively, switch on) the signal to stop the train arriving, as well as switch off (respectively, switch on) the transit signal for the train arriving, related to the SA function "signal to the train unavailable track" (respectively, signal crossing permission to the train).

Note here the choice of separating the transit authorization and stopping instruction functions, which may seem redundant: this is a design decision related to security, because failure of a single signal would have catastrophic effects that justify this redundancy.

The two SA functions "detect crossing by the train leaving" (respectively, arriving) will be described in the LA by three functions: detect the train departure from the platform, detect a train arriving in the distance and detect the train passing the level crossing, direction, track; the latter function is common to both SA functions (and shows that the LA is not a refinement of the SA).

Another functional structuring decision that has to be made in the LA is how to perform the services requested in SA and called "stop (respectively, release) vehicle traffic". To increase the security of blocking, both visual and physical, the design choice will incline to include a traffic light, a visual barrier and a ground device that physically prevent transiting. Hence, the functions created in the LA (and related to previous SA functions) are: switch road signaling to Red (respectively, green ones); activate the visual safety barrier; activate the crossing prevention device.

It should be noted here that each of these last two logical functions responds to the two SA functions.

Design choices also lead to responding to the SA function "Verify the absence of vehicle in the crossing", through two separate functions: detect a vehicle accessing the track and detect the vehicle exiting the track (this is thus a choice in favor of the detection of dynamic motion rather than the detection of a static presence).

Another functional design choice is the will to improve the fluidity of road traffic, to anticipate traffic jams, and for this purpose to add functions for the observation of traffic approaching the crossing, the functions "detect approaching vehicles" and "Detect length of vehicle queue" are also added to this end.

***

The SA need function "supervise the departure procedure" is carried out by several functions in the LA: launch a departure procedure (or not), supervise delayed departure, monitor the nominal starting procedure, to which two functions – stop (respectively, release) road traffic – have to be added.

The function "supervise the arrival procedure" is performed in a similar way, but then again, it shares with the departure procedure the functions "stop (respectively, release) road traffic".

***

Functions related to safety, which respond to the SA function "monitor the operation", are designed to work independently of the traffic control itself:

– three main functions are defined: detect conflicting accesses to the crossing; detect and secure a vehicle stopped on the track; test the proper operation of the system;

– in order to verify the operation of the system, they must resort to functions, specific to the SA, for verifying the state of the various bodies (whose generic name is "verify the state of ..."). These functions, like all the previous ones, must be related to the SA functions by way of traceability and justification links;

– an emergency train stop function "shut down the power supply to trains" is also added, following security analyses.

***

Finally, the LA must remain at a description level just sufficient to highlight previous major design choices, but with no further detail. For example, at this level we will decide to merely describe the interaction of the system with operators by way of direct exchanges between processing functions and operators (see Figure 7.1). It is only in the physical architecture that human–system interfacing functions will appear, at the time when they will be subjected to allocation to physical components.

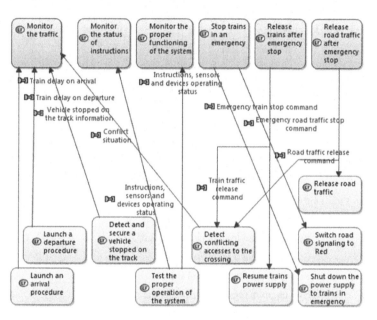

Figure 7.1. *Logical architecture interface operators*

Had the functional analysis approach followed not been top-down (through successive decompositions) but yielded a number of basic functions, then it would have proved helpful to structure these features to build a synthetic view of the behavior thus defined (this is then considered as a bottom-up functional grouping approach).

Here again, it should be noted that there is no compulsory requirement to structure LA functions in the same manner as in the SA: these behaviors can satisfy different criteria, for example more related to areas of responsibility, non-functional constraints (security, for instance), etc.

EXAMPLE.– *A possible functional hierarchical tree in the LA is presented in Table 7.1.*

Control rail and road traffic
    Control the power supply to trains
        Shut down the power supply to trains in an emergency
        Resume trains power supply
    Detect conflicting accesses to the crossing
    Detect and secure a vehicle stopped on the track
    Ensure the proper functioning of the system
Control vehicles crossing
    Control road traffic.
        Release road traffic.
        Stop road traffic.
    Control road devices
        Activate the visual safety barrier
        Activate the crossing prevention device
        Switch road signaling to red
        Switch road signaling to green
Control train movements
    Switch off the arriving train stop signal
    Switch off the train departure signal
    Switch off the train arrival signal
    Switch on the train arrival signal
    Switch on the train departure signal
    Switch on the arriving train stop signal
Control the road traffic status
    Detect vehicles stops before the barrier
    Detect length of vehicles queue
    Detect approaching vehicles
Implement the arrival procedure
    Launch the arrival procedure
    Monitor the nominal arrival procedure
    Supervise delayed arrival
Implement the departure procedure
    Launch the departure procedure
    Monitor the nominal departure procedure
    Supervise delayed departure

Verify the status of devices
Verify the status of road devices
Verify the status of barriers and devices
Verify the status of vehicle detectors
Verify the status of traffic lights
Verify the status of rail track devices
Verify the status of train emergency stop commands
Verify the status of train detectors
Verify the status of vehicle on the track detectors
Verify the status of train signals
Control movements on the track
Detect a vehicle accessing the track
Detect the vehicle exiting the track
Detect the train departure from the platform
Detect the train passing the level crossing, direction, track
Detect a train arriving in the distance

Table 7.1. *Functional tree hierarchical structure in the logical architecture*

Unlike the essentially functional organization of SA, in the present case in the LA, the organization criteria of functions are diverse: separate rail from road traffic (as in SA), but also separate control functions from regulation ones; group all movements on the track, whether road or rail vehicles; group the verification functions of devices status, regardless of what they may be, but separate them from monitoring and testing functions that make use of them; etc.

This organization also achieved on functional exchanges by grouping them into categories, then allows that a high-level, synthetic view of the design be provided (Figure 7.2).

Naturally, functional dependencies between previously identified functions and associated functional exchanges must benefit from the same type of design thinking process, by responding to need elements originating from the SA. At any time, each function created must be analyzed as such, through several considerations.

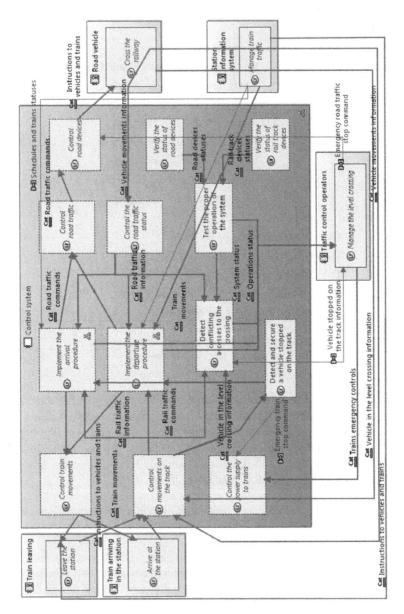

Figure 7.2. *Logical architecture functional synthetic view*

We initially consider the functions and requirements of the SA to which it is connected through traceability links, in order to verify that it properly satisfies some of the need of each function or requirement under consideration, and to make sure that the contribution that is expected thereof is correctly identified. Symmetrically, we will verify that every system needs function or requirement is properly integrally taken into account by the functions defined in the LA related thereto.

The next step is to search for a possible function already defined in the LA, which could also play the role of the function considered, rather than creating a new one or to have defined two similar ones; this makes it possible to minimize the number of defined functions, to maximize the genericity and to greatly simplify the model.

Finally, we verify or define which inputs this function needs to achieve what is expected of it; where these inputs can come from; what the function can and must provide and to whom; this results in creating, reusing or modifying functional exchanges also inherent to the LA.

We will also determine where will its complexity reside, what is its content (subfunctions, requirements), which non-functional constraints it must convey, which genericity it will have to use or bring forward (reuse of already defined functions, implemented common factor), etc.

***

For each scenario and functional chain associated with a capacity identified in the needs analysis (SA), functional chains and scenarios should be defined in the LA, taking those defined in SA into consideration. Traceability links will have to be maintained between them. Additional capacities can also be added to account for needs related to design decisions or to the choice of product line, for example, or in view of structuring integration.

EXAMPLE.– *Therefore, the functional chain described in the SA in Figure 6.12 is repeated and detailed in the LA; an excerpt is indicated hereafter (Figure 7.3).*

In light of the choices made for the preliminary design that the LA enables, the modes and states defined for the system must be revisited, completed and their expectations or impact on the functions defined in the LA determined, as well as the events that govern their transitions.

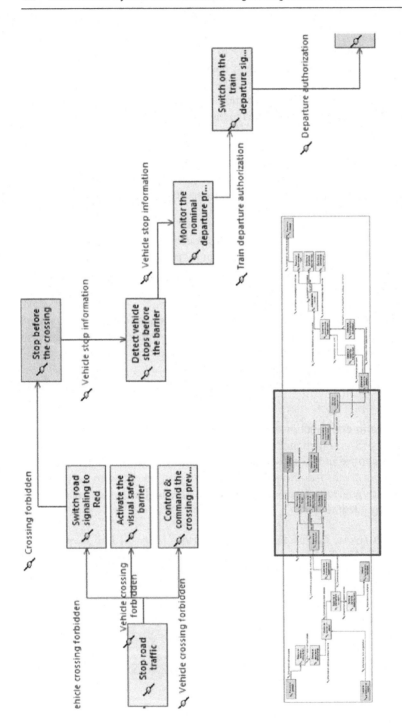

Figure 7.3. *Departure procedure logic functional chain (excerpt)*

EXAMPLE.– *The modes described in the SA overall remain unchanged in the LA in our case of the traffic control system. However, the allocation of functions to each mode is of interest because it raises questions. For example:*

– must we give instructions, switch lights, etc., before exiting the emergency stop mode, or after entering the road traffic mode?

– should the departure or arrival of trains be blocked in addition to shutting down the power in this mode?

These decisions will be manifested according to the functions deemed to be available in this mode or not.

In addition, the conditions of transitions between modes are this time considered in the functional analysis and the design of the LA, and are thus more specific, and differ from those identified in the needs analysis.

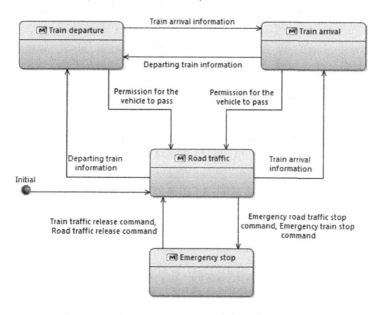

Figure 7.4. *System global modes in the logical architecture*

The next step consists of building a complete and coherent global description using these behavioral elements: to combine them, to assemble them based on their contribution to need, to modify them if necessary and to complete them in order to cover the totality of this need. The traceability with the SA also has to be finalized.

***

Behavior alternatives must also be looked for according to needs and constraints to be satisfied; they must be characterized by their potential properties and metrics and will have to be compared during the selection of the alternative architecture offering the best compromise.

EXAMPLE.– *For example, the definition of the required behavior of the traffic control system reveals various possibilities or alternatives:*

– traffic monitoring can be directly achieved by operators, visually, or by displaying this traffic in operator monitoring stations, based on detections carried out by the system (which is more expensive but allows for more freedom when it comes to the location of the control station);

– similarly, monitoring the status of instructions (open or closed barrier, etc.) by operators can be done by visualizing the associated transmitted commands, or rather by designing detection devices of the status of each instruction, independently of commands, and returning the state observed rather than the command (which is preferable in terms of safety, incurring though higher costs);

– detecting whether a vehicle is present on the track can be achieved by a presence sensor (magnetic loop, for example), but this requires that a road device be installed on the track, which can raise difficulties (responsibilities, maintenance, etc.). Preference will thus be given, as already mentioned earlier, to dynamic motion detection, which requires no installation on the track;

– monitoring the correct functioning of the system should be ensured by the system; however, the responsibility to define whether a failure is critical and if the traffic must be interrupted or not can be assigned to the system incurring very high cost and security constraints, or more probably to operators.

***

It should also be specified that this construction work is iterative and carried out jointly and in interaction with the component-based structuring hereafter.

It is absolutely possible to start by laying out the components (especially when a system or existing components drive the definition of the architecture), and to then directly allocate the required functions in progressive manner.

In addition, the functional analysis may have to be reviewed for each alternative definition of components, for example to split a function that should be distributed between two components, to separate functional data paths to be segregated (for safety or confidentiality reasons, for example), to make functions generic to optimize the architecture, to replicate portions of behavior in redundant chains, etc.

7.4. Construction of component-based system structuring alternatives

This step should reveal a number of principle solutions, describing the preliminary structure of the system, built on the basis of the previous behavior, incorporating both non-functional associated constraints and the factors and design choices underlying it.

The system is broken down into principle components called logical components. The term "component" is understood here in the general sense, as a constituent of the system at this level; it can later be implemented as a subsystem (or several), equipment, one or more mechanical parts or assemblies, one or more electronic cards, a software program itself eventually distributed or even a human contributor. The components will then tend to mainly constitute the base unit for the definition and allocation of development and outsourcing; for the integration, reuse, management of the product line; the management of configuration items; etc. (but other criteria will be taken into account to define the limits of these elements, from the perspective of the physical architecture).

EXAMPLE.– *The components that make up the LA of our traffic control system are presented in Figure 7.5. Rail facilities as well as road facilities comprise traffic detection and signaling components and specific mechanisms (road barriers, train emergency stops); a management system ensures the control of the system and security.*

Logical components are represented in blue, in the same color as the system.

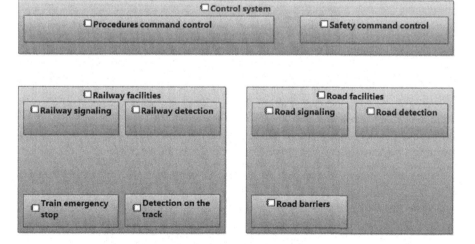

Figure 7.5. *Logical architecture components*

The component building process consists of grouping together or segregating the behavior functions previously defined, according to the constraints and criteria imposed, in grouping sets that thus constitute the components. These latter can themselves be structured by subcomponents, according to the same types of criteria if necessary.

Each viewpoint defined previously is likely to impact this grouping, thus prompting us either into grouping correlated functions according to this viewpoint (functional coherence, strong interaction or complex interfaces, same variability need, etc.), or instead into separating them (functions with different levels of criticality or confidentiality, highly resource consuming functions that have to be distributed, etc.). It is recommended to submit each choice of functional grouping to the multi-viewpoint analysis[2], in order to remove as quickly as possible erroneous groupings according to a major viewpoint. Similarly, because grouping/segregation criteria can be different or even contradictory, all these viewpoints must be confronted to and reconciled with each other; several trade-offs are generally possible, yielding various alternatives of candidate architectures.

EXAMPLE.– *The decomposition criteria of the previously mentioned components are as follows:*

– *the separation of rail and road facilities, because they relate to different authorities, equally in terms of installation, maintenance responsibility and civil responsibility;*

– *the inclusion among railway facilities, however, of means for detecting vehicles on the track, due to issues related to localization and maintenance constraints (such as required traffic stop);*

– *the separation between signaling and traffic detection (common principle systematically applied), both for functional and technological reasons (sensors on one side, actuators on the other), but also to simplify procedures and means of integration (required for stimulation on the one hand, or for the analysis of instructions on the other);*

– *the same choice regarding the separation of "hard" traffic control mechanisms: emergency stops in trains, road barriers, also for segregation reasons for safety purposes, these elements being critical from this viewpoint;*

– *the isolation of the management system, for geographical constraints (it can be positioned elsewhere than close to the tracks), and flexibility in positioning operators workstations;*

---

2 More details are given in Chapter 10.

– the segregation, in two different components within the control station, between the control command of departure and arrival procedures, and safety control, because they have different criticalities and should present no common failure mode.

***

The (preliminary) definition of interfaces between components (or with external actors) can be done at this level (or be postponed until the definition of the physical architecture): they are built based on the functional exchanges linking the functions allocated to these components or actors, and exchanges data (and exchange elements) that these exchanges convey; data and exchanges are mainly grouped according to semantic proximity or usage considerations. The actual exchanges between components are also achieved by way of grouping functional exchanges; combined with the capability to hide subcomponents in order to consider those of first level only, this also constitutes a level of synthesis or even of abstraction able to hide the complexity of functional exchanges, and to reason on several levels of detail.

EXAMPLE.– *Exchanges between components properly synthesize the nature of the interfaces required between them, as shown in Figure 7.6. They are grouped here based on functional proximity criteria (states, detection information, commands, etc.).*

It should be noted that at this stage, it was not deemed practical to define component ports (the white rectangles with a directional arrow here) on aggregating components (control system, rail and road facilities), with possible delegations of any of them, because this does not contribute much to the understanding of the architecture and unnecessarily overloads the model.

The exchanges between components are represented by blue arrows between white component ports.

The component interfaces must follow good practice guidelines that should be defined in advance. In general, the list of interfaces of a component should provide a representative overview of its features and capabilities, a sort of "manual of instructions" of the component; criteria for grouping exchange items should be: facilitate the understanding of how to use the component (main types of services performed, of data available or required, of implementation constraints, etc.); hide the internal complexity of the implementation; be generic enough to be suitable for the largest number of possible usages (and such that it will not be dedicated to a particular type of usage only, for example); etc.

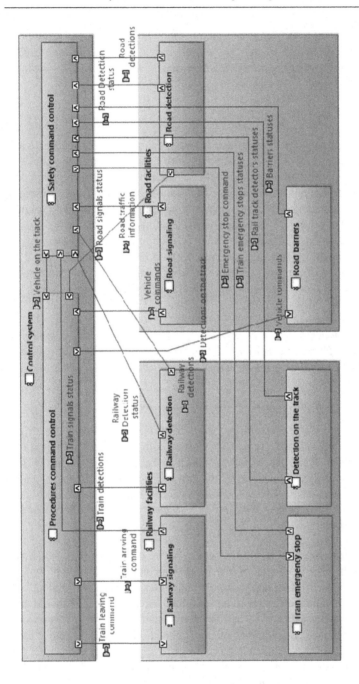

Figure 7.6. *Components and exchanges in the logical architecture*

EXAMPLE.– *Consider the interface between the procedures command control component and the information system of the station. According to the functional analysis, this interface should provide the component with schedules and train statuses, in addition to the information related to the train leaving.*

An analysis of the information needed by the functions of the component making use of this information will lead to define the following types of information:

 – *A train movement will be described by:*

  - *its identifier (train number);*

  - *its planned departure or arrival schedule;*

  - *its estimated departure or arrival schedule (in case of delay);*

  - *its status (on time, delayed or canceled);*

  - *its track number;*

  - *its status at a given time (at the platform or not, ready or not to leave).*

 – *Two lists of train movements, arrivals and departures, will be defined; the movements of trains of each list will be described as mentioned previously.*

A formalization of this information is given in Figure 7.7. Dotted arrows represent the relationship between a list and one of its items; solid arrows are associations, specifying that a planned schedule and an estimated schedule are associated with a train movement, both described by the same type of schedule.

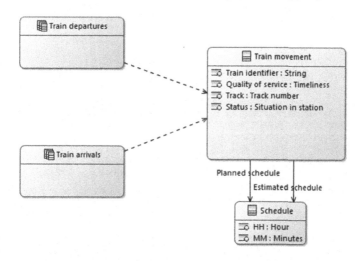

Figure 7.7. *Information about the movement of trains*

In addition to the definition of the information exchanged, it is also necessary to define the conditions of their transmission. The group of information simultaneously transmitted during an exchange is called an exchange item. In this case, two exchange items will be defined:

    – The update of the train schedule, which should simultaneously transmit:

      - the list of train departures;

      - the list of train arrivals;

      - the publication time of the information;

      - the time of the next publication.

    – The information related to the train leaving, in this case train movement information for the train under consideration.

Figure 7.8 illustrates these groupings. The rectangles are exchange items; dotted links are links reflecting what constitutes an exchange item.

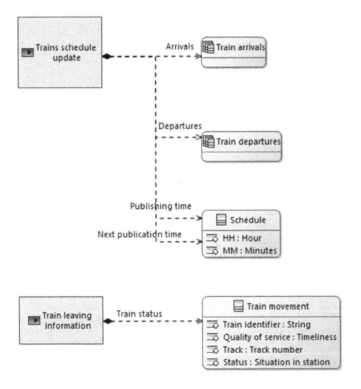

Figure 7.8. *Exchange items of the movement of trains*

These items remain to be linked to the functional analysis conducted so far:

– the functional exchange "schedules and train statuses" will convey the exchange item "train schedule update";

– for its part, the functional exchange "departing train information" will convey the exchange item: train leaving information.

The consistency of this expressed interaction need still has to be verified, with the actual information provided by the information system of the station (external actor); the set of interface constraints that an existing external system can impose on our system or component also remains to be implemented, as well as their real provision conditions as they were imposed. For this purpose, several additional model elements will have to be defined (Figure 7.9):

– a behavioral exchange is defined between the component and the actor (named train schedule or timetables service); it, for example, conveys the constraints and conditions of transmission (e.g. an RSS stream over HTTP);

– this exchange will convey the exchange item actually provided by the actor (update train timetables);

– a physical link expressing the communication medium required to obtain this information is created (e.g. representing a Wi-Fi network).

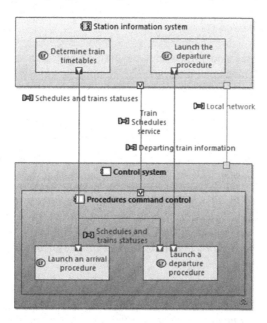

Figure 7.9. *Interface with the station information system*

Here again, this detailed definition is justified in the LA only for expressing structuring design choices related to the exchanged content, or for securing the use of an external system. For example, it will be possible to define the principle of decisions related to delayed trains at this stage, and we will probably need to verify that the content of the information received from the station correctly provides the elements necessary for making this decision.

***

This static definition of interfaces most often must be accompanied by a dynamic definition, by creating scenarios at the boundaries of the components, and if necessary state and modes machines associated with each contributor to exchanges, and managing this dynamics of interfaces. This is also a method for verifying consistency with the previous functional analysis and the behavior then defined, for detecting missing exchanges, functions to be added, modifying or moving one component to another, etc.

EXAMPLE.– *The system need scenario in Figure 6.7 (part 2) is detailed in Figure 7.10 by resorting to functions of the solution on the one hand, and by introducing the main system components involved on the other hand, which illustrates the implementation of their collaboration and their interfaces. From left to right, we can identify the actors "road vehicle" and "train leaving", then the components "management system", "railway facilities" and "road facilities", and finally the actor "station information system".*

Furthermore, states and modes can be defined and allocated to components, based on those implemented at the system level in the previous behavioral functional analysis, and consistent with them. Justification links should be preserved to formalize this consistency.

EXAMPLE.– *For the procedure command control component, we will distinguish:*

– an absence of rail traffic mode, in which functions "launch a departure/arrival procedure" are available;

– a departure mode, in which the functions "stop/release traffic", "launch a departure procedure", "monitor the nominal departure procedure", "supervise delayed departure" are included; the transition condition of this mode is the launch of the departure procedure by the station information system via the "leaving train information" functional exchange;

– the departure mode is broken down into two sub-modes: nominal/delayed departure; in addition to the previous condition, each of them requires a delayed or deferred departure command originating from the function "launch a departure procedure", in order to be activated;

– the operation is similar for the arrival mode, with activation when receiving the "arriving train approaching information" exchange item;

– switching back to the absence of rail traffic mode is carried out when the release traffic command is issued.

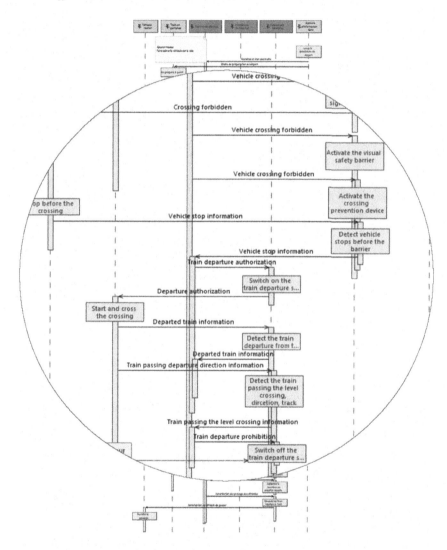

Figure 7.10. *Components scenario – nominal train departure (excerpt)*

These component modes are consistent with train arrival/departure and road traffic system modes, defined earlier, and allow us to take them into account in the architecture.

Figure 7.11 shows the formalization of these component modes.

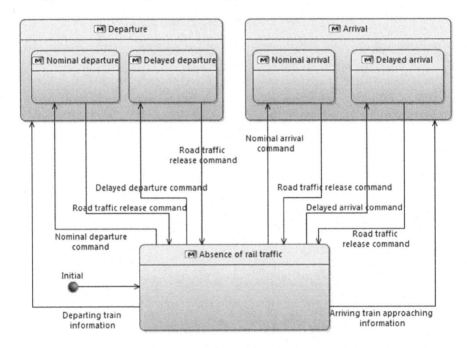

Figure 7.11. *Procedures command control modes*

The security control component mainly manages three modes:

– the nominal mode;

– the vehicle stopped on the track mode, conditioned by a vehicle driving on the track for more than 1 minute;

– the ongoing conflict mode, conditioned by a detection returned by the function "detect conflicting accesses to the crossing".

Returning to nominal mode is achieved when a command is issued by operators: train traffic release command.

The three functions provided by the components "detect and secure a vehicle stopped on the track", "detect conflicting accesses to the crossing" and "test the proper operation of the system" are present in every mode but their behavior and their commands are different depending on the case.

These component modes are consistent with the management of the previously defined emergency stop system mode and enable us to take it into account in the architecture.

Figure 7.12 presents the formalization of these component modes.

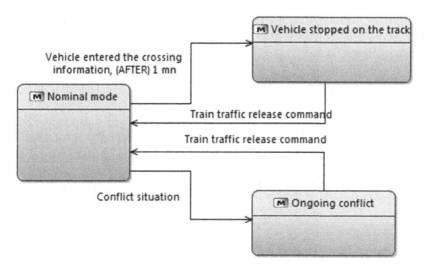

Figure 7.12. *Safety command control modes*

The functional chains defined in this functional analysis are also compared to the structure of the components; new chains can eventually be created to clarify or complete the behavior at the boundaries or within a component. The same happens for scenarios.

***

Requirements and non-functional constraints are also allocated to components by way of indirection, through the links that connect these requirements to functions, and allocation links of these functions to components. This can lead to re-decomposing a requirement to specify its impact on each component; the same occurs for an expected non-functional property (e.g. a maximum latency budget on a functional chain from end to end will be distributed between the components that it traverses, each receiving part of the budget on a subchain that is allocated to it).

As indicated earlier, this work of structural definition is iterative and carried out jointly with the previous definition of the behavior; functions and components can in turn be decomposed to better adjust, and the behavior should be namely specified at the component boundaries.

Similarly, these works can be restricted to most promising alternatives and detailed only as choices become clearer.

EXAMPLE.– *For example, the functions appearing in Figure 7.2 have been organized by grouping functions that belong to the same component, and broken down, in order to be able to offer a synthetic view per component, such as the one hereafter (Figure 7.13).*

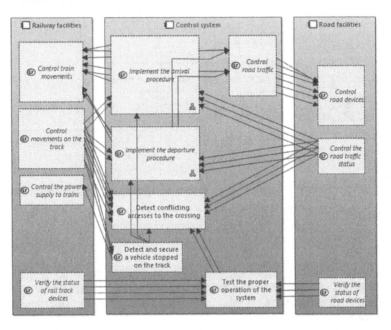

Figure 7.13. *High-level components and functions*

Finally, although the LA is required to preserve a certain level of abstraction, it may be necessary in order to verify feasibility or manage technical risks, to take the analysis further beyond that level, for a limited part of the need or of the system. In this case, it may be desirable either to detail a little more the LA, or preferably, to achieve a (separated) foreshadowing of what will be the physical architecture for these parts (e.g. in case of performance problems according to the assumptions about the computational power available).

7.5. Selection of the architecture alternative offering the best trade-off

The purpose of this activity is to find among previous candidate architectures the one that represents the best trade-off with respect to all viewpoints under consideration, and to justify its compliance to the need.

The evaluation of the architecture in the broad sense is beyond the scope of this book, therefore we will here mention only the multi-viewpoints analysis (detailed in Chapter 10), which constitute one of the components of this evaluation. Each alternative has in principle been evaluated based on the major viewpoints impacting it – and their relative importance – during its definition; the inadmissible non-conformities have been eliminated, but as the evaluation is rarely binary, the point is therefore now to compare the "merits" of each candidate in a multi-criteria quantitative analysis, of which previously identified viewpoint analyses, priorities and metrics are key elements.

Naturally, the compliance to previously determined design choices should also be verified.

***

The verification of the compliance of each alternative to the need relies on the traceability links developed during its definition, to ensure the coverage of the required functional and non-functional capability need. It may be necessary or desirable to thus backtrack up to the operational and capability need, by following traceability/justification links, both from the viewpoint of use cases and implementation scenarios, as well as activities and functions to be considered.

7.6. Summary

The LA perspective formalizes the first design choices of the architecture of the solution: first, through an internal functional analysis describing the behavior chosen for the system, then through the identification of the principle components implementing these solution functions, integrating therein the non-functional constraints that have been chosen to address at this level.

The functional analysis performed at this stage should not be regarded as a simple refinement of the SA, but as the result of the system design in terms of its behavior in response to this need.

The LA is developed following a constant to and fro between functional behavior and structural decomposition.

Following are the main activities to be undertaken for the definition of the logical principle architecture:

– to define the factors impacting the architecture and the analysis viewpoints;

– to define the principles underlying the system behavior;

– to build component-based system structuring alternatives;

– to select the architecture alternative offering the best compromise.

7.7. Exercise

LA of the door is shown in Figure 7.14.

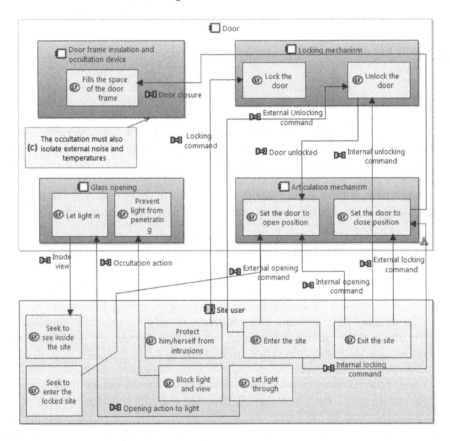

Figure 7.14. *Logical architecture of the door*

8

Definition of the Finalized Architecture or Physical Architecture

8.1. Principles

The finalized architecture, commonly called physical architecture (subsequently abbreviated as PA), defines the solution at a sufficient level of detail to specify the developments and acquisitions of all subsystems (or components) to be implemented, and to define and orientate the system integration, verification and validation (IVV) phases.

It must contribute to mastering complexity by promoting the separation of concerns, in terms of separability of components (so that they can be developed and tested separately), to facilitate and alleviate assembly and integration, constraints containment, the development capacity or reuse by third parties, etc. As such, a good architecture is not only key to the quality of the system and its usability, but also a decisive factor for the mastering and the efficiency of engineering.

It is often at this level only that choices and constraints are introduced related to implementation and production technologies, to existing elements to be re-used. Any ambiguities or inaccuracies that could still exist in the logical architecture (LA), if they did not impact its structuring, should this time be resolved, in order to constitute clear development contracts for the identified components.

For all these reasons, the level of detail of the PA is generally finer than that of the previous LA.

All the figures in this book are available to view in color at: www.iste.co.uk/voirin/arcadia.zip.

The definition of PA (an activity often – and abusively – known as "physical architecture" for convenience) is very similar to the previous LA definition concerning the general design approach; the reader is invited to refer to it.

In addition to the objectives and the level of detail specific to the PA mentioned previously, it adds to the LA the concepts making it possible to define and to determine the sizing and performance of resources and materials necessary for the implementation of the specified behaviors of the solution. It constitutes the main contribution to the definition of the product breakdown structure that describes its components and their hierarchy.

Finally, as we will see in Chapter 13, the PA is the privileged place of co-engineering with subsystem engineering and software or hardware components.

***

The main activities to be undertaken for the definition of the finalized PA are the following:

– to define the structuring principles of the architecture and behavior;

– to detail and finalize the expected system behavior;

– to build and rationalize one or more possible system architectures;

– to select, complete and justify the system architecture retained.

8.2. Definition of the structuring principles of the architecture and behavior

Factors impacting or constraining the definition of the architecture, as well as the viewpoints and structuring design choices mentioned earlier (Chapter 7, section 7.2), equally apply to this level of architecture and are to be taken into account in a similar way.

Nonetheless, one of the major objectives of the PA being to minimize complexity through rationalizing, a number of practices in this direction are to be considered, including some examples mentioned here, for purely illustrative purposes.

***

One of the most commonly used means of rationalization consists of reducing diversity and heterogeneity within the solution, by searching for similarities and therefore possible architecture invariants (sometimes called "patterns") that can be applied more than once in the same manner – or configurable. These may be generic common behaviors – or data, interfaces, unified protocols or services, which allow them to be reused as often as possible – or components replicated because they are utilized several times in different contexts (redundancy, load or processing or flow balancing, etc.), or because generic and used by several processing chains.

The gain obtained by this "factorization" is all the larger in that it simplifies the definition of the solution (and thus the construction/use of the models that formalize it), the implementation, the integration, the subsequent logistics, etc.

The adoption of industry standards, when properly chosen and relevant in the targeted context of usage, also contributes to reducing diversity, and mostly makes it possible to rely on design elements, components, tools, etc., predefined or existing on the market, *de facto* reducing the scope to be developed and implemented.

EXAMPLE.– *For example, we will define a replicable element "track signal command", which will be replicated in triplicate per track (departure, train arriving stop, arriving train crossing). Only the aspect (form, color, position of lights and panels) of signals will change from one to another, but not the control organ itself.*

Moreover, the control board of the lifting barriers also happens to have the same functions and expectations than those of the crossing prevention devices; therefore, here again a replicable component will be defined that will be employed in quadruplicate (one on each side of the level crossing, for each type of device). In these two cases, the main interest lies indeed in the design choices intending to share a common part between subsystems that were not a priori identical.

Regarding standards, we can mention the need for communications between the station information system, the processing circuits ensuring the monitoring of the system, and the station(s) operators. The choice of an Ethernet connection (which in addition could also be imposed by the station information system) also has the advantage, as it is a standard, of being able to use a commercial network router.

***

Another classic way to overcome complexity is based on the separation of concerns and their containment within parts of the architecture as separate as possible from each other. These concerns may be of very different kinds: for example, functional (e.g. by separating the core of a process or procedure on the one hand, and its monitoring on the other, separated from its control) or technological (separating the implementation functions of sensors, from data processing, and from the interface with operators, etc.), or involving the containment of variabilities (distinguishing between generic behavior and behavior specific to a customer or need, and separating them into disjoint components to localize the adaptations to each customer; or still, defining generic interfaces for general use, and creating adaptation components or layers in view of adapting to a specific interface, which will be the only ones impacted by a change of interface).

EXAMPLE.– *A separation criterion already mentioned is safety, to avoid the common modes of possible failures, but also to minimize the certification costs of critical components.*

Another criterion may be industrial: operator interfaces, real-time or critical constrained processing components, the hardware architecture being used, electric or hydraulic subsystems, etc., are often entrusted to specialized teams, therefore distinct, which results in turning them into separated components in the system architecture as in the development.

***

Similarly to factors and viewpoints, the structuring principles of the architecture should be classified by relevance or priority, in order to be able to arbitrate between them in case they lead to antagonistic solutions or when it will be necessary to release certain constraints to find an acceptable compromise.

It should be noted that the previous elements may as well affect the behavior as the solution structure.

8.3. Detail and finalization of the expected system behavior[1]

The goal is to precisely define the expected behavior of the system, to a level of detail and validation enough so that each of its components can be implemented (or selected and purchased), without any further risk or major questioning; this definition must of course demonstrate compliance with constraints, especially non-functional constraints, by which the system will have to abide when being used under operational conditions.

The development approach is that of functional analysis. In addition, it is also similar to that implemented for the definition of the behavior in the LA (Chapter 7, section 7.3), whose principles are applied in the same way. Only a few additional concerns that have to be accounted for are mentioned here, without prejudice to their order of execution.

---

1 The recommended approach is described in Chapter 4.

In particular, the finalized behavior should not necessarily be considered as a simple refinement of that defined in the LA: certainly, more detail is required, particularly to clarify ambiguous or incomplete processing, often just outlined in the LA, to clarify the deployment conditions of the selected technologies, etc. However, beyond this level of detail, the finalization of the chosen behavior in fact often constitutes a re-designing, which must result from the comparison between the principle behavior of the LA, and the implications of the principles chosen in the PA: technological choices and adoption of standards, previous structuring principles, in particular.

Another source of potential questioning of the principle behavior is related to the reuse of an existing component that contributes with its own behavior; this existing component must be described and evaluated with respect to the principles originally defined in the LA. This can lead either to replacing the originally intended behavior by that of the component being reused, or a development thereof, or even by not reusing the component at all.

This also applies when we introduce the state-of-the-art technologies, technical choices and practices, which are likely to constrain the behavior, and which at least add additional functions related to their implementation: for example, communication functions to add, coupling conditions between two machines and the associated operation, as well as technical functions and services such as the management of the lifecycle (start, stop, etc.); the supervision and monitoring of each system component, and the management functions of reconfigurations; observation or stimuli functions for testing purposes, etc.

EXAMPLE.– *If the LA function "detect a train approaching at a distance" is implemented by means of a trivial sensor that detects train movements, regardless of whether they leave or arrive, then in the PA the function will be named "detect a train in motion" and specified as such; the functional exchange in the PA will also be different from the one in the LA, because it will transmit a simple information from the detection of a train in motion.*

New functions may also appear in the PA, to specify behaviors for which further detail was unjustified in the LA, for example. In our case, we had chosen to represent operators/system interactions in the LA by simple functional exchanges. In the PA, it will be necessary to detail the expected functional content (geographical representation, trains and vehicles positions, etc.), interaction mechanisms (screens, keyboard, mouse, etc.), etc. Furthermore, these functions can then be allocated to components responsible for implementing them. They can be placed between system processing functions and those assumed by operator actors, to ensure the mediation of the interaction.

In order to simplify, we here make use of three operator interface functions:

– process operator commands;

– display the map situation of the traffic and the system;

– display traffic and system alerts.

It is interesting to compare this definition (Figure 8.1) with that established in the architecture shown in Figure 7.1.

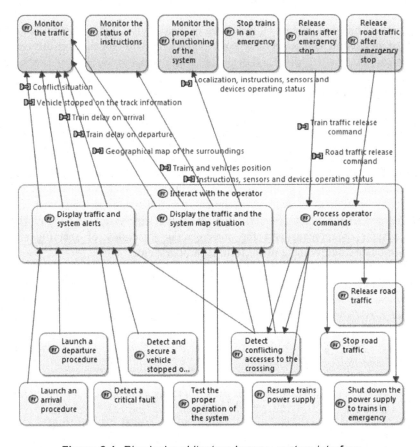

Figure 8.1. *Physical architecture human–system interface*

EXAMPLE.– *In another area, if we look into the hydraulic subsystem that will command the crossing prevention devices, then a logical analysis could give a decomposition of the function "activate the crossing prevention device", such as the one hereafter (Figure 8.2), which gives a summary view of it.*

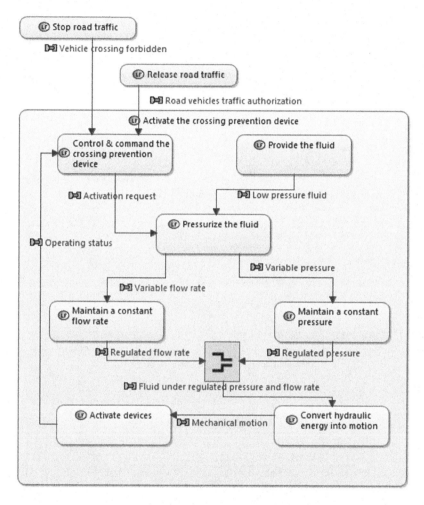

Figure 8.2. *Decomposition of the function "activate the crossing prevention device" in the logical architecture*

In the PA, in order to be able to determine all the organs necessary to the hydraulic system, the analysis has to proceed much further. Figure 8.3 gives a detailed vision to be able to describe the associated PA (see further).[2] The functions in bold help to differentiate from those of the LA.

---

2 It should be recalled that the models provided do not intend to exhibit absolute technical accuracy and are merely given as examples to illustrate the form and not the substance of this modeling.

The functional exchanges between functions "convert hydraulic energy into motion" and "activate ground obstacles" in particular should be taken into consideration: in a direction, a force; in the other, a travel velocity.

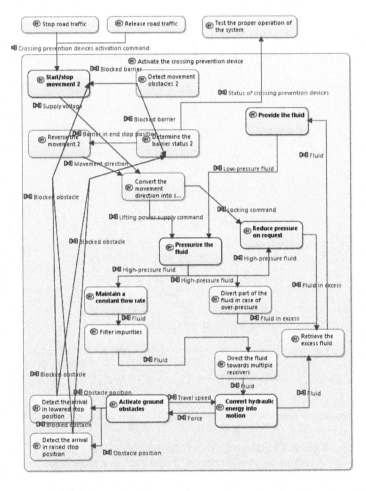

Figure 8.3. *Decomposition of the function "activate the crossing prevention device" in the physical architecture*

Similarly, the interfaces should this time be defined with accuracy, as it is based on their definition that subsystems suppliers will rely for their development or supply.

EXAMPLE.– *The nature and characteristics of the hydraulic fluid are accurately defined by data indicating:*

– the physical nature of the fluid (viscosity, operating temperatures, applied standards, etc.);

– the physical state at a given time (pressure, temperature).

The units in use (degrees Celsius and hectopascals, for example) should also be specified, in addition to the ranges of values being considered.

These two previous pieces of data are grouped into an exchange item named "fluid under pressure", which represents the use of this fluid at a point of the hydraulic circuit.

This exchange item is transmitted through the functional exchanges mentioned in Figure 8.3.

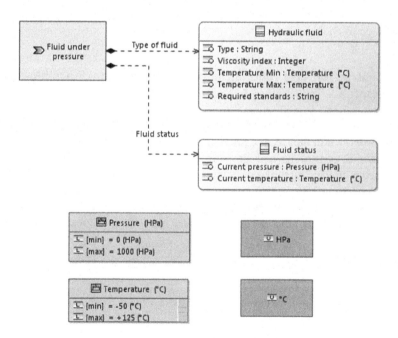

Figure 8.4. *Characterization of the hydraulic fluid*

Moreover, the construction of the architecture and the identification of its components, which if we recall are carried out jointly with the finalization of the behavior and iteratively, lead to modifying this latter: the scope of functions can vary depending on their allocation, according to the state of the art or to technologies and off-the-shelf components or equipment available; it can also depend on multi-viewpoint analyses, which may require a reappraisal of the components as well as of their functional content and their behavior. Moreover, different production and implementation options can also lead to a reappraisal or to multiple alternatives of this behavior.

EXAMPLE.– *In the LA, a function detecting train departure from the platform had been defined. An analysis of existing systems to finalize the PA results in preferring a presence detection system (using a magnetic loop, for example); the function will remain the same as in the LA, but the information provided will no longer be an event notifying the departure, but a presence status (Boolean); the function(s) using this information will therefore have to be accordingly adapted with a different departure detection algorithm.*

Finally, the traceability of the chosen finalized behavior must be ensured with that defined in the LA, in order to verify the consistency, completeness and the justification of choices made.

8.4. Construction and rationalization of one or more possible system architectures

This step is intended to define one or more solutions reflecting the structuring principles defined in the LA, the previous finalized behavior, satisfying the expected non-functional constraints and applying technology and reuse choices decided in accordance with the structuring principles adopted.

It specifically defines behavioral components (with principles similar to LA components), enabling the desired behavior, by way of allocating functions to components.

EXAMPLE.– *Compared to the components defined in the LA, a similar decomposition can be observed (with a few exceptions described later), including more details and design choices that will subsequently be discussed (Figure 8.5).*

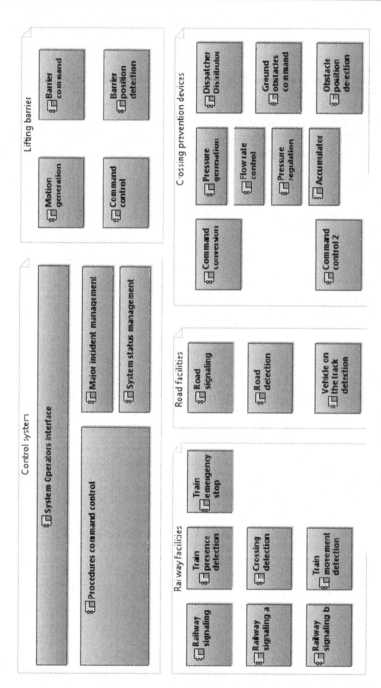

Figure 8.5. *Behavioral components in the PA*

The approach for building behavioral components is very analogous to that implemented for structuring the system in the LA (Chapter 7, section 7.4), whose principles are applied in the same way: grouping or segregation of functions, structuring into subcomponents or grouping into parent components, definition of component interfaces (integrating therein the constraints related to selected standards), dynamic behavior allocation (scenarios, states, modes, etc.), possible refinement of requirements and allocation to components involved, and jointly with the finalization of the behavior. Subsequent additions will be especially made for all these activities at the boundaries between components (e.g. to define communication protocols between them).

EXAMPLE.– *An exchange item "train passing the level crossing information", between the "crossing detection" and "procedures command control" components, will include:*

– *a track number;*

– *the time of crossing;*

– *the traffic direction.*

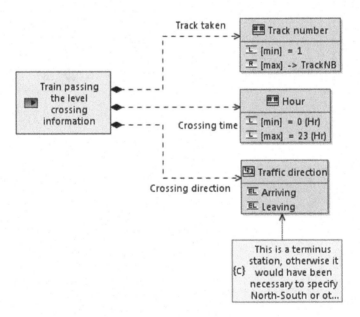

Figure 8.6. *Train passing the level crossing information*

In the simplest cases, or in systems with a physical or electrical dominant, the exchange items are often simple in their description and usage at this engineering and modeling level. However, for more complex exchange items, involving large numbers of exchange contents elements, it is desirable to be able to structure a list of exchange items that can be extensive, by grouping them by type of service achieved, for example. This is the role of the concept of an interface (also mainly present in software design). The associated definition approach is described in the following example.

EXAMPLE.– *For illustration purposes, if the station information system explicitly provides two separate services for the movements of trains in general and for the train leaving, a "station movements interface" will then be created, which will group together the exchange items "train leaving information" and "train schedules update", as defined in the LA (Figure 7.8).*

This interface will be allocated to the port of the actor station information system, as the provided interface, and to the corresponding system port, as the required interface.

A more detailed and comprehensive example of interfaces is given in the following for the vehicle detection radar.

In the PA, behavioral components must in addition meet decomposition criteria defined in the LA (exceptions will have to be justified), while detailing and refining them; they can also be duplicated to meet deployment constraints, and completed by technical components related to implementation choices, for example. They are connected by traceability and justification links to the logical components that they implement.

EXAMPLE.– *In the LA, a component was defined to perform the detection of vehicles on the road, and another to detect them on the railway. However, an analysis of available technologies shows that a radar could implement both roles. In addition, it would allow us to assess the speed of the vehicles and to define their precise position. Finally, two radars being necessary (each pointed toward one side of the road while covering the railway), they both provide redundancy in detection on the railway, which is a real benefit for safety.*

In this case, the architect can make the decision to group sensors for detecting presence/stops at the barrier, the length of the waiting line and approaching vehicles, as well as sensors for the detection of vehicles entering and leaving the rail track into a single sensor, which will be a radar. This is thus an exception, in the PA, to the rule that stipulates that the decomposition done in the LA has to be respected; but this exception is legitimate as soon as it satisfies the constraints and structural principles of the architecture.

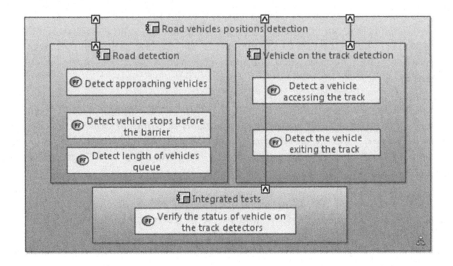

Figure 8.7. *Behavioral components and functions of the road traffic detection radar*

In Figure 8.7, the behavioral component "Road vehicles positions detection" is broken down into three subcomponents: road detection, vehicle on the track detection and integrated tests, each implementing the functions that it must execute. Ports in behavioral components are defined in each component, characterizing its "instruction manual", then connected to the rest of the system by behavioral exchanges. It should be observed that there are delegation links between the ports of the aggregating parent component and those of the components it contains.

It also should be noted that the two functions for the verification of the status of sensors existing in the LA are replaced by a single function in the PA, because a single device is used.

∗∗∗

In order to interface this component with the rest of the system, the functional exchanges that concern it should first be defined (Figure 8.8).

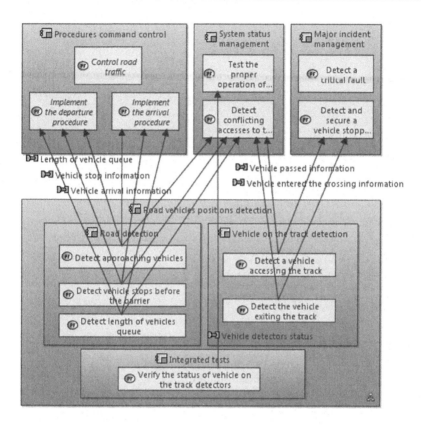

Figure 8.8. *Functional exchanges of the road traffic detection radar*

Then, ports and behavioral exchanges between components will be defined by grouping functional ports and exchanges.

The behavioral exchange "road detections" includes the "length of vehicle queue", "vehicle stop information" and "vehicle arrival information" functional exchanges. The behavioral exchange "detections on the track" includes "vehicle arrival information" and "vehicle passed information". Road detection status, for its part, contains only the functional exchange "vehicle detectors status".

These groupings are represented at the port level by allocation links of functional ports (red and green in Figure 8.9) onto behavioral ports (white), these allocations being indicated here by dotted lines.

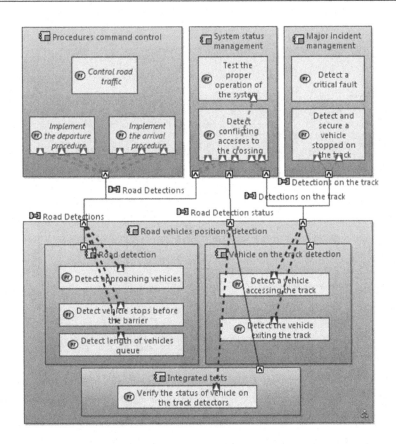

Figure 8.9. *Behavioral exchanges of the road traffic detection radar*

In general, the contents of each functional exchange are defined, in the form of an exchange item, which aggregates data or information. For example:

– the functional exchange "vehicle arrival information" transmits the exchange item "approaching vehicles", defined by a list of vehicles (along with their distance from the crossing and their speed), the relevant side of the crossing and the precise detection time;

– vehicle stop information, transmits "stopped vehicles", defined in a similar way (with a speed equal to zero);

– length of vehicle queue, transmits the "number of stopped vehicles", defined only by their number.

The grouping of functional ports and exchanges into behavioral ports and exchanges will also lead to grouping the exchange items into interfaces:

– an interface "presence of vehicles on the road" will include the previous exchange items and will be associated to the appropriate behavioral ports.

This information can be formalized by a more accurate notation, such as the following one, provided solely for illustrative purposes. The first element is the interface, the exchange items are on the left, the data that they transmit on the right.

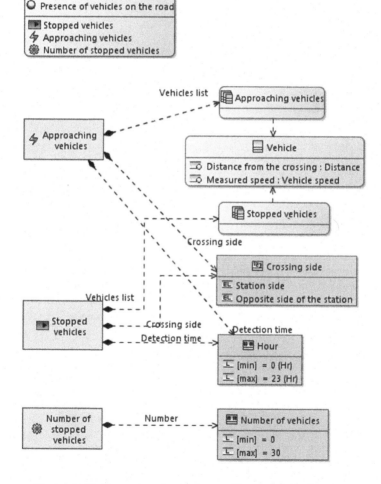

Figure 8.10. Presence of vehicles on the road radar interface

Analogously, the "presence of vehicles on the track" interface comprises the exchange items "vehicle on the track" and "vehicle out of the track", both transporting a datum describing the "crossing side" and the "access time (time of crossing)".

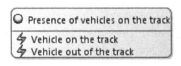

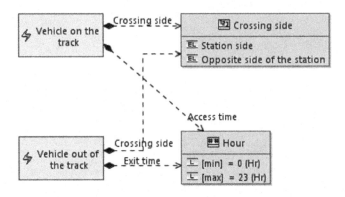

Figure 8.11. *Presence of vehicles on the track radar interface*

The "radar diagnosis" interface will be reduced to a Boolean specifying whether it is operational or failed (in reality, it would probably be wiser to define a more detailed diagnostic, but it has been decided here to comply with a procedure providing standardized diagnostics identical across all equipment).

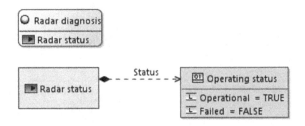

Figure 8.12. *Radar diagnostics interface of the radar*

The PA complements this behavioral description by way of the definition of implementation components, or hosting physical components, containing behavioral components and forming the infrastructure of the system; the behavioral components are deployed on these host components, which provide necessary resources for their behavior and hardware vectors (links) for their communications. It may thus consist of high-performance computers, resources for digital or analog processing, mechanical systems, evaporators, furnaces, chemical reactors, etc.

Hosting physical components are themselves connected by physical links, reflecting the media that channel exchanges between behavioral components (a cabled network, a satellite link, a pipe or a mechanical shaft, for example).

The same rationalization processes have to be performed for hosting physical components as for the behavior and behavioral components, in compliance with the established structuring principles.

EXAMPLE.– *The radar, at this engineering level, is considered to be a single host component, without being more detailed, because this detail would be the responsibility of the engineering of the radar itself. For its part, the control subsystem is constituted of a cabinet (or a rack) that contains two electronic processing circuit boards – a commercial one for the control of departure and arrival procedures; the other specific because it will have to satisfy particular constraints of operation safety and integrity, given the criticality of the processing it hosts – namely the management of the system state and processing of major incidents. Moreover, it is also for this reason that the fine detail of the two circuits is considered and represented at this engineering level. The three are the hosting physical components.*

The main physical link between the two subsystems mentioned previously consists of Ethernet connections. These connections are channeled through a router (also used in the connection with the information system of the station).

Furthermore, as stated earlier, the correct operation diagnostics of the radar is forwarded through a discrete link, due to consistency concerns with other equipment.

Figure 8.13 represents behavioral components in blue, including their behavioral ports in white; the previously mentioned host components are described in pale yellow and their physical ports (connectors, for example) in darker yellow. The deployment of a behavioral component on a host component is expressed by the fact that one contains the other. The physical links between physical ports (such as Ethernet or discrete cables) are in red. Behavioral exchanges and ports are allocated to the physical links and ports that convey them; this is pictured in

Figure 8.13 by way of the allocation links between behavioral (white) and physical (yellow) ports.

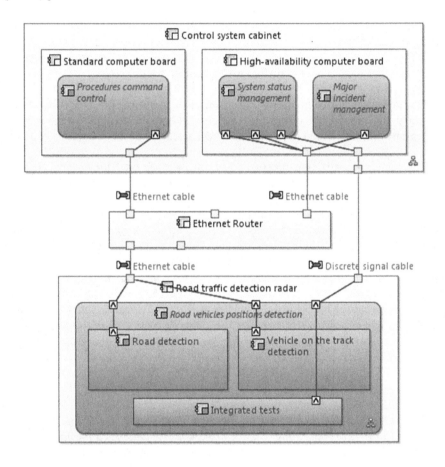

Figure 8.13. *Components and implementation for the road traffic detection radar*

However, in the case of the radar, in particular, the physical path is not necessarily reduced to a single physical link: for example, road and railway detection must go through the router. Consequently, a physical path is defined, consisting of links that connect the physical departure port to the arrival port, to which each behavioral exchange following this path will be allocated. The physical paths of the road traffic management and road traffic control (toward the components of the control system) are illustrated in blue and red in Figure 8.14; the black portion is common to both paths.

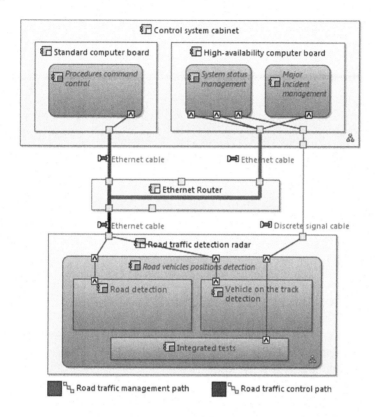

Figure 8.14. *Physical paths for the road traffic detection radar*

EXAMPLE.– *The architecture of the lifting barrier presented in Figure 8.15, still using the same representation conventions, highlights the co-existence of the three functional (in green), behavioral (in blue) and physical implementation (in yellow and red) layers or viewpoints, as well as their links (the allocation links from functional ports to behavioral ports are however omitted here to improve readability).*

We should particularly note the different nature of the functions (transform a voltage into mechanical torque), of behavioral components (motion generation) and implementation hosting physical components (electric motor).

Similarly, the engine and the transmission exchange at the functional level a couple in one direction, a velocity of rotation in the other; the corresponding behavioral exchange consists of the engine driving the transmission; the associated physical link being the rotation axel of the motor.

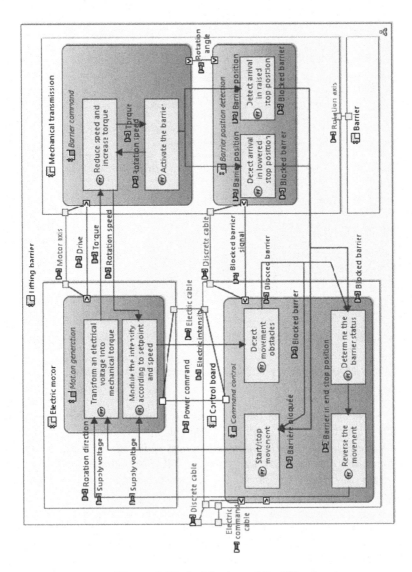

Figure 8.15. *Architecture of the lifting barrier*

EXAMPLE.– *The crossing prevention device shows another way of using the model, because exchanges are of a hydraulic nature.*

Host components represent the physical constituents of the hydraulic circuit, in which behavioral components define the behavior: namely a power generator integrating the pump generating the pressure and the fluid accumulator, the circuit controller incorporating the pressure regulator and flow controller, the distribution, actuators, etc., connected by pipes or hoses. It should be noted that the distinction between high- and low-pressure hoses relates to their physical characteristics (capability to withstand these high pressures), and not to the pressure of the transported fluid (which would be a characteristic of functional or behavioral exchanges transported by the hose).

Behavioral exchanges are mainly exchanges of hydraulic fluid and system commands (Figure 8.16).

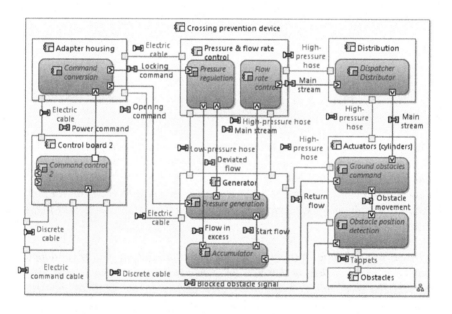

Figure 8.16. *Components of the crossing prevention device*

In order to clarify the operation of the hydraulic system, let us add functions and their functional exchanges within the components that implement them. Functional exchanges mainly transport the fluid, and at the interface between hydraulic and mechanical systems, a force in one direction, and a velocity of movement in the other. The fluid itself can be described by an exchange item, both in terms of nature and of physical parameters at a given moment and place, as illustrated in Figure 8.17.

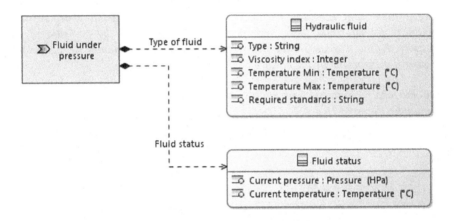

Figure 8.17. *Characterization of the hydraulic fluid*

It should also be noted that, to illustrate the iterative and global character of the construction of the solution and due to the choice of architecture, the control circuit employed is similar to that used for the lifting barrier (this can be seen in Figure 8.18, in which the number "2" is represented next to each control function, because it is a second copy of the reused function, in addition to that of the lifting barrier).

This is a good thing in terms of architecture but leads to adding an adaptation component. In effect, for the barrier, the command is unique, each new command reversing the direction of rotation of the barrier. In the case of the crossing prevention, the command is sent to raise the obstacle off the ground (by supplying the pump), but another command is necessary to make it return to the ground (by reducing the pressure so that it goes down by simple gravity effect). The adaptation component thus makes it possible to convert a single command accompanied by a movement direction into two separate opening and closing commands.

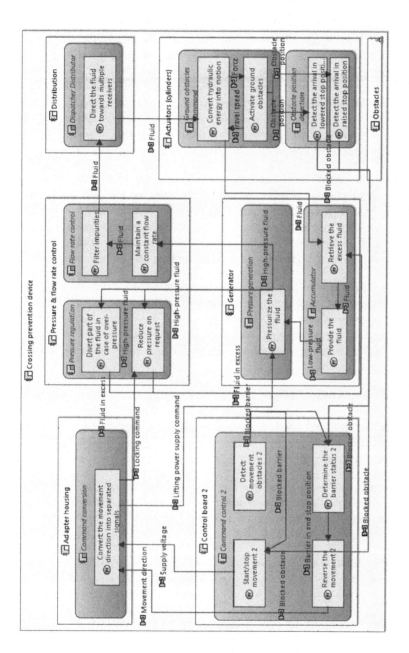

Figure 8.18. *Components and functions of the crossing prevention device*

NOTE.– *Components in the PA are intended to define the product breakdown structure, as well as configuration items, interfaces and the integration strategy (see Chapter 9). Unlike the LA, any component (within the meaning given by Arcadia) created here should therefore have a physical existence, in terms of interfaces, deployment, development, procurement, integration, verification, etc., and thus in particular have its own ports and interfaces (to be used and integrated "as a black box") eventually delegated to its subcomponents, and not be distributed over multiple host components. An exception is a single behavioral component defining the behavior of a host component, but which has no actual separate existence.*

Behavioral components or hosting physical components should not be used to structure the decomposition tree, for purely documentary or synthesis purposes, or still as simple grouping elements. For this matter, logical components already assume this function, as they aggregate physical components via traceability / justification links and provide a high-level vision of the architecture; and at a different level, configuration items, also group components based on their particular criteria.

EXAMPLE.– *For example, the control system cabinet does actually exist as a physical component, in addition to being the host to computer boards and power supply, among other things. The same happens for the lifting barrier and the crossing prevention device (chassis, bodywork, etc., but which will be described at other levels of engineering and with different models such as 3D mechanical models, for instance).*

Similarly, the behavioral components of the control system cabinet – procedures command control, system state management, major incident management – do actually exist as software components separately developed, each with its own lifecycle and to be integrated with other components (high-performance computational circuit boards, etc.).

Nonetheless, in the case of the electric motor of the barrier, for example, the behavioral component "motion generation" has no physical reality or existence outside of the motor host component; as a result, it does not show up in the product breakdown structure.

On the other hand, there should be no components for the purposes of grouping in the PA, such as "rail and road facilities", "rail or road signaling and detection", etc.

8.5. Selection, completion and justification of the system architecture retained

This last stage of the construction of the architecture of the solution (at the engineering level under consideration) must finalize the choices among potential alternatives, and verify that the retained alternative satisfies, possibly by means of an acceptable trade-off, all of the needs and constraints that have been imposed thereon.

The approach is similar to that carried out in the LA. Similarly, the evaluation of every architecture or design decision, and of each considered alternative, bearing in mind principles, factors and design viewpoint, must be carried out continuously, so as to eliminate as quickly as possible non-viable alternatives.

For example, the implementation resources available may not be sufficient to support an expected behavior or associated properties (computational load too high for a given process in computers supporting it, temperature and pressure too high for a given pipe, etc.). This will lead to a redesigning of the architecture, including a redecomposition and a different distribution of behavioral components, or the use of other implementation resources (more powerful computers, more robust pipes).

At or before this time, and in order to mitigate the risks that can subsist about the design of the solution at this level, behavior, performance and main non-functional assumptions must be confirmed by more specific and detailed analyses (but this can also be done at each previous step, to test a particular local hypothesis, for example). This approach is described in the section dedicated to the multi-viewpoints analysis (Chapter 10).

8.6. Summary

The PA perspective defines the solution at a level of detail sufficient to specify the developments of its subsystems or components, and to drive system IVV phases.

It describes the designed solution at a degree of precision and completion far more significant than the previous LA, with which it must however remain consistent. It integrates in particular technological and environmental issues among others, and hardware resources required to ensure the expected behavior.

All components must have, at this point, a physical existence for engineering at all levels (development/acquisition specification, configuration, contribution to integration).

The main activities to be undertaken for the definition of the finalized PA are the following:

– to define the structuring principles of the architecture and behavior;

– to detail and finalize the expected system behavior;

– to build and rationalize one or more possible system architectures;

– to select, complete and justify the system architecture retained.

8.7. Exercise

PA of the door is shown in Figure 8.19.

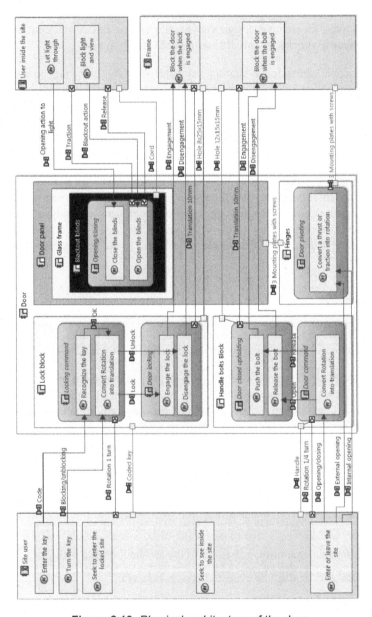

Figure 8.19. *Physical architecture of the door*

Definition of Implementation, Development, Acquisition and Integration Contracts

9.1. Principles

Being the final stage of system design strictly speaking, this definition of the Product Building Strategy (BS) prepares later development, implementation, production, acquisition stages of subsystems or components identified in the physical architecture, and their integration, up to the qualification of the system in an operational environment. We will refer it in the following by BS.

The definition of the architecture of the system – implemented and formalized in the previous perspectives and stages, in particular in the physical architecture, forms the basis of this perspective oriented toward the detailed specification and the integration of the system components previously identified.

The product breakdown structure and the implementation contract of each constituent have their roots in the physical architecture, from which they derive for the most part.

The integration, verification and validation strategy and the basis of testing campaigns that will support it also rely on this physical architecture and they will have the responsibility to implement it into the final product ready to be delivered to the customer.

All the figures in this book are available to view in color at: www.iste.co.uk/voirin/arcadia.zip.

The main activities to carry out for the definition of development, acquisition and integration contracts are the following:

– to define the product breakdown structure;

– to finalize the development contracts of components to be implemented;

– to consolidate the definition of components to be acquired;

– to define the integration, verification and validation strategy and processes.

9.2. Definition of the product breakdown structure

The product breakdown structure lists the set of all of the concrete elements, to be created or acquired, constituting the system as previously defined, and that will be the subject of the integration phase.

These elements are here limited to the components defined at this level of engineering. Those among them that will be designed and produced (and not simply acquired) will then in turn themselves be potentially broken down, within the context of subsystem (or software, hardware, mechanics, etc.) engineering, and will thus complete the product breakdown structure initialized here.

Each item will have to be managed as part of configurations in order to identify its configuration state: its version, its parameters or potential adaptation, etc., in each of the system definitions to which it contributes. These elements are part of the product breakdown structure.

The main constituting elements of the product breakdown structure are structural elements of the previous physical architecture: host components, physical links, physical ports, etc., or a more detailed description if needed (for example a strand of cables, a linking piece, etc.). Behavioral components may also appear, insofar as they will be acquired or developed separately from host components in which they are inserted (for example software components, computer programs or parameterizing of programmable components, etc.).

In general, each element is mentioned once; if it appears in several copies, then its cardinality (that is, the number of copies used in the product) is indicated.

Additional items are sometimes added to this tree structure, such as a configuration element for grouping purposes, easier to manipulate or to subcontract than a set of separate elements, and having a unique version identification.

However, the product breakdown structure is not enough on its own to describe the final product: it lacks the "assembly rules" which can be found in the physical architecture. It must refer to it at all times. The product breakdown structure remains a partial representation, but it is convenient, for example to calculate the price of a product.

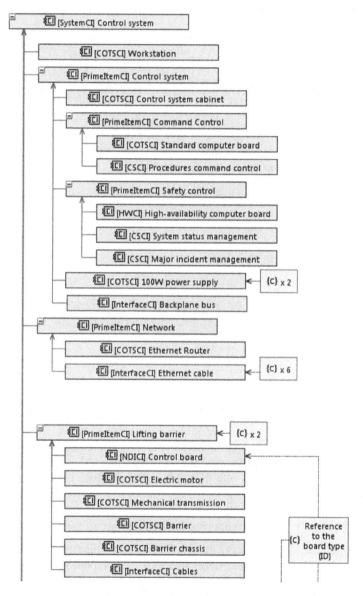

Figure 9.1. *Product Breakdown Structure (part)*

EXAMPLE.– *Figure 9.1 presents part of the product breakdown structure of the traffic control system. The elements of the tree (Configuration Items [CI]) are typed according to their nature:*

– Prime item: grouping element;

– COTS : commercial-off-the-shelf (commercial product);

– CSCI: computer software CI (software program);

– HWCI: hardware CI (hardware piece of equipment);

– Interface CI: used for connections (hoses, cables, etc.);

– NDI CI: not developed item, used here for references to an item not developed in the context of the relevant grouping element (for instance control circuit board reused by the barrier and the crossing prevention).

The constraints (in yellow marked with a (c)) indicate the cardinality, which is the required number of copies.

9.3. Finalization of development contracts of components to be implemented

The development technical contract of each component describes what is expected of its supplier by the system engineering team, so as to satisfy the definition of the physical architecture produced and to secure later integration validation verification stages.

In principle, compliance with this contract should ensure that the IVV of the system will be performed without problem, and that functional as well as non-functional needs will be satisfied.

Similarly to the product breakdown structure, this development contract is based on the physical architecture for the most part, and should have been the subject of negotiation or coengineering with its supplier. We will also refer to Chapter 13 for more details.

Mainly, for a behavioral component it describes:

– the functions (or services) that the component must perform in its system environment, and their internal exchanges inside the component;

– interfaces with its environment (other components, actors external to the system), defined by the nature of the exchanged elements (data, signals, information, material flows, physical quantities such as torque or calories, etc.) and sources/destinations of these exchanges (for functions and the component). It may make sense to distinguish between components or services that it requires (which are essential thereto) to perform the service expected;

– the expected dynamic behavior, within the component and at its boundaries (shown by functional chains, scenarios, states machines, etc.), in particular internal states and modes imposed by the system level, the communication protocols with its environment, the contribution to start, stop, or reconfiguration procedures;

– the different versions of the component to be delivered throughout the IVV, their functional content and associated system integration versions (dated); mainly the functional content and non-functional expectations (limited performance, released constraints) of each version must be specified based on previous elements;

– the expectations from the IVV specific to this component may also be requested in the form of scenarios or functional chains to be demonstrated, for example (which, it should be noted, assumes that scenarios, functional chains, etc. providing these expectations in the system physical architecture, are derived and allocated to each component, even if it means that they have to be decomposed accordingly);

– interfaces with the host component in which it is inserted (for example the ports of this component that previous interfaces will utilize);

– the amount of resources of this host component and communications media that are allocated thereto (processing capacity, memory for a software system, metrics and physical quantities such as flow rate, maximal torque or volume not to be exceeded, etc.);

– the potential contribution of the component to the global data model of the system, in connection with previous interfaces, and its internal data if necessary;

– the non-functional constraints to which it will have to comply; for example, we shall mention the performance (such as the duration of the execution of an operation, of a functional chain, of a scenario; the precision, the quality of service associated therewith), the safety of operation (failure scenarios, criticality, feared events, or the admissible failure rate), security (classification of sensitive data, authentication constraints, attack scenarios and feared events), cost (of development, of production or of series), etc.;

– the possible product line constraints (optional parts of services and associated conditions), in the form of a variability tree associated with the component, and the characterization of the elements of the component for each of these variabilities;

– eventually, an extract of the conditions of operational service focused on the context of the component (in the form of an operational analysis dedicated to the component);

– textual requirements, allocated to the component, and its accompanying definition above. These requirements can be resulting from the refinement or the decomposition of system requirements during the construction of the logical or physical architecture, or added to these stages at most at this point, either because the content of the architecture is not suitable for the formulation of these requirements or because they describe in more detail a previous item (a function, for instance).

And for a hosting resource component it describes:

– links, ports or hardware interfaces with its environment (other hosting resource components, actors external to the system), defined by the maximal capacity of elements to be conveyed (such as data sizes and flow rates, signal frequencies, volumes of information, material flow, physical quantities such as maximum pressure, temperature, flow rate, or torque, etc.);

– links and interfaces with the host component containing it, if necessary (for example physical links, means of power supply, cables or pipes);

– the resources that it has to make available to behavioral components as well as their maximal admissible sizing, with possible consumption patterns (per phase, over time, or according to system modes, etc.);

– the associated environmental and regulatory characteristics (extreme operating conditions such as pressure, temperature, humidity, or vibrations; the requested resistance to damage, the consumption of external resources, heat dissipation; or the maximum weight, etc.);

– textual requirements, allocated to the component and accompanying its definition above, either because this definition is not adapted to the formulation of these requirements or because they describe in more detail a previous element (for instance, a physical constraint for example);

– the constraints of the product line (see above).

9.4. Consolidation of the definition of components to be acquired

The definition of the previous contract should in principle also apply to components that are not meant to be produced but acquired, and this can also apply to preexisting off-the-shelf components.

It is strongly tempting to consider that since the component already exists, the design is already done and validated, and therefore the previous analysis does not have to be performed in this case. However, then, there is no guarantee that this component will be adequate to the use that the system will make of it, both from the functional and non-functional perspective. Therefore, it is strongly recommended to give as much importance to the analysis of existing components (acquired or reused) as to others, following the previous approach, most especially in the physical architecture.

In this situation, the contract above will rather thus be a technical contract of the integration of the component, mainly used to possibly formalize the contractual content of the acquisition, and at least to verify that the component delivered is properly consistent with the expectation transcribed in the physical architecture. It will therefore be possible to verify, by appropriate means of analysis or tests, the consistency of its interfaces, capabilities, usage conditions (services performed, scenarios of use, available functional chains, etc.), performance and non-functional properties, based on the elements that have been allocated thereto in the physical architecture.

Moreover, in the case of an acquisition, the capability to adapt the component if it does not respect the integration contract is very small or even non-existing. It is therefore essential, first, to secure the conditions of its usage and, second, to study the impact of the component failing to comply with the contract, at least on major issues: an impact assessment must be conducted if discrepancies are found or apprehended, and may even lead to adapting the system architecture accordingly, taking containment precautions, degraded modes or alternative solutions, or even to discontinuing this component.

9.5. Definition of the IVV strategy

The IVV strategy defines the order in which operational and system capabilities will be delivered and verified, the order in which components and their functions will be integrated and tested, and the conditions to achieve this: namely, the nature of verification, the content of testing campaigns and required test means and testbeds.

The approach for the definition of this policy is described in Chapter 12. Only a few elements, in interaction with the stages and perspectives of the architecture above and of the supporting model, are mentioned here.

The nature of the verifications demonstrating the adequacy of the system or product with the need is often characterized by the acronym IADT, for Inspection, Analysis, Demonstration and Testing. The means of inspection are multiple and fall outside the scope of this book; on the other hand, a certain number of analyses can be performed on the architecture model, especially through the use of multiple viewpoints (Chapter 10). Demonstrations and tests will bring forward the demand exerted on the system by scenarios that will rely on those described in the model; the expected behaviors that the IVV will have to verify will be partially characterized by this same model, particularly by following the functional chains and the behavioral description that it comprises; similarly, the model provides invaluable help to the investigation, analysis of identified defects and their localization.

Provided that contracts destined for subsystems or components can and should be constituted based on the model, in the same way, test means and testbeds can be specified relying on the functional content of the environment of each constituent or subset of the system (functions requesting it or functions making use of its outputs, for example) for each step of the IVV. This allows a functional and non-functional specification of these test means and testbeds, whose functional content can be versioned and spread out in time according to the IVV strategy, which leaves much more flexibility to the engineering of these enabling systems.

Finally, in a number of cases, the optimization of the IVV will require feedback into the architecture design in order to make it more suitable for stimulating, observing and analyzing the functioning, but also for the progressiveness of tests or for facilitating the localization and containment of errors and defects.

9.6. Summary

The perspective defining the construction strategy of the product, or Building Strategy, defines the expectations about each of the components of the system, and then the conditions of their integration up to the product validation verification.

The main activities to be carried out for the definition of development, acquisition and integration contracts are the following:

- to define the product breakdown structure;

- to finalize the development contracts of components to be implemented;

- to consolidate the definition of components to be acquired;

- to define IVV processes.

PART 2

Method in Action: Using Engineering Models

10

Mixing Viewpoints: Analysis and Specialties

10.1. Justification

In most cases, systems architecture cannot be built solely on functional criteria. One of the main difficulties architects encounter is finding the best compromise that meets all the constraints the finalized solution must meet, particularly those known as "non-functional". For example, the following concerns and dilemmas (of course, it is not an exhaustive list) are likely to impact the architecture to some degree, depending on the domains considered:

– functional coherence;

– performance (e.g. reaction time to external events or inputs, number of elements or volume of material to be processed etc.);

– interface complexity;

– safety of goods and people, operations safety, fault tolerance;

– security, protection against attacks (confidentiality/non-disclosure, authentication/non-repudiation, protection against denial of service, etc.);

– human factors, ergonomics;

– reliability, availability, maintainability, testability;

– weight, volume and dimensions, energy consumption, thermal dissipation;

– environmental protection;

– dependencies and ease of integration;

All the figures in this book are available to view in color at: www.iste.co.uk/voirin/arcadia.zip.

– flexibility, modularity, scalability;

– product policy;

– reuse of legacy parts;

– availability of technologies;

– available resources;

– ease of subcontraction;

– recurring and non-recurring costs, delays in supply;

– competencies available in development and deployment; required training;

– logistics footprint, deployment constraints, lifecycle, withdrawal from operations;

– ...

Each domain in engineering of course has its own concerns and constraints and priorities influencing trade-offs between candidate solutions and the search for the best compromise.

To the difficulties resulting from the solutions' often contradictory constraints and orientations, can be added the fact that expertise on each of these concerns is generally the preserve of specialists, from the viewpoint of the problems to be addressed, the professional standards and expertise to be respected, procedures, solution techniques and associated tools (which we will group here under the term "specialty engineering").

Moreover, specialty analyses often do not take place in the same cycle and the same timescale as the architect's decisions, as they require work that is often very detailed and so potentially time consuming. Here, it is therefore a matter of finding a compromise not only between constraints, but also between different actors in engineering. It can be seen that this work, although most often placed under the control of the architect, should really be collaborative, in a coengineering approach between all the actors involved.

Finally, it is necessary to study different alternative architecture solutions before finding the most acceptable, which necessarily means working in a short-loop to evaluate, quickly, the comparative merits of each alternative, and with multiple viewpoints, to evaluate its adequacy with all these different viewpoints. The aim is therefore to provide help in evaluating architecture in these conditions, relying on the model's analytical capabilities (automatic if possible).

10.2. Principles behind the approach

At each level of engineering, several stages and types of work should be considered to progressively draw out the compromise expected between all the constraints and actors to be satisfied (see Figure 10.1):

– during development of needs analysis (OA and SA), the constraints required for each viewpoint are captured in the model each time it is possible, by enriching operational analysis and system needs analysis;

– during the initial architectural solution building (LA and PA), taking account of these constraints requires trade-offs and choices in design. Each design decision can be impacted or conditioned by each viewpoint, and sometimes in contradictory ways. It is therefore imperative to be able to analyze the impact of these diverse viewpoints simultaneously and in a short loop, to be able quickly to draw, evaluate and keep or eliminate all the alternatives to be considered. This short loop, aiming to draw out, little by little, the best compromise between the different viewpoints, thus makes it necessary to mechanize analysis of the architectural model, simultaneously by different relevant viewpoints, which makes it possible to evaluate each significant design choice immediately, from each viewpoint. The architectural model is analyzed according to the rules of the art, to check that it fully respects them, and that it satisfies the constraints identified previously, for each viewpoint. Analysis can also most often help identify the causes behind non-conformity, as well as where they are found;

– to finalize the solution architecture and the contracts for development (PA, BS), a detailed, in-depth analysis should be carried out for each major viewpoint to confirm the initial evaluations and selections made at the previous stage. This new analysis (which can be started in parallel to the previous ones) finely details and completes the previous models, relying on metrics defined throughout the design, by adding elements to viewpoints considered (a fine description of behavior for performances, dysfunctional transformations for safety, etc.), and so requires more time than the previous short loop analysis. It is therefore carried out by specialty engineers, for each viewpoint, most often independently of the others. It also generally uses different methods and techniques to those used in the definition of architecture: simulation, finite element analysis, formal proof, etc.
It is also often at this stage that "proof" and contractual and regulatory justification elements are created for each specialty (fault trees, for example). This can also be the time to refine and update characterization of viewpoints from the architecture model by more precise metrics and values;

– if the results of fine analysis call into question the architectural choices made previously for one or more viewpoints, then it is imperative to repeat these last two stages, correcting faults or shortcomings revealed in the architecture studied, then subjecting it again to multiple viewpoint analysis to check that the new compromise is still acceptable for all of these;

– in integration, verification, validation (IVV), it is necessary to check that the constraints identified in OA and SA have really been taken into account effectively in the product's design and development and production. This happens in the classic way, but by defining scenarios appropriate to checking each viewpoint, or by making use of analyses or inspections, some of which may be based on analyses of the engineering and specialty models developed previously.

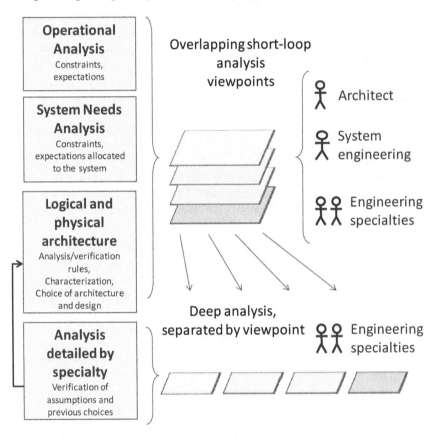

Figure 10.1. *Analysis approach from multiple viewpoints*

As each viewpoint is likely to create one or more specific fine analysis models, it is also necessary to guarantee coherence between the general architectural model and these fine models. To do this, it is recommended, if possible, to have only one reference architecture description, which can be partly carried by the architectural model, and partly by the models of each specialty engineering, but without either redundancy or duplication. For example, the architecture model should be usable as the (sole) description of the system's structure and its internal and external interfaces, completed or detailed for each component in the fine viewpoint models.

NOTE.– *Despite this, we must not confuse that this requires refining analysis, i.e. elements of modeling on the "specialty concerns" axis, with the refinement that will be carried out by subsystem engineers to detail the needs for these and their design.*

Each of these stages and each engineering perspective are likely to contribute to multiple viewpoint analyses and the associated choices, from operational analysis to physical architecture. Consequently, each specialty viewpoint is transverse to previous architectural perspectives (from OA to BS) and contributes to or uses each of them.

EXAMPLE.– *For example, for a space launcher, a feared event described in OA might be an inability to follow the predicted trajectory (it could be linked to an operational activity, for example).*

Then, at SA level, the system's required functions such as vector propulsion will be associated with feared events such as trajectory calculation error and the vector thrust function malfunctioning; both these feared events should be linked to that defined in OA.

Finally, in LA and PA, functional chains and components ensuring the fulfillment of these functions should be subject to a dysfunctional analysis and its consequences: the functional chains, for precision in calculation for example, the components for checking that the redundant calculation chains have no shared mode, which can lead to simultaneous failure, a link whose probability of failure is too high for initial demands.

Moreover, in-depth studies of algorithms, trajectography, failure and fault tolerance, reliability, etc., will confirm the hypotheses and choices made, or call them into question if the specifications' performance for following the trajectory or probabilities of failure are poorly adapted; this could then necessitate a modification in choices of architecture and a new evaluation of alternatives, carried out again on all viewpoints.

***

Each viewpoint formalizes expertise from the specialist profession involved, which will enrich the models describing the requirements and the solution, and uses these models to check the major design choices:

– addition of new notions to the previous modeling (e.g. at the level of needs: expected performances, feared events, possible threats to security, and at the level of the solution: resource sizing, physical capacities for resistance to solicitations, reliability, unitary cost, etc.);

– associated principles of behavior or architecture and architectural styles (e.g. customer-server, redundancy and majority vote for safety, firewall protection against IT attacks, servo principles, etc.);

– metrics, professional standards and expertise, algorithms for model analysis with a view to checking the architecture properties (e.g. calculating precision in data, calculating latency, pressure or electricity consumption; checking the absence of shared failure modes of failure between critical, redundant functional chains etc.);

– criteria for trade-off or for reconciling viewpoints making it possible to choose the most acceptable compromise (which should be privileged, for example: reliability, cost or performance?).

***

The approach described here is likely to involve all levels of system and subsystem engineering, potentially as far as the elementary components. It should therefore be applied to each of these levels, but the dependencies and consequences of the analyses and choices of architecture should also be considered between levels.

Thus, the system's operation safety imposes constraints to subsystem design and development; but conversely, a subsystem's properties and safety constraints can call into question or influence analysis and security policies at the system engineering level; a subsystem's or software's modes of failure are influenced by those of the system (failures in computing or input resources for example), but the subsystem's/software's modes of failure should be integrated into system level analysis (consequences of internal software failure, for example).

10.3. An illustration of some viewpoints

This section describes a scenario for taking account of viewpoints dealing with performance, the safety of goods and people, and protection against attack, in engineering a software-dominant system. This consideration should rely on algorithms and tools, specialized for each viewpoint, which will enable analysis of each alternative architecture captured in the model to verify its pertinence to constraints and expectations. Existing or additional concepts of modeling brought into play in the viewpoint are *mentioned in italics*.

EXAMPLE.– *For the traffic regulation system, various considerations, particularly safety, have been mentioned throughout the presentation of the main perspectives in the method. Only a brief mention of some concerns and considerations linked to these viewpoints is made here, in addition, for the purposes of illustration.*

10.3.1. Operational analysis

General case:

– identify the viewpoint's *operational constraints*;

– from this, deduce the characterization, the sizing parameters and expectations of the *entities or actors* involved, their working conditions, the *operational activities and processes* at play as well as *operational scenarios*.

From the viewpoint of performances:

– identify the *time constraints* on the *operational processes* and critical *activities*;

– list the *action or reaction times* expected by users;

– identify the *scenarios* conveying the superposition and simultaneity of these constraints.

From the viewpoint of the safety of goods and people:

– identify the potential dangers and associated *feared events* with their *criticality level*;

– list the *operational processes* and *scenarios* in which these occur and their operational consequences;

– define degraded *operational modes* (or modes of protection) expected in these scenarios.

From the viewpoint of protection against attack:

– identify the *operational vulnerabilities* and the *critical elements or activities* to protect;

– list the *types of attack* feared and associated *scenarios*;

– identify *response strategies* and *operational processes* with which to react to these attacks to minimize the consequences.

EXAMPLE.– *For example, for the traffic regulation system, determine the maximum blocking time acceptable for the road traffic.*

Identify feared events, such as the presence of a vehicle on the line when a train departs or arrives, the approaching train's inability to stop in time, an incorrect instruction to depart, or failures (accidental or malicious) in observing traffic conditions and promulgating orders to regulate it.

10.3.2. System needs analysis

General case:

– allocate *operational constraints* to the *system* and its environment;

– characterize expectations upon each element in the system needs (*functions, exchanges, functional chains, scenarios,* etc.) accordingly, depending on the sizing parameters decided;

– define the *system's* (and *user*) contribution to the scenarios envisaged and the potential *degraded modes* that it will have to manage.

From the viewpoint of performances:

– for each operational process, define the *functional chains*, which are critical from the viewpoint of their *latency,* traversing the system;

– attribute the previous *time constraints* to these chains and distribute them between *users* and the *system*;

– define the *priorities and* maximum *latencies* acceptable, as well as the *scenarios* dimensioning the system's processes or production.

From the point of view of the safety of goods and people:

– identify the *scenarios* or *functional chains* likely to be at the root of a *feared event*;

– from these, deduce *criticality* of each contributing *function's, data's or exchange's* contributing *criticality;*

– define functional responses appropriate to feared events (*the roles* of surveillance, reconfiguration, etc.) required from the system;

– eventually, complete the list of feared operational events with new events linked to the system's functional content or user behavior.

From the point of view of protection against attacks:

– identify the critical functional chains to be protected and the possible functional vulnerabilities or exchanges-related vulnerabilities;

– from this, deduce each *function, data or exchange's* contributive *criticality*;

– define the *functional safety barriers* required (e.g. required encryption and authentication) and *scenarios* involving protection against or reaction to attacks (e.g. disconnecting the network).

EXAMPLE.– *Identify the critical time for stopping road traffic circulation; determine, in the scenario where the arrival of a train is delayed by a vehicle on the track, the maximum time admissible between detection of the vehicle and signal actuation, depending on the maximum speed limit for the train, and adjust the needs accordingly.*

Identify information on train movement as critical, and communications with the station's information system as presenting a risk for computer security.

Add the monitoring functions needed for the system to perform correctly, and emergency shutdown of train power supplies.

10.3.3. *Logical architecture*

General case:

– propagate the needs' constraints and characterizations on the defined solution;

– characterize elements of the architecture accordingly (*functions, exchanges, components*, etc.);

– implement the principles of architecture and several alternative candidates to satisfy them;

– analyze the pertinence of these choices and choose the alternative providing the best compromise between the different viewpoints considered.

From the viewpoint of performances:

– evaluate the *complexity of the functions* to be carried out, the *size of the data* exchanged, the associated *flows*;

– study the contribution of each *component* to critical *functional chains*;

– identify potential difficult points regarding performance;

– envisage initial adaptations linked to performance (e.g. *components breakdown*, functions *and exchanges distribution and parallelism,* etc.).

From the viewpoint of the safety of goods and people:

– define the possible *failure modes* on the architecture (failing *components* or *exchanges* that cannot be performed, for example associated *scenarios*);

– identify the associated propagation conditions (*defining dysfunctional transformations* linking unavailable or corrupted inputs and the outputs of each *function,* for example);

– according to these failures, define the appropriate safety barriers (e.g. redundancy of critical *components,* majority vote);

– check for each alternative architecture that the probabilities of feared events defined in the previous perspectives (OA and SA) are acceptable;

– possibly, complete the list of feared events with new events linked to the system's design choices (functional and structural).

From the viewpoint of protection against attacks:

– define the possible vulnerabilities on the architecture and *modes and scenarios* of attack (e.g. access to sensitive information or functionalities, identity theft, denial of service, network intrusion or partial takeover of control);

– identify propagation conditions (e.g. *functions or data* accessible in case of intrusion, intrusion perimeter);

– depending on these failures, define the appropriate security barriers (e.g. *functions* or *components* for encrypting *data* and *communications,* firewalls, managing passwords and private keys);

– check for each alternative architecture that the probabilities of attacks succeeding defined in the previous perspectives (OA and SA) are acceptable;

– eventually, complete the list of vulnerabilities with new elements linked to the system's design choices (functional and structural).

EXAMPLE.– *Estimate the time between generation of an order forbidding road traffic circulation, and the lowering of barriers and devices; sequence orders to trains accordingly.*

Add data protection functions issuing from the station IT system for protection from hacking via its communications links. Suggest firewall components.

Define the functions, components and resources for detecting that all devices are functioning properly, and also for detecting conflicts in access to the tracks and processing incidents. Determine the distribution of roles between operators and system for processing incidents, shutting down power to trains and then releasing them.

10.3.4. Physical architecture

General case:

– similar to work carried out in logical architecture;

– integrate the hosting physical components providing resources and physical support for communication.

From the viewpoint of performances:

– as in logical architecture;

– add the performances of *hosting physical components* providing *resources* for the behavioral components (e.g. the processing power and memory capacity of computing resources, bandwidth for communication means);

– define the rules for calculating global performances by comparing the functional complexity metrics to those of the available resources;

– estimate the resulting performances (e.g. compare the complexity of the sum of functions allocated to a *component* to the processing capacity of the *resource* hosting it; compare the volume of data exchanged per unit of time between the functions allocated to the two components and the bandwidth available for the *communication means*; from this, deduce the latency of a *functional chain*);

– analyze and locate deviation from the constraints expressed in the needs perspectives.

From the view point of the safety of goods and people:

– as in logical architecture;

– add a resource characterization (e.g. component reliability, mechanical resistance, failure conditions);

– define the rules and conditions for propagation of defects linked to physical resources;

– analyze the global failure conditions associated with feared events, fault trees and associated minimal cuts;

– place physical security barriers to reach the safety objectives imposed (e.g. redundant *physical paths or resources*, highly reliable *components*).

From the view point of protection against attacks:

– as in logical architecture;

– add a characterization of types of attack and vulnerabilities linked to the choice of resources used (e.g. depending on the operating system, communication standards or business software used);

– define the rules and conditions for propagation of defects or vulnerabilities linked to *physical resources*;

– analyze the global *failure conditions* linked to attacks that can be envisaged, the fault trees and associated minimal cuts;

– place physical security barriers to reach the security objectives imposed (e.g. certified and secure operating systems, hardware cryptography, biometric authentication).

EXAMPLE.– *Check that the power and characteristics of the electric motors and the hydraulic system's latency and power are fully compatible with the time needed to put the required barriers and anti-crossing devices in place.*

Choose a secured operating system for command and control, and a firewall configuration appropriate to the dangers identified.

Choose a high availability host computer card to accommodate the software components for system state management and major incident processing, which is involved in safety management.

Add functions for detecting critical failures and relaying warnings to operators.

To ensure that the presence of a vehicle on the track is detected, apply a classical, redundancy type architectural style including surveillance component: the two radars either side of the track can each give information on the potential presence of a vehicle; but the addition of a component comparing the two detections and detecting potential incoherence is also needed to reduce the risks. Moreover, it must be verified that the two radars are independent of each other (particularly by analyzing physical architecture): no shared power supply, no operational or communications cables with shared control system, for example.

Then, on the basis of this architecture, the appropriate specialty engineering will make calculations on global reliability and the likelihood of failures, the safety engineering will make detailed analyses of modes of failure and their effects, as well as fault trees and minimal cuts, etc.

10.3.5. Contracts development

General case:

– allocate constraints and design choices above to each component;

– define means of analysis, inspection and *test scenarios* on the integrated global system, making it possible to verify the properties and constraints defined during the needs analysis and the effectiveness of corresponding architecture and design choices;

– if these constraints cannot be supported by the available components, repeat the previous process.

From the viewpoint of performances:

– define the *capacities and resources* that each *hosting physical component and physical link* should provide (e.g. calculating power, memory space, bandwidth);

– allocate each *behavioral component* the maximum resource consumption *budget* allowed;

From the viewpoint of the safety of goods and people:

– define for each component the *criticality and reliability level* required, the *behavior* expected in case of failure (e.g. *functions* for failure detection and confinement, reconfiguration, degraded *modes*);

– verify residual vulnerability and the consequences of constraints and choices in taking account of safety when the components are assembled by propagating them at the system engineering level.

From the viewpoint of protection against attacks:

– an approach similar to that carried out for the safety of goods and people.

EXAMPLE.– *The software components with a role in managing safety will be specified, with the highest level of quality assurance required. Radar engineering will report the risks linked to detection errors or false alarms on a presence on the track and the precautions taken in response. The engineering responsible for the barrier and anticrossing device will allocate functional chains at their subsystem ends, carrying the maximum permitted opening/closing times.*

10.4. Summary

To best meet the expectations and constraints identified, the architecture should result from an acceptable compromise between various concerns, each brought by a specialty in its profession (safety, security, performance, product lines, cost, logistics, human factors, etc.).

The model can form an essential support for this coengineering between specialties, each bringing its own constraints to the needs, checking that they are met in the solution, and so helping the architect to evaluate the merits of each alternative architecture.

An iterative approach should be carried out, first with multiple viewpoint analysis in short loop to select the most likely alternatives, then from each viewpoint in detail, to validate the hypotheses and repeat if necessary.

11

Requirements Engineering and Modeling

11.1. Limits of engineering based only on informal requirements

Today, informal requirements (e.g. "the system should provide such and such a function", "...should meet such and such a performance", etc.) are still, in most engineering practices, the main vector for managing technical contracts with customers: the customer expresses their needs in the form of customer requirements or User Requirements (UR); the supplier analyzes, refines, specifies or completes these requirements and from them deduces the System Requirements (SR), drawn up in relation to the URs, and which form the "technical contract" describing the expectations of the solution system, then the component's subsystems, must meet.

But very often, these requirements[1] are also the main (or indeed the only) vector for the formalized system definition, described simply by allocating each requirement to one or more constituents or subsystems; each configuration item in the decomposition tree produced is also linked to the requirements it should meet, just like test campaigns, drawn up in relation to the requirements that they are meant to make it possible to verify; the faults records and requests for change benefit from this same traceability with the requirements.

Unfortunately, this requirement-centered approach shows significant lacunae, likely to weaken the engineering in a high-complexity context. In fact, they are not described formally and are subsequently open to ambiguity and multiple interpretations, and cannot be validated by formal methods or automated analysis. Moreover, they are not fit to describe a functional architectural solution precisely and in a shareable way, and are unsuitable for supporting design (studying and

---

All the figures in this book are available to view in color at: www.iste.co.uk/voirin/arcadia.zip.

1 Hereafter, unless otherwise stated, the single term "requirement" will be used to describe these informal requirements, which are mainly textual.

characterizing alternatives, verifying properties, justifying definitions, etc.). Finally, the process of creating traceability links mentioned above, itself unclear and impossible to formalize, is consequently difficult to validate, which makes using the links a delicate matter.

The most visible limits for requirement-centered engineering appear in integration, verification and validation (IVV) since, in such an approach, this is the first moment when it is really possible to verify the global design hypotheses (unlike the opportunities for anticipated verification that the model approach and multiple viewpoint analysis offer). The faults thus engendered, shown recurrently in these IVV stages, are especially:

– poor mastery of the integration stages and their complexity (as the requirements selected for each stage are not homogenous in terms of complexity);

– missing components when we need to run a test verifying a requirement (in default of a rigorous identification approach to functions and components contributing to satisfying the requirement, resulting in a lack of links between requirements and the product breakdown structure);

– difficulty mastering behavior, especially non-functional behavior (start-up, configuration changes, non-nominal states and modes, etc.) due to lack of functional vision from end to end;

– high complexity in defining, organizing and optimizing non-regression tests (for the same reasons);

– difficulties in locating faults and analyzing impact (as requirements do not describe the solution's operation nor its structure), etc.

These problems will increase with the systems' complexity, products and projects, and of course with the size of engineering teams.

***

In the articulation between system and subsystem engineering too, the use only of informal requirements proves to be ineffective and even risky. In fact, the need to re-express system design in the form of informal requirements aimed at subsystem engineering is both pointless and expensive, but is also a source or errors and misunderstandings, since informal requirements do not provide the expressiveness and rigor required in the description. And in another sense, the subsystem engineering team will have to reconstruct their own needs perspective for their subsystem from these informal elements alone, without any guarantee of conformity with the vision, non-formalized and untransmitted, of the system engineer. The informal diagrams that sometimes accompany textual requirements can certainly be an aid to this mutual understanding, but one that is increasingly insufficient as the level of complexity increases.

11.2. Using models as a support for expressing requirements

Engineering approaches using models such as Arcadia seek (among other things) to palliate these limits to the traditional approach using models as the main engineering vector (formalized "model requirements", but not "formal" requirements), rather than the informal requirements[2]. Figure 11.1 gives a brief view of this.

The needs are mainly formalized in a model, more especially in operational analysis and system needs analysis (SR) in a verifiable form that can be shared and analyzed; model requirements are thus defined, each being formed of a model element or a group of elements identified as contributing to the same requirement; functional requirements in particular are conveyed by operational activities and the functions required of the system, as well as the exchanges, data, scenarios, operational processes and functional chains, modes and associated states; non-functional requirements are also, if possible, conveyed by model elements, for example by functional chains (which convey latency constraints or associated feared events) or data characterized by their confidentiality level, etc.

The requirements that the model has proven unsuitable for expressing are in this case recorded in the textual requirements that arise from completing this model. These can, for example, be environmental requirements (temperatures, corrosion etc.), norms and standards to apply, or a required maintenance period. It is, moreover, recommended not to create "artificial" functions to convey such requirements (such as a hypothetical function of "ensuring a lifespan of 20 years", for example), which makes the model complex without bringing about an associated

---

2 Requirements labeled as informal – most often textual – can, however, be structured in chapters for example; each is generally identified in a unique way, endowed with attributes making it possible to characterize it with a view to its usages (operational importance, criticality, maturity and status, etc.), and linked, for example, to elements of the product breakdown structure and tests. But unlike model requirements, it does not use a description language endowed with a formal grammar and semantics limiting ambiguity of expression, and they are most often not linked to one another by semantic links, as is the case for model requirements.

This being the case, it must be specified that the language supporting Arcadia models (described in the third part of this book) is absolutely not a "formal" language supporting rigorous capacities for testing or verifying mathematical properties, but a simple description language to which can be applied a method of constructing, justifying and evaluating, what informal requirements do not allow. To summarize, the model requirements are (like the model) formalized, and not formal in the strict sense of the term.

benefit, but rather to keep the functions in textual form for example, if this is most explicit.

The solution is formalized by the logical and physical architectures model; it is traced and justified in relation to the needs by links between functional (and non-functional) analyses of the needs and the solution.

The model (rather than the requirements) is linked to configuration elements and to the product breakdown structure by means of components in the physical architecture. Links between the "model requirements" and these elements are obtained via needs-solution traceability links and links for allocating solution functions on the components.

Similarly, tests campaigns are preferably linked to capabilities, functional chains and the scenarios describing them, but also more generally to all the model elements forming requirements that should be verified by these tests: a set of system modes, for example, or an exchange contributing to an interface definition to validate.

Finally, as discussed in Chapter 13, articulation between levels of engineering, the model requirements for each subsystem or component to be specified, identical in nature to those described above, result directly from the physical architecture of the system model, and so are linked to it by traceability links between elements of the system and subsystem model, generally one for one.

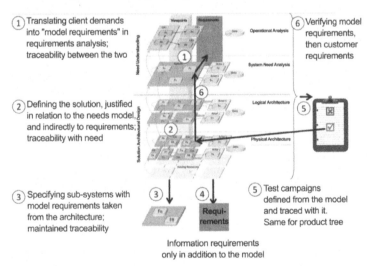

Figure 11.1. *The model, the principal support for requirements*

Consequently, all types of link between requirements and other artifacts in engineering remain, since they are an important support for this; however, these traceability links this time rely on a formalized, unifying model, and an explicit and verifiable process, which secures their usages and thus the engineering.

If the customer wishes, textual or informal requirements remain the main vector. The functional description is, for the customer, an explanatory addition and/or a support for developing the specifications. Therefore, at the system needs level, only those additions that the customer really needs to know and approve, are to be added to informal customer requirements, relying on the model as a support in negotiations.

Within the engineering, on the contrary, modeling thus hosts most of the description of the needs and solution. Anything that can well be expressed in the model is thus formalized in the form of "model requirements". In this case, it is useless to create or refine informal requirements that would be redundant with these model requirements.

Textual, internal requirements can be added where necessary to express a constraint or an expectation more precisely than does the model or to express constraints or expectations it cannot. Customer requirements remain traced in the model and the engineering artifacts for justification. It will be verified later that these requirements have been covered and met indirectly through the model (see Chapter 12, section 12.4).

11.3. Link between informal and model requirements

As the model becomes the main vehicle for the system's requirements, informal requirements received from the customer should, whenever possible, be "translated" into model elements, with which traceability links should be created, to indicate the model elements that formalize each requirement. These "model requirements" are mainly functions of system needs analysis or operational activities, as well as exchanges, data and interfaces, scenarios, modes and states, functional chains, or non-functional properties of these, or sets (grouping elements) of such elements: for example, the link from a requirement to a functional chain or a scenario that illustrates it is often enough, as it is a means of verifying the requirement directly, and this also makes it possible to limit the cost of traceability and its use.

Most often, a customer requirement is taken into account by several elements in the model, and reciprocally for example, a function can contribute to expressing several customer requirements.

Thus, if a requirement relies on data to be exchanged between two functions, it would be more accurate to link it to the exchange concerned itself, as this exchange is likely to carry the definition of the associated data; we could, for example, find requirements mentioning data much more easily by going back from these data to the exchanges that host it and from there to the associated requirements; if it is only the functions that host the requirement, this is impossible to do simply by analyzing the model. But if the requirement focuses on the more global interaction between the functions on either side, at the moment of defining tests for verifying the requirement, then both functions of the two "sides" of the interaction should be considered (and therefore linked to the requirement, and provided during the IVV).

***

Moreover, some customer requirements can also be allocated directly to elements of the solution model (and consequently traced), especially in physical architecture: for example, if they are related to a choice of technology for design or implementation, to production constraints or to respecting norms. It is useless to link them to the needs model in this case (so as not to be led to create artificial functions without any other object). These requirements can also be attached in physical architecture to the components, ports, exchanges or physical links involved.

Finally, informal customer requirements that cannot be modeled are maintained in parallel with the model, and consequently without links to it. The important thing is that after requirements have been taken into account, each of them should be allocated either to a model element, or to another engineering item (simulation, study, etc.), or to a subsystem.

***

Just as the engineering completes the needs model and designs the solution, it can be led to add informal requirements to the model that are complementary to it, to express industrial constraints (choice of reuse, of technology, etc.), development, acquisition or production constraints, and also to prepare and complete the specification for the subsystems; they can also be attached to any element in the physical architecture, including components, ports, exchanges or physical links.

The traceability of informal requirements, especially customer originated, to engineering artifacts (product breakdown structure, tests, etc.) remains available if necessary; it is simply obtained indirectly, via the model, by following the links: requirements ⇔ model ⇔ artifacts.

NOTE.– *The approach to allocate derived requirements to subsystems is described in Chapter 13.*

11.4. Structuring requirements and the model

The first structuring imposed on all requirements is separation, between customer requirements, the SRs formed in response to this expression of customer needs and finally requirements added or derived from engineering, in view of the specification of subsystems and components to be developed or provided. These three requirement bodies follow different life cycles and should be managed (especially in configuration) separately, but correlated, given the links maintained between them.

Within these three requirement bodies, those requirements conveyed by the model are naturally structured by the concepts that the model implements: in preference, by the associated capabilities, functional chains and scenarios, both because they represent different use contexts and the customer's main operational expectations, and also because they will structure the strategy for integration, verification and validation, as detailed in Chapter 12. Another structuring axis, that will complement the previous one, is the product policy to regroup requirements conveyed by the part of the system shared by all the product alternatives and to regroup or segregate the others according to the variabilities they involve.

In parallel with this first structuring, in logical or physical architectures, components provide another natural axis for regrouping requirements, which will be used especially in the articulation between system and subsystem engineering.

These two structuring axes are particularly useful, not only for the intelligibility of the system definition, but also to process more easily the reuse of components or capabilities, management of separate configurations, product policies based on the assembly of reusable parts, etc.

The same benefits may be extended for structuring informal requirements: each time it is possible, they should be structured based on their links with the model (by capability, or by reusable component, for example). This can, of course, lead to reformulating, cutting, refining or duplicating requirements to allow this allocation.

11.5. Summary

In the model-based engineering approach that Arcadia promotes, the principal vector for requirements is the model itself. It conveys system needs requirements in operational analysis and in system needs analysis; it supports requirement traceability links with implementation, tests campaigns and test cases, and the product breakdown structure.

Textual or informal requirements remain, to capture the contractual customer needs if necessary, but also to take account of expectations that the model itself cannot formalize. These requirements can also be used to contribute to specifying subsystems, complementing the model that remains their principal specification vector.

12

Integration, Verification
and Validation Approach

12.1. Defining and implementing the test strategy

12.1.1. *Principles*

Beside securing the engineering and anticipating the verification of design choices, one of the great benefits of model-based system engineering is the support to Integration, Verification and Validation (IVV) of the system (or more generally of the solution fulfilling the expressed needs).

Here, we will specify our definition of these terms, which aim to give well-differentiated objectives for the three concepts, and to show them in relation to Arcadia's different perspectives on engineering.

System integration aims to ensure that the global system operation conforms with the behavior chosen during system design; this is the design described in the system's physical architecture. It is therefore an activity internal to engineering, which verifies the global coherence of the system behavior as designed.

To do this, the system integration activity gradually builds the system by composing (or assembling) its constituent parts, verifying at each stage that the behavior of each and their local interactions conform to their specification; this specification for each component comes from its description in the system's physical architecture and from the contract for development resulting from it:

All the figures in this book are available to view in color at: www.iste.co.uk/voirin/arcadia.zip.

– Verification aims to demonstrate that the system satisfies the requirements (functional and non-functional) for which it has been designed; this need is described in the system requirements and in the system needs analysis perspective of the model. Here, the system is considered as a whole, without prejudging of its structure or its internal functioning (system is seen as a "black box" with no vision of its inner contents). Validation aims to demonstrate that the system, in real use, fully meets the operational expectations and conditions of use of customers, users and other stakeholders in its operation; these expectations are described mainly in operational analysis (as well as by the customer requirements), and involve all aspects of this operation (for example deployment, use, conditions for withdrawal, environment, etc.). This time it is a more open or external activity, often involving final users.

∗∗∗

To build an IVV strategy, a traditional approach involves drawing, from informal requirements, traceability links with configuration elements (CE) of the product breakdown structure (components to be integrated), and creating test campaigns meant to verify each of the requirements, by integrating the CE linked to this requirement.

Experience shows that when the complexity of the needs and solution increase, the previous traceability links are unreliable and questionable and are difficult to verify/justify. On the other hand, the way of building test campaigns remains informal and subject to error. Finally, in the absence of a precise and detailed vision of the system architecture and behavior, it is consequently very difficult to localize precisely the flaws and changes required and to optimize the test strategy and non-regression tests.

Previously, we saw that engineering support models such as those offered by Arcadia better formalize the needs and solution in the least ambiguous and most justifiable way, as well as the traceability links and the justification between them. The IVV approach will therefore mostly rely on these models.

The needs description (OA and SA) will be the main vector for validation with the customer, and for the definition of the functionalities that will be provided to him/her in each delivery. It will also make it possible to define the validation tests in particular.

The functional description of the solution (functional analysis in LA and PA) will make it possible to define the test campaigns for integration and their content to verify the expected behavior that it formalizes and the functionalities made available. It will also be the support for defining successive integration versions in terms of the capabilities and functionalities offered.

Articulation of this functional description with the structural component description will make it possible to define the order of assembly and the logic for integrating these components, the functional contents associated for each component to be integrated, as well as the test means required at the boundaries of the system parts integrated at each stage. Finally, this is a major support for localizing and identifying the defects found and analyzing non-regressions.

12.1.2. Defining the strategy for testing and integration

The first stage for the test strategy is defining *the strategy for delivering operational and system capabilities*, functional chains or scenarios, which should be verified and made available, and especially the order in which they are integrated; this order depends first on the dependencies between capabilities, those which use other capabilities should be integrated and verified after those capabilities they use. The customer may also wish to get some capabilities first according to his/her own needs.

We should also take account of the dependencies between functions that functional chains and capability scenarios involve; it is therefore good to check that the functions providing data to these functions are already integrated during the previous stages – or if not, that simulation means are available for these. We thus define a *functional versioning* that defines the functional content of the successive versions.

This originally functional scheduling may however need to be rearranged, taking account of *analysis of the architecture constraints*: first, some components may not be available as soon as desired, which can jeopardize the order in which the functions are integrated. To carry out this analysis, beside the links between the previous capabilities and functions, the model will make it possible to know the list of components to which are allocated the functions considered in the desired capabilities. If a component is lacking, it is possible to navigate up to the functions, functional chains, scenarios and capabilities concerned, as it will not be possible to test them at this stage.

Then, the dependencies linked to the resources and hosting physical components should also be taken into account: it is clearly not possible to integrate behavioral components before the IT computing resources they need to operate, for example unless there are means of emulating or simulating these resources; similarly, resources for electrical power supply, refrigeration, pressurizing hydraulic fluid, etc., should be available and integrated before the components that need them; these physical dependencies should also be analyzed in the model. It is the same for other types of technological dependencies, such as starting up a server before the clients it supplies for example – there again, test or simulation means can temporarily palliate these problems. Finally, managing risks can lead to tests on a particularly critical component or functionality being put in place as early as possible.

The three previous activities, influencing one another, should be carried out in parallel and iteratively.

$$***$$

The next stage for definition of the test strategy is *determination of the integration configurations*, describing components and elements of architecture to be supplied for each previously defined version, based on the functional versions defined previously and on a time planning compatible both with customer expectations, the availability of components and test means, and the workload associated with verifying each integration version.

It is beyond the scope of this book to describe these activities; however, the engineering model can still, here, guide and secure *dimensioning the IVV plan*.

First, starting from a version's functional definition, analysis of the model (potentially from a dedicated viewpoint) makes it possible to determine components to integrate in order to form this version, and more precisely the functional content (which may be partial) that each of the constituents should provide for the version (integration configuration): this is the *definition of components' functional contents*, required for each version. The contract for development for each component will therefore possibly include the functional contents that it is required to provide to each version of the integration plan. Additionally, for each component, it is possible to determine on which other components its operation depends, by following the functional dependency links, which sometimes lead us to revisit the purely functional initial strategy, and to add these components to the planned integration contents.

Finally, (even if this can and should be done throughout the previous work), it is also necessary to *dimension the IVV plan* to appreciate its complexity at each previously defined stage. The model gives a fairly precise idea of the work that each integration version presents through the functional content, the number of interfaces at work, the number of scenarios and functional chains or components to be tested, etc. This makes it possible to dimension the associated effort through objective metrics, and especially to verify that the successive predicted stages are fully compatible with the project resources and constraints: one could, for example, seek to balance the efforts of one version as closely as possible with another, or on the contrary to adapt them to a progressive increase according to a growing staffing of the integration team.

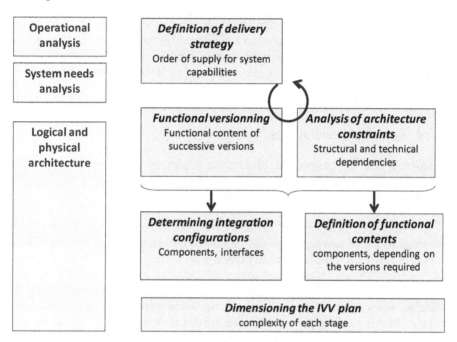

Figure 12.1. *Defining the strategy for testing and integration*

12.1.3. *Optimizing multilevel IVV*

As a continuation of coengineering between system engineering and subsystem engineering, a joint optimization of multilevel IVV (between the systems and subsystems that form it) becomes possible by relying on the organization and links between models of different levels.

On the one hand, it is possible to specify the IVV expectations to the subsystems in the same way and at the same time as specifications expressed by the model:

– the expected versioning (list of successive versions and the functional content of each thanks to the links between the functions allocated to the subsystem and the capabilities present in each of the versions to which they contribute);

– the desired validation scenarios and the functional chains allocated, both at the subsystem boundaries (section 12.3), etc.

On the other hand, when the test campaigns and strategies have been defined at each engineering level, it is possible to optimize them by detecting the tests that are complementary or redundant by defining tests for a group of subsystems at system level that rely on those at subsystem level, etc. This approach relies on the intermodel links between the system and subsystem: for example, if a functional chain in the system can be allocated to a single subsystem, then it should rather be tested at the level of this subsystem; a system scenario can be lightened of all the verification details belonging to the subsystems, if these have already been accomplished in subsystem tests.

12.1.4. *Specifying test means*

In most test campaigns, the system, or a part of it, should be stimulated depending on the chosen test scenarios, and the results provided by its operation should be analyzed and compared to the expectation.

It is therefore necessary to define test means able to provide these stimuli according to the chosen scenarios and functional chains, and to analyze the system outputs to verify that they conform to expectations.

In addition, at each IVV stage, not all of the required components may be available, whereas the integration logic and risk assessment…, justify tests from this moment. In this case, temporary means are needed to replace real components, with functional or non-functional content that is evidently limited and simplified compared to the final components.

In current practices in requirements-based engineering, the specification of test means appears very late, almost at the end of the detailed design or indeed development stage; in fact, in the absence of a precise vision of the content and detailed configurations for the integration stages, one should most often wait for the first design elements of each subsystem or component to be able to define the associated test means; since it is very difficult to define the functional content required at each stage precisely, this means that a large proportion of these surrogate means should be provided in their entirety from the start of the integration.

In the approach proposed by Arcadia, it is possible to specify precisely a large proportion of the test means on several aspects: this means identifying, in the model, for each version and for each test scenario envisaged previously, the components that shall actually be provided, and those that should be simulated or replaced temporarily by test means, as well as the data and parameters to be verified and the associated observation means; it is therefore possible to specify the expectation regarding test means, from this definition stage, with the same principle for the versions and functional content expected for each; this would in particular release constraints on engineering these means and make it possible to extend its deliveries over time.

When part of the architecture has been defined (according to the approach above) so that it can be integrated into a given version, the first stage of functional definition for test means includes, at least, the functions outside the perimeter defined as the version content, but which interact with the perimeter's functions; these initial functions required for the test means (or also built-in test functions integrated into the system) can be obtained directly by following the functional exchanges entering or exiting the perimeter of the model considered. We will therefore create a grouping element in the model (we call it the "test means needs" rightly), which will be initialized with this first lot of functions, including exchanges with the system components being tested.

Then, if necessary, it falls to system engineering to add to these needs regarding test means, additional functions, which may be of several types: system model functions linked to the previous ones by functional dependency links (i.e. by exchanges) and required to specify the behavior expected of the test means; functions to replace some system functions, to simplify them in the test means or adapt them to these; additional functions belonging to the test means, for example to manage particular stimuli, to use and analyze results provided by the tests considered, to give control of the tests to test operators or to extract data present in the system and necessary for the tests. We note that in the latter case, this can lead to the addition in the system architecture itself of stimuli injection points, and observation points, with the sole aim of enabling test means to be connected.

The above-mentioned functions, provided by the test means, can be grouped into components that will structure these means from the viewpoint of the system engineering, for example for reuse (including several successive versions) or to define successive simulation variants (which are increasingly rich in their functions for example or some of which will be implemented on standard commercial off-the-shelf hosting resources before using dedicated means) or also to manage more easily the different versions and therefore the configuration contents for the corresponding test means.

Finally, it may be necessary, in the IVV strategy, to define several configuration states for the different versions and the system components: some can first be replaced by dummies, by simulation or emulation means (to simulate the real weight of a subsystem that has still not been supplied for example, or use a commercial off-the-shelf calculator while waiting for the final calculator to be installed) , or by requirements less stringent than those to be applied in the final system (calculation function with lower precision, communication with reduced flow, etc.). In this case, we will create different components and functions for the test means, potentially in several successive versions, which will be substituted temporarily with the final components as described in the physical architecture, and should be linked to them by justification links.

All these choices will therefore be formalized with the help of elements of the "test means needs", as well as associated functions and potential components; it can be useful to characterize all these elements by an attribute characterizing their nature, describing if they belong to the test means, or if they replace elements of the final system. The "test means needs" should be versioned with regard to the IVV strategy – so possibly defined for each IVV version.

***

As a result of this work on defining test means needs, a needs model, also versioned, will be generated automatically as an input for their own engineering, as will the models for the subsystems (see Chapter 13).

This articulation will occur in the form of a "multicomponent" type transition, since the engineering system will probably already have structured these components at a high level. In this specific case, in the needs model focused on test means that will be formed, the elements defined as "test means needs" will be transmitted as forming the specification of these means; as for the system elements, these will be represented by actors external to the test means with which they must interact.

12.1.5. *Optimizing progress of the integration*

The first means of optimizing integration is to define the IVV strategy very far ahead, at the earliest during the architecture design phase, to verify the ease of testability that the defined architecture presents, and to adjust this architecture to integrate it as easily as possible.

For example, if a component requires huge unitary integration effort due to its functional richness, it can be sensible to break it down into subcomponents, more easily testable, more easily observable, easier to locate flaws, as well as favoring simpler non-regression tests.

It may also be necessary to add system functionalities dedicated to tests, for example to test a communication between two functionally complex components that are distant from one another: simple self-sufficient communication verification functions could be useful to check first their quality and integrity, before beginning complex test procedures. This also makes it possible to verify, progressively, the expected behavior, and to identify the origins of failures more precisely.

Similarly, the architecture's testability and observability may lead to the addition of observation or stimulation points, means of isolating one part or another to test it separately to the rest of the system, even if it means reviewing the breakdown into components here too.

***

In the daily activities of IVV, the first benefits of modeling are linked to better mastery of the system architecture, better understanding of its operation and greater precision in localizing flaws; as a matter of fact, the model enables better comprehension of the system's functioning and the contribution made by each component, it makes it possible to see the impact and imprint of each scenario or functional chain on each to compare the behavior observed with that provided by the model and so to localize deviations and their sources. Often, it even makes it possible to design additional test scenarios to refine analysis and localization of flaws, which are much more accurate and pertinent than without the model.

But from day to day, another important benefit arises from a much more effective and greatly facilitated management of ups and downs. As an example, if a component or subsystem is provided late, or if its functional content does not conform to the expectation, the model is able to identify operational capabilities or functionalities that would not be available as a result (by following the allocation and traceability links back); the model can also help to identify tests it would be useless to run without the expected component or functional content (this time following back the components/functions/scenarios links), since they would not be able to perform the expected but unavailable functionalities. We will therefore define "available" integration versions, from the confrontation between the desired integration versions defined in the integration strategy, and the functional contents and availability of components. On this basis, the associated test campaigns will be reviewed and readjusted depending on the discrepancies compared to the desired integration version.

It is the same for a defect seen during IVV, in which the consequences may be finely analyzed in the same conditions: identifying and localizing this defect on functions, functional chains and components concerned, makes it possible to deduce its consequences on other functionalities and capabilities at work, and therefore on the operational maturity of the associated version or delivery. Moreover, the functional or interface maturity of each component can be estimated from the different defects associated with it (which often results in the "degree of confidence" that the integration team give it), which is a valuable invitation to, potentially, reconsider the initial integration plan.

Non-regression tests can also be optimized, given that their definition relies on the functional content that has evolved between two versions or corrections of defects. It is then easy, thanks to the model, to identify the tests that involve a suspect component, and so to use them as a non-regression perimeter when the component is provided in a new version correcting the defects identified.

Of course, these operations and uses of models for IVV are to be assisted or automated by modeling viewpoints and tools, and more generally by the engineering workshop.

12.2. Verifying model requirements

12.2.1. Principles

The definition of requirements responds mainly to two concerns: on the one hand, the description of what is expected from the system (the expectations) and, on the other hand, in response to these expectations, provision of "proof" that the solution provided meets them correctly (here we will talk of verifying [satisfaction] requirements).

The description of the expectations conveys what the customer wants from the solution supplier; Arcadia suggests formalizing this through the needs model description (model requirements), and the additional informal requirements that this model cannot express simply or effectively.

Provision of proof by the supplier should respond to and be coherent with the previous description of the expectations: it will therefore involve model parts (and informal requirements) describing the needs that we will seek to verify in the system, its design and realization, to demonstrate that they conform fully to the expectation.

This proof is generally provided in several possible forms, and with the help of various concrete means of verifying them: the activities of Inspection, Analysis, Demonstration, Test (IADT). Let us see how the model can be brought to contribute to IADT.

12.2.2. Inspection

First of all, inspection of the model itself can be an extension to inspection of traditional engineering documents to verify that all the requirements (including model requirements) are taken into account fully during design and IVV:

– verify that all the informal entry requirements are properly traced (referenced) by the model, or if this is not the case, to the design justification, evidence and test campaigns;

– verify that each model requirement is properly traced from the solution model, and taken into account in the contracts to subsystems (both in the model part of these contracts, but also in the part for the derived requirements, if there is one);

– verify that each model requirement is properly associated with one or more verification tests (or a verification means), and that it is the same for operational processes and scenarios, regarding the validation;

– later ensure that the results of all these tests are conclusive (on this subject, see section 12.2.4).

Naturally, the task of inspection cannot be reduced to verifying the previous links, but should also and above all ensure that semantically, the account taken in the solution and tests are coherent with the needs. The model's conformity with the expectations is a necessary condition, but it does not contribute to verifying the system itself, of course.

12.2.3. Model analysis

Aside from functional coherence between the needs and solution thus evidenced by prior inspection of the links between them, the verification that requirements are satisfied, especially non-functional requirements can already be partially accomplished through multiviewpoint inspection and analysis of the model. This time, it is a matter of verification if the design of the architecture itself meets the functional and non-functional constraints expressed, particularly in the needs model. The approach followed is the one detailed in Chapter 10.

From this analysis, it is possible to draw proofs contributing to the justification and certification files of the system solution, such as fault trees, their minimal cuts and the associated analysis for example, in the domain of the safety of goods and people.

However, it is important to note that this does not here mean a "formal proof" of the model, which would verify properties by applying mathematical techniques in particular: on the one hand, this would require a much more complex formal language and a substantial enrichment of the model and its complexity; on the other hand, for this analysis to form a real proof in the proper sense of the term, this would also suppose that the remainder of the tool-supported process up to the system production would guarantee that these hypotheses could no longer be questioned at any later stage (for example automatic generation and certification of the software code, as well as the code generation compilation chain, and associated properties of calculators running the code).

In other words, viewpoint analysis verifies system design, but not the properties of the system produced itself. This is a matter for IVV, which will follow through demonstrations and tests.

12.2.4. Demonstration and tests

The activities of demonstration or test involving the system can be defined partly by relying here again on the needs and solution model(s).

Some elements of the system expectations described in the model can be considered to be directly verifiable through demonstrations or tests: scenarios and functional chains at the system boundaries. In fact, the required capabilities of the system, its inputs/outputs, the actions on it and its expected answers/results, which are representative of its use, are defined and illustrated in the scenarios at its boundaries, just like the expected functional content, in the functional scenarios and functional chains, and the associated non-functional constraints. Scenarios and functional chains therefore convey very well the system usage conditions that are representative of the expectations placed on it. Moreover, the test procedures that classically form IVV test campaigns are entirely of the same nature, and should therefore be built, at least in part, by detailing and extending the model's scenarios and functional chains. The conditions for their definition and use are described in more detail in section 12.3.

***

Scenarios and functional chains also make it possible to confirm, this time indirectly, that the system fully satisfies the other model elements that they run: functions and exchanges, states and modes, external interfaces and more generally grouping elements identified as model requirements.

For example, if a function is involved in some functional chains (or functional scenarios), if these are representative of the function's diverse uses[1], and if its major incoming and outgoing exchanges are thus properly performed too, then the function can be considered verified, when all the scenarios and functional chains are verified.

In the same way, a set of exchanges and the interfaces they carry will be considered verified if all the scenarios and chains that mention them are representative of their uses and themselves verified. A mode's or state's incoming and outgoing transition conditions should appear in at least one scenario.

Strictly speaking, this indirect verification principle thus assumes there is detailed analysis during the construction of scenarios and functional chains destined for verification validation: it is a matter of ensuring that each use of any model requirement is covered by at least one of these scenarios or chains, and that all those that mention a model requirement are fully representative of its uses. Here, this meets model-based testing, which formalizes a system use model, independent of its internal design.

Similarly, this also assumes that during analysis of test results, a model requirement is only considered verified if all the scenarios and functional chains that mention it have really been verified themselves.

Just as for informal requirements, model requirements can be defined in all needs and solution perspectives (from the OA to the PA), but system needs analysis (the SA) is clearly the major place for defining them. As we will see in the following, they are verified through their projection into the solution architecture, by means of scenarios and functional chains, which support the tests. Once these have been successful, the associated scenarios and chains are considered verified, which makes it possible, by following the traceability links from the solution back to the needs, to propagate this verification to needs model requirements, in a way similar to traditional practice between system and customer requirements.

12.3. Definition and use of scenarios and functional chains in IVV

Scenarios and functional chains form the natural and preferred support for defining test campaigns in IVV, with the condition; however, they ensure a good coverage of other model requirements, as discussed in section 12.2.4.

---

1 The function's use should be taken here in its most general sense; it can, for example, materialize in an expectation of services or processes carried out by the function, expressed in the form of a textual requirement potentially linked to it, and by the different incoming and outgoing exchanges of the function involved.

On the other hand, directly using the *needs scenarios and functional chains* described in system needs analysis to feed verification activities and tests is not enough, as most of the time the detail of interfaces, associated protocols, operator interfaces or indeed the detail of functionalities really present in the system produced are only defined in the physical architecture (indeed in some cases only in subsystem engineering and models). This is even truer in the use of operational processes and operational analysis scenarios, which should guide validation activities, but cannot be used as such, since they are not even supposed to mention the system.

It is therefore necessary first, for each scenario, operational process or functional chain defined in operational analysis or system needs, to "transpose" it to the logical, then the physical architecture: by following the functional traceability links put in place between the needs and solution perspectives, we first reconstruct a scenario or chain involving the corresponding functions in the architecture, as well as the detailed exchanges added during design of the chosen functional behavior; from this, we deduce scenarios that are no longer functional but structural, i.e. involving interactions between system components carrying these functions and external actors; finally, they are completed by exchanges internal to the system, between the components involved, which also makes it possible to verify the validity of the exchanges identified, and to complete them if needed. We thus obtain *needs verification scenarios*, in logical or physical architecture, traced and justified with the previous needs scenarios.

EXAMPLE.– *This transposition has been made, for example, between the need scenario, as shown in Figure 6.7. System needs scenario -- Nominal train departure – Part 2 and the corresponding scenario in logical architecture are shown in Figure 7.10. It is the same for the functional chains shown in the same Chapters 6 and 7.*

Verification of the operational and system needs analysis scenarios and chains is then carried out by "following back" traceability links between needs and solution – including traceability links between needs and needs verification scenarios (respectively, functional chains) – consolidating at needs level the results of tests carried out on the scenarios, functions and solution.

***

These scenarios and functional chains for verifying needs will for the most part support *system verification and validation* in relation to the needs expressed, but they should be completed by other scenarios and chains; this time illustrating the detail of the design choices and of the chosen behavior, and that will structure verification of good system operation in relation to its design. These *operation verification scenarios and chains* are added in logical and physical architecture, and form part of the normal solution definition. This second type of scenarios and chains will, therefore, this time support *system integration* activities.

It is however most often necessary to define, in addition, *scenarios destined for partial integration* more especially, as the logic that governs it can differ from verifications and validations, which illustrate global use and operation conditions: it is a matter of defining the content of different integration stages using dependencies between the elements to be integrated (functional dependencies, dependencies on required resources, technical dependencies between a client and an IT server for example); in particular, we will define *partial integration scenarios* that will make it possible to carry it out progressively; they will therefore be focused and limited to this or that part of the system, which is subject to a test campaign in the course of the integration strategy.

Furthermore, for the purpose of the subsystem specification and optimization of IVV between engineering levels, it is necessary to define scenarios and functional chains focused on each subsystem, which will define both the behavior expected of the subsystem in operational conditions (resulting from dimensioning scenarios defined especially in the needs), and the tests that are delegated by the engineering system to the subsystem engineering, as a prerequisite for its integration into the system itself. These *scenarios allocated to subsystems* will in particular be the vector for *validation of each subsystem*, as expected by the system engineering.

Figure 12.2 illustrates all of these scenarios and their use in IVV activities. The functional chains show the same differences and expectations.

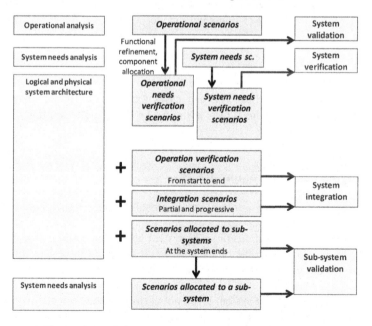

Figure 12.2. *Different types of scenario and their uses*

Finally, specification of test means is also carried out relying in part on the definition of component or subsystem interfaces, but also on the previous scenarios, which characterize the dynamic behavior and use of these test means.

Of course, the additional informal requirements that can arise from a demonstration or test should themselves be verified, in parallel with the model's use.

***

Remember, too, that test campaigns are built especially from the capabilities they should validate, or the components that should be integrated at a given instant. For each capability, the scenarios and functional chains involved are used to define the test cases associated with the campaign. Similarly, for each component to be integrated, the scenarios and chains that use it are candidates for test case definition.

The test cases governing the IVV are therefore built from the model scenarios and functional chains mentioned previously; however, not all of their detailed content is described in the model, as this would pointlessly overburden it. Rather, for each scenario or functional chain described in the model and pertinent for IVV, it is necessary to refine it and complete it to construct more detailed and complete case tests, while still respecting its content (functions, interfaces, etc.): these test cases will in particular integrate alternatives for operation, an exploration of the value margins for parameters and outside the limitations, unlisted uses, degraded operational conditions, etc. For one single model scenario or functional chain, test campaigns will include several test cases, which will be linked to it by traceability links.

To summarize, each test campaign is linked to the capabilities it should show and the components it verifies. The test cases that describe it are linked to the scenarios and functional chains it uses in the model – and to the additional informal requirements.

12.4. Verifying informal requirements

The principle of verifying informal requirements depends on their nature.

Informal requirements (at customer or system level) that could not be expressed effectively by model requirements are verified in the traditional way through the IADT approach described earlier. They are beyond the scope of this book.

Informal requirements (at system level, not customer requirements), which detail model requirements (for example that describe the non-functional behavior or characteristics expected of a function or functional chain), should themselves be taken into account by an IADT-type approach. When they can be verified by tests that also verify the associated model requirements, then they follow the same verification rules as the latter; in the opposite case, they should be subject to separate tests, to which they will be linked by traceability/justification links, and verified directly from the results of these tests.

Finally, informal customer requirements conveyed by model requirements are verified indirectly: this kind of requirement is considered verified when all the model requirements to which it is linked are verified.

Of course, there may be intermediate cases, where verification of a requirement should be obtained both by its direct links with the tests and indirectly through the model.

12.5. Summary

Arcadia suggests basing the system IVV mainly on use of its model as a needs and solution description to guide and structure the IVV strategy and its implementation.

Traditional informal or textual requirements are "translated" into model requirements in OA and SA. These are traced, through the model construction, from the solution (LA and PA) by justification links.

Capabilities, scenarios and functional chains structure integration and delivery versions and test campaigns, and they ensure verification of model requirements.

Informal requirements remain where the model is not appropriate for representing them.

13

Articulation between Engineering Levels

13.1. Principles of the coengineering approach

One of the principle means used in system engineering to master complexity consists, as we have seen, of "dividing and ruling", i.e. cutting the system into a number of subsets or subsystems that may then be designed and developed separately from each other, before being integrated with one another by the system engineering[1]. This of course requires defining the role of each subsystem and the interfaces between them precisely, and verifying that the sum of the contributions of each one fully meets the global objectives fixed for the system, from the functional as well as the non-functional viewpoint.

The approach to defining system architecture mentioned above meets this expectation, with the benefit of reducing the complexity of the problem and solution design by limiting it to only the level of detail and preoccupation required for this level of engineering – i.e. enough to make proper decisions required at this level, but no further. Once this first level of design is validated, the engineering system can "hand over" to the engineering of each subsystem, which takes on the task of designing the subsystem with a finer level of detail but a reduced perimeter as

---

All the figures in this book are available to view in color at: www.iste.co.uk/voirin/arcadia.zip.

1 This approach can be applied recursively at any level in the system or engineering breakdown structure (so between a subsystem's engineering and the associated sub-subsystems' engineering for example). For convenience, in the rest of this chapter, as before, we will use "system level" to designate the higher level of collaboration considered, and "subsystem" level for that of one of the higher level components.

compared to the system; this makes it possible to limit the complexity to be processed in each engineering and to distribute the responsibilities properly: each engineering is responsible for designing its own part as far as its verification and validation are concerned.

However, when the system engineering defines the architecture and the distribution of roles between subsystems alone, on its own, experience shows that the resulting design is often far from optimal, without mutual understanding between the engineering of both levels, and without conciliation between the different constraints that govern their needs and design choices.

***

Arcadia, therefore, advocates a joint definition, at least of the system's physical architecture (PA), "coengineering" between the system-level engineering and the subsystem or component engineering teams (or mechanical, thermal, software, electronic, etc., engineering teams) involved. Responsibility for definition at this level remains with the engineering system, but each brings its own constraints and vision to find together an optimum acceptable for all its parts:

– system engineering defines the principles of operation and architecture of the solution, it guarantees the feasibility of the whole, of operations and global qualities, and adequacy in response to the need; it potentially arbitrates between contradictory constraints or propositions between subsystems;

– each subsystem engineering expresses and verifies its constraints in the system solution design and suggests optimal solutions from its viewpoint; in doing so, it also imbibes the requirements, constraints and choices belonging to the system, and their justification, which keeps its own design to respect them more easily;

– the system engineering, for its part, can better understand the subsystems' constraints, but also their possibilities: the technologies used, the opportunities for reuse and their conditions for example; because of this, the system engineering is better able to define, in full knowledge, interfaces between subsystems and the role of each. This especially reduces the number and duration of successive iterations and feasibility studies;

– finally, this joint approach eases respect for stop criteria appropriate to the responsibilities of each, and especially limits the risk of overspecifying a subsystem by the system engineering: one of the roles of subsystem engineering teams in this coengineering approach is indeed also to ensure that the contract defined by the system engineering remains only at the subsystem need specification level, rather than being the start of the subsystem design; as a matter of fact, this design would probably be non-optimal since it is outside the field of competencies and responsibility for the system engineering, and it would limit the margins for designing the subsystem engineering.

If in the rest of the development, a difficulty or impossibility appears in a subsystem engineering, bringing into question the definition of the system architecture defined previously, then of course the subsystem engineering involved can (and indeed should) renegotiate the conditions for interfacing and inserting its subsystem into the system.

However, most often this should entail a global questioning and reassessment of the system architecture for the system engineering: this modification of expectations on the subsystem will have consequences; these may produce modifications in other subsystems, and very probably an impact on the system's IVV strategy and running. Similarly, the architecture's global properties (such as operation safety) may need to be reconsidered. In these conditions, the previous coengineering process should be followed again, focused this time on the difficulty encountered and its consequences.

13.2. Responsibility and limits of each engineering

More precisely, when should engineering at a given level stop? How far should it define the breakdown of its system, and at what moment should it "hand over" to the subsystem engineering teams? The principle criteria are, of course, architectural and technical, but the distribution of roles and responsibilities is also involved.

The architects at a given engineering level are responsible for the detailed definition of the system architecture, at the appropriate break down level. This engineering level is also responsible for integrating the components it describes, and for verification and validation of the whole set that they form. To be able to define the IVV strategy, the associated test means, the test campaigns, etc., surely, precisely and durably, this architecture definition should be fairly finalized to be stable, and should not be later questioned substantially, especially during subsystem design. It is the capability (or lack of it) to assume these responsibilities that should determine to what level the engineering breakdown system should go:

– if the engineering of a given system level chooses to define (and so impose on the subsystem engineering teams) the intercomponent architecture to a certain level of detail, then it should assume their definition and integration to the end: guarantee the definitive allocation of functions to components (with respect to constraints: performances, operation safety, security, weight, consumption, feasibility constraints, etc.); consolidate interfaces to their finest level of detail for production or acquisition; specify the detailed dynamic behavior expected in interactions between components, etc., such that these are not later questioned. It should also ensure integration of what it has defined, and so itself integrate the components defined with one another and verify their global behavior;

– if the system engineering does not have the competency or means for this finalization, then it must imperatively delegate it to the subsystem engineering teams, rather than impose a breakdown that will later be questioned, or which will be a source of useless constraints. *The system level engineering should therefore stop at the grain of the components it can fully specify and integrate in a finalized way, and allow the subsystem engineering teams to decide the refinement of each, as well as to ensure their global IVV.*

It should however be noted here that "delegate" does not mean no longer having any right to oversight and mastery or control: system level engineering can impose separability constraints on the subsystems (for example for the purposes of modularity, reuse, operation safety, etc.), observability or interchangeability, and can validate their design and internal breakdown in relation to its own architectural constraints, etc. Depending on confidentiality and intellectual or industrial property constraints, it is also free to access detailed models of the subsystems, and to carry out any global analysis involving several of these models.

It is now time to define how the different engineering levels are articulated. This articulation depends especially on the nature of the "contract" between the two levels, first the technical contract (in the form of informal or model requirements) and the industrial contract too, depending on the relationships and role distributions between customer and supplier.

13.3. Articulation by informal requirements only

This approach is applied only in the case where a subsystem or production engineering does not use the Arcadia approach, and there is little or no modeling of its design and architecture.

In this case, the technical "contract" that the subsystem engineering should respect will be defined for the most part by informal requirements (and enriched by all useful additions, such as prestudy results, simulations, dummies and mockups, definitions or interface files, etc.).

Each customer or system requirement, identified during the system level engineering, should be analyzed to determine which subsystems it involves, and how it is refined, specified or restricted for each subsystem involved. A requirement for the system's reaction time to an event, for example, should be transformed into as many requirements as subsystems involved, mentioning the maximum reaction time expected from each subsystem.

The requirements linked to the system model, as we saw above, can be transmitted from the system needs analysis (SA) to the logical analysis (LA) and physical analysis (PA), following the requirement traceability links – SA elements – LA elements – PA elements (for example solution functions responding to a needs function that conveys the initial textual requirement; it will be the same for functional chains, scenarios, etc.).

These system requirements undergo the process of allocation to subsystems and refinement described above; the model can then make it possible to determine the subsystems that a requirement involves, there too by following the traceability links: thus, a requirement placed on a functional chain in SA, for example, should probably be allocated to the components implementing the functions that traverse the functional chains of the PA, which are traced in relation to this needs-level chain: either communally (if it specifies a criticality or confidentiality level for the propagated data for example) or by particularizing it for each subsystem (if it specifies a system reaction time for example, which should be distributed between the subsystems).

We also note that some requirements appear from the outset to involve only one subsystem. In this case, it is possible, indeed desirable, to take account of them only in the subsystem engineering on condition that they clearly have no influence on the definition at the first system engineering level (such as contribution to one or more transverse system functions, the need for distribution between several subsystems, an unanticipated need for input data, etc.). The same questions should be considered if a requirement can be verified entirely at a subsystem's IVV level.

***

Moreover, in a model approach, a substantial part of the expectation for subsystems is contained, as we have seen, in the model itself, which carries the "model requirements". If the contract with the subsystem engineering does not include the model, then the model requirements at system level should also be "translated" into informal requirements (most often textual, sometimes illustrated in the form of explanatory tables describing interfaces, etc.), which represents a non-negligible effort, and the risk of error, incoherence or incompleteness.

To summarize, it is the functional allocation to subsystems and components that guides allocation of informal requirements to these by following the model's traceability links and by completing these requirements to describe, through them, the expectation of the subsystem.

13.4. Model-based articulation

We saw in Chapter 11 the limits of an articulation only by requirements, especially in the continuity and coherence of definition between the different engineering levels involved. The translation of model items into informal requirements destined for subsystems is a source of inefficiency, indeed errors (given the manual nature of the work), and misunderstandings between engineers.

The use of models, both as a major expression of need for the subsystems, but also as a support for transmission of this need, is a very important source of improvement, since it brings about a reduction both in ambiguities, deviations, failures of understanding and transmission, but also less effort in engineering and in rewriting requirements. This is why Arcadia advocates relying on the system model defined in coengineering to generate automatically the contracts for the subsystems, themselves in the form of models.

Arcadia therefore recommends separating the models corresponding to the different engineering models, responsibility and details, with a separate model at each level, but also a formalized articulation with traceability and justification links between them.

Various strategies are, however, possible, depending on the engineering context.

13.4.1. *Single component transition*

The definition of the PA of the system in its associated model (which should be performed in coengineering) defines the contour and the content of each subsystem in the form of a behavioral component, potentially hosted by a hosting component, as well as the non-functional properties it should respect. This definition therefore forms most of the system engineering needs expression for each subsystem (see Chapter 9).

For maximum efficacy, when conditions permit, each subsystem's engineering applies the same approach and method, relying on the subsystem modeling, to benefit from the same advantages; Arcadia is therefore applied recursively to different engineering levels and to the architecture definition of each constituent component identified.

It is therefore possible to extract (automatically) from the model of the system PA, a needs model for each subsystem (SA); this needs model will thus, this time, initialize the model of the subsystem engineering, and will form most of its input contract. This operation is commonly called "(vertical) model transformation".

This subsystem needs model is therefore formed in the following way:

– the "system" boundaries are that of the subsystem itself;

– the functions allocated to it are those of the subsystem in the PA system;

– the other system components, the subsystems at the same level as the subsystem considered and which communicate with it, are transformed into actors external to this subsystem. It is the same for system actors interacting with the subsystem;

– the functions allocated to them[2] are those resulting from their contribution in the system PA, potentially restricted to those functions in direct interaction with the subsystem;

– the exchanges and physical links, scenarios, functional chains, states and modes, data and interfaces, etc., of the system PA, involving the subsystem, are also propagated in its SA, and potentially restricted to the immediate vicinity of the subsystem;

– all the non-functional properties expressed by these model elements in the system PA are also included in the subsystem SA model (for example a latency on a functional chain, here allocated to the subsystem);

– the system operational analysis (OA) can be transmitted directly as it is to the subsystem, or expurgated, or made more precise, detailed or completed (this time manually), if needed;

---

2 This functional vision, broader than the boundaries of the subsystem itself, is necessary, first to specify the dynamic behavior of the interfaces with its environment (communication protocols, for example); it also makes it possible to express the integration, verification and validation conditions: scenarios and test procedures, and functional specification of test means at the subsystem boundaries, which involve functions either side of the subsystem boundary.

– the variability constraints for product line management are also transmitted with the model elements they characterize, as well as the potential part of the associated variability tree (feature model);

– expectations on the subsystem integration, verification and validation are transmitted too: expected versions and characterization of associated model elements, dedicated scenarios or functional chains, etc;

– traceability links are maintained between the two models, so as to support further impact analysis and multilevel navigation between these models.

EXAMPLE.– *In the traffic regulation system, the System Operators Interface component and its environment are described in this system's PA, as shown in Figures 13.1 and 13.2, extracted from the PA of the traffic regulation system model.*

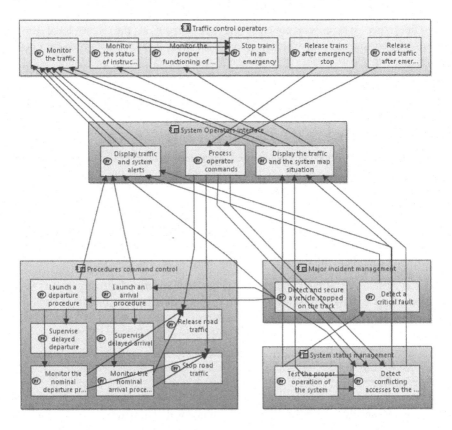

Figure 13.1. *System Operators Interface and functional exchanges*

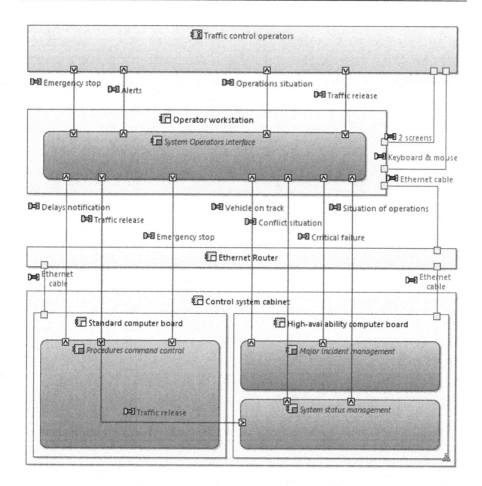

Figure 13.2. *System Operators Interface and components*

If the system engineering considers this component as a subsystem to be subcontracted to allocated dedicated engineering team, the transformation creating the needs model for the System Operators Interface subsystem will give the following result in the subsystem model's SA (not the system SA) (Figure 13.3).

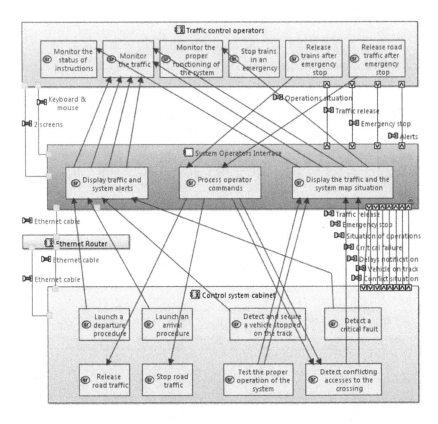

Figure 13.3. *Needs analysis of the System Operators Interface subsystem*

In the majority of articulation cases, the system engineering therefore represents the subsystems it subcontracts in the form of leaf components (i.e. those not broken down into subcomponents), which it defines in its PA (a behavioral component and the hosting component it hosts). Each leaf component description in the system PA gives rise to a model for the subsystem involved, as discussed previously.

13.4.2. *Multicomponent transition*

There are, however, cases where a subsystem's subcontracting (or acquisition) boundary exceeds that of a single leaf component. For example, for a software-predominant system, a software distributed over several execution nodes or servers will in reality be formed of several behavioral components, communicating with one another in the system PA, but it will in fact be subcontracted as a whole. Similarly, the associated computing infrastructure will be formed of a set of networked hosting physical components for software implementation, and will probably be subcontracted as such, i.e. as a set of hosting components, and also behavioral service components, for administration, security, etc.

Consequently, the contract defining the expectation on the subsystem is no longer limited to a functional, non-functional and interface description as before, but it also extends to the definition of the components that should implement these functions, with their own interfaces, connections, etc. In this case, it is therefore really the system engineering (in coengineering with the subsystem engineering teams involved) that defines precisely and once and for all these components and their external interfaces with one another. Logically, these components should therefore appear as such in the subsystem's logical and PA, and their definition by the system engineering should not be questioned there (they are considered in the subsystem model as "read-only", i.e. not modifiable by the subsystem engineering, except with express agreement from the system engineering, and under its control).

The articulation approach in this case initializes a subsystem model with more details and wider scope than in the previous case, by adding the contract part regarding the structural constraints and components; it includes:

– the subsystem needs (SA) described above (thus including in particular all the system PA functions allocated to the subsystem's perimeter);

– the subsystem's logical architecture (LA), initialized with the behavioral components defined in the system PA for the subsystem, their associated exchanges and interfaces, data models, states and modes, etc.;

– the subsystem's PA, initialized with the hosting physical components defined in the system PA for the subsystem, their associated physical links, etc;

– still in the subsystem PA, the behavioral components defined in the system PA for the subsystem, their associated exchanges and interfaces, data models, states and modes. This term of the contract can however be optional; if the system engineering authorizes the breakdown of the component it defines, provided that it preserves the interfaces and functional allocations;

– an allocation contract link between each function in the sub-system SA and component in the sub-system LA and PA that should carry it;

– a hosting contract link between each software component of the subsystem LA and the hosting component that should host it in the subsystem PA, if the system engineering authorizes the component breakdown.

The "read only" components thus created in the subsystem architecture in this way impose on the subsystem the structure chosen for it in the system engineering, and the contract links make it possible to verify respect for the allocations and hostings in the subsystem model. As a matter of fact, each SA function is linked by traceability to one or more LA and PA functions; following the links down to the component to which the latter are allocated, we can therefore verify if these links are really coherent with the direct contract link between the SA function and the component that should take account of it.

EXAMPLE.– *The description of the liftable barrier in the PA of the traffic regulation system is shown in Figure 8.15. From this description, the multicomponent transition will initialize the three perspectives, SA, LA, and PA, of the subsystem level model of the liftable barrier, as shown in Figures 13.4–13.6 (with, additionally, allocation contract links, not visualized here).*

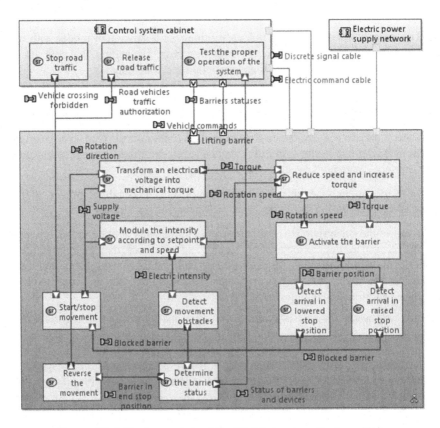

Figure 13.4. *System needs of the liftable barrier after transition*

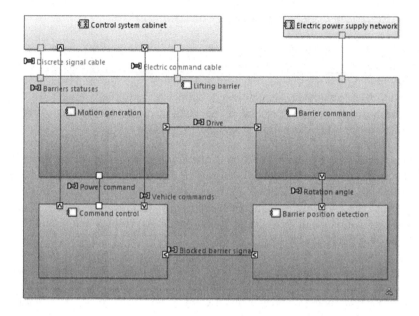

Figure 13.5. *Logical architecture of the liftable barrier after transition*

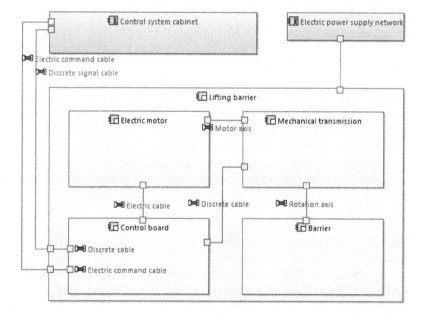

Figure 13.6. *Physical architecture of the liftable barrier after transition*

13.4.3. Reusable component-based construction

The purely "descending" approach shown above is not the only one: it is common for all or part of the system to be formed by assembling existing components "on the shelf" (see Chapter 15). In this case, the previous process is reversed: each subsystem engineering builds a simplified model of those components to be reused, destined to be integrated into the system's PA (this simplified model is therefore itself at system PA level).

This model is a "synthetic" version of the engineering model of the component or subsystem, as its level of detail conforms to the system engineering's concerns, which does not need the detailed and precise description required to design the component. The assembly of component models by the system engineering as they are designed would result in a system model much too complex and voluminous to be usable at this engineering level.

Depending on the cases, it may be preferable to provide either a basic model per component – the system engineering being in charge of assembling the components – or rather a global model of preassembled components, if the rules for assembly are complex and if the number of assembly combinations remains limited.

Finally, traceability links should, however, be maintained between the two models to verify that coherence is maintained between the two all along changes on both sides.

13.4.4. Transition to design and development engineering

Each design, development, production engineering has its own specifics, processes, formalisms and tools, which require an adapted and for much of the time non-generalizable response. We will consequently limit ourselves to citing some examples of articulation, and the use of Arcadia engineering models made. It should however be noted that in the majority of cases, a single model is likely to feed several development and production engineering teams at once, for different parts coexisting in the system and which should interact with one another.

Generally, the product breakdown structure should be reused within the organization management and production system: it initializes a part of its nomenclature and product configuration items. This part of the model is linked by traceability and navigation links to the product reference database (Product Lifecycle Management) for example, and the PA (and possibly other parts of the model) can also be referenced in technical problems report databases, feedback from logistical support, requests for changes, etc.

EXAMPLE.– *When the system includes an electric or electronic subset, for example, the PA describes the connections between the hosting physical components; a viewpoint dedicated to wiring can enrich the model with information for defining cables, connectors and their pinout, signal routing and electric lines, grouping in strands, defining motherboards, packplanes, etc., from which the specialist tools and the production and assembly files can be initialized automatically. Here, it is therefore a model transformation that makes the link between the engineering teams.*

In the case of a mechanical structure, however (including the support structure for the electronic sub-set above, boards, racks, cabinets, etc.), the link is looser, as there is a clear rupture in representation between the engineering model and the digital 3D models; these models add connecting parts for example: most often, articulation is limited to navigation and traceability links, for example between the system model's components or exchanges, and parts or sets in the 3D model. It can however be useful sometimes, when the structural engineering model is complex, to initialize, automatically, the digital 3D model by an initial breakdown into parts, or to create, automatically, the 3D components representing the connections or assembly described in PA, this time using an initial transformation between models; of course, no geometry or other information can be extracted from the engineering model, which therefore provides only the nodes of the digital 3D model and their links at a high level.

The case of a software subset is particular, as, on the one hand, Arcadia can be used to define and justify its architecture itself (with viewpoints dedicated to the software domain or course) and, on the other hand, the Arcadia language can describe design elements that can be directly integrated in the software design models, or the code itself in some cases.

Here, we take up the hypothesis where the software architecture is designed using Arcadia. In this case, at least the definition of the software interfaces, and the associated data model, can most often be generated automatically in a form directly usable by the software code, in the appropriate target language.

EXAMPLE.– *In the case where the software development relies on an approach based on components, it is most often possible to go further and generate automatically:*

– the definition of each component (its "container") with its interfaces, provided and required services, especially:

- the description of the assembly of software (behavioral) components with one another (via behavioral exchanges),

- and the description of the deployment of software components on the execution computing nodes via the hosting components.

In this case, it remains only for the designer to write the detailed design of each component's applicative behavior.

To go further, if the software technologies chosen permit it, scenarios, state(s) and mode(s) machines, non-functional properties, etc., allocated to components, as described in the Arcadia model, can also be reused to generate the corresponding software artifacts.

Finally, depending on the case, these transformations from the Arcadia software architecture model can target the standard code in the target programming language, application code generators, or software design models (in UML for example), which will then generate the code required.

13.5. Articulation with the customer

The use of engineering models as a major support for customer needs specifications is still very far from being the rule. It also poses numerous questions, including on the contractual and legal level, which largely exceed the scope of this book. However, different (non-exhaustive) scenarios can already be considered in the technical conditions for their use.

We will distinguish in particular the case of a final customer (the specifier and recipient of the solution to be provided), and that of a lead system supplier, who is the project owner or integrator of the whole, and delegates parts of work to the subsystem engineering or subcontractors considered.

13.5.1. *Articulation between final customer and lead system supplier*

The final customer, when they adopt a modeling approach, uses it most often to support an activity that frames and analyzes its general need[3].

This analysis is followed, for the customer (potentially jointly with the lead supplier), by seeking the solutions in principle to this need, and choosing those that

---

3 By the way, note that this customer need goes far beyond the perimeter of the system of interest: also to be considered are the required capabilities and their conditions for acquisition and deployment over time; organizational aspects; doctrines, operational rules and processes; resources, competencies, training; logistical footprint and associated means; etc., and this over the whole deployment and lifecycle of the required capabilities. These elements are, however, beyond the scope of this book.

represent the best global compromises. But the definition of the solution(s) retained is still very general (we talk about the solution's "orientation"), and not sufficient to form a complete specification of the system or solution to be designed and developed. The specifications are at a level of definition that is still preliminary and not finalized (User Requirements (UR) or Technical Need Specifications (TNS)).

When customer models come to formalize some of these elements, these models form some of the inputs into the supplier's system engineering. The descriptions thus made and the underlying concepts are supported mainly by Architecture Frameworks languages such as NAF. Although their scope is much larger than that embraced by Arcadia, these descriptions include concepts and principles similar to Arcadia's initial perspectives, OA and SA. But the associated analysis is still not yet sufficiently advanced to be able to build input requirement for the system to be designed, it should therefore be refined, consolidated and finalized by the system engineering.

***

From these inputs, the engineering analyzes and defines the detailed need (in OA and SA) assigned to it to produce System Requirements or System Specifications.

We therefore have two models, the orientation model developed and provided by the customer, and the engineering model that forms the response proposition by the supplier. These models are described at different levels of granularity, detail and finalization. Traceability/justification should be created and maintained between the two worlds for models as for informal requirements. The proximity of concepts on both sides is evidently a factor facilitating this traceability.

13.5.2. Articulation between the lead supplier and a subsystem supplier

When the customer is themselves the lead supplier of a solution to which the subsystem subject of the engineering contributes, then the lead supplier must create their own system engineering. The approach should therefore become closer to that described above (section 13.4).

In a hypothesis where the customer chooses a real coengineering with subsystem suppliers, this can lead to a joint definition of the subsystem specifications detailed enough to form the subsystem requirements directly. The customer model, developed jointly, is then at the same level as the subsystem's SA.

If the customer also uses Arcadia, then the single- or multiple-component transition as described above can be applied, and this is clearly the simplest and safest situation. In the opposite case, it is necessary to attempt to bring closer the customer's modeling language and that of Arcadia, to be able to apply a secure model transformation, which would directly initialize the Arcadia subsystem model. This is possible in a number of cases where the proximity of concepts permits (frameworks architecture in particular), but work remains to be carried out on a case by case basis. It is essential, in this case, not only to seek semantic correspondences between concepts in the two languages, but also in the principles of building models themselves, in the processes of building and using models.

In fact, two partners do not necessarily share the same modeling objectives, the same levels of detail, the same engineering constraints, etc. The differences between engineering and modeling methods, the semantics of the concepts they use, uses of models, concepts, rules and modeling practices, etc., and of course the associated tools can therefore be significant.

If it is not possible to bring approaches and concepts closer in this way, then it is generally preferable not to constrain the modeling either side, thinking to simplify the transition by doing do, as this would detract from each partner's tooled approach. The minimum to be ensured is therefore to maintain traceability between the two partners' models, between requirements and coherent management both of versions and configuration. It is also often possible to transmit at least the definition of the subsystem interfaces in a formalized way.

***

In the hypothesis where a real coengineering is not possible however, then it is probable that the customer need is at a preliminary level of defining User Requirements, and requires additional refinement to build proper subsystem requirements. As mentioned in section 13.5.1, the supplier's system engineering will have to analyze this need and deduce the detailed need from it (in OA and SA) to produce System Requirements.

The two models, the one at global system level by the customer and the other that builds the response proposition by the supplier, will therefore be linked only by traceability/justification links, as informal requirements are today.

13.6. Summary

The articulation between system engineering and subsystem engineering teams begins with (coengineering) collaboration between them for developing the system PA.

This coengineering makes it possible to establish each party's limits and responsibilities, and from this to deduce the level of detail appropriate to each for designing their own model.

The use of engineering models offers the opportunity to formalize the technical contract between stakeholders and to automate the transition from one to the other, with scenarios dependent on roles, organizations and business processes.

14

System Supervision, States and Modes

14.1. Introduction to supervision

The notion of the system supervision considered here covers several aspects:

– management of the system's and its components' modes and states;

– monitoring the system's correct operation and detecting potential failures;

– potential dynamic reconfigurations to be made during operation, especially for failure recovery;

– starting and shutdown of the system and its components.

The general engineering of a system's supervision is a very broad and complex subject and is often underestimated; here, we will only consider its relationships with the architecture definition as driven with the help of the model, and the engineering approach it underlies. But the approach discussed in the following already gives a good idea of the complexity of what must really be considered a full-fledged specialty engineering.

14.2. Principles and concepts

Note that unless stated otherwise, the notions introduced here can be applied just as well to operational entities, actors, the system of interest and its components, even though the approach discussed in the following will be presented from the system's viewpoint.

The definition of the system's expected behavior (or therefore, of one of the elements mentioned earlier) in situations decided from the design is captured in the form of system *modes*[1]; each mode is characterized principally by the functional content expected of the system in this mode (as a mnemonic, we talk of a "mode of life" to express the different expectations, priorities and activities in a life, and a "mode of transport" to indicate the means of travel). A mode can convey various concepts, such as a mission or process stage, a particular behavior required of the system, conditions of use such as a test or maintenance mode, a training mode, etc.

EXAMPLE.– *As its principal modes, the traffic control system will naturally have the modes characterizing the principal situations it should manage: train departure, train arrival and road traffic.*

To illustrate another domain, if we consider the case of an avionics system, it could have principal modes such as aircraft parking, taxi-ing, take-off, climb, cruise, descent, approach and landing.

Passing from one mode to another corresponds generally to an explicit decision, for example changing the system's use to respond to new needs or new situations; it is therefore conditioned by choices made by the system, users or external actors, through operating a functional exchange or activating a particular function for example. In addition, only some transitions from a mode to one or more others are significant.

EXAMPLE.– *A direct transition between taxi-ing and take-off is possible, but not between taxi-ing and cruising for example.*

For all these reasons, formalization of modes uses the notion of oriented *transition*, linking two modes to indicate that a transition from one to another is possible. The transition is also characterized by conditions for passing from an initial mode to a subsequent mode (operating a functional exchange for example)[2]. A set of modes and the transitions that govern them will be described in what we will call a "modes machine" (see note 1).

EXAMPLE.– *Transitions triggering passing in the mode "Train arrival" will, for example, be triggered when arriving train passes a train detector (this will be*

---

1 The detailed definition of states and modes and their modeling is specified in Chapter 18. It should be noted that the definition and use of modes and states systems in the literature and industry are varied and sometimes contradictory, as expressed, for example, by [OLV 14, WAS 11].

2 The formalism most often used in this formalization is called a finite state machine; we will avoid the term later to avoid confusion with states as mentioned in the Arcadia method, since for the method, modes, as well as states, use this formalism.

a functional exchange from the train actor, to the passing detection function) (Figure 14.1).

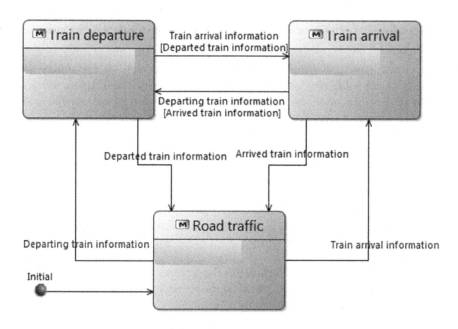

Figure 14.1. *Traffic control modes*

The transition between a plane's taxi-ing and take-off will be triggered by receipt of permission to take off from the control tower (which will without doubt have materialized in the model through a functional exchange coming from the control tower external actor). On the contrary, transition from the cruising to the descent stage will most often come from an automatic pilot command, so from a functional exchange internal to the system.

***

In the course of its life and use, the system also passes through some states it undergoes (we say "What a state you are in!" and we speak of a "state of alert or of emergency" to indicate an unexpected situation). Most often, a state characterizes mostly structural elements (presence or absence of a component, availability or breakdown, integrity or lack of it, availability of an external actor or loss of connection with it, etc.).

EXAMPLE.– *The level crossing can be found in a state occupied by a vehicle stuck on the track, or on the contrary, free (as expressed by the states of the control system itself). This situation is of course foreseen, but not on the initiative of the system, so it is undergone by the system, which must consequently react.*

Another example: our airplane can also be in states of filling different tanks, which change during the flight independently of the actions of the system itself (which does not mean that the system has no influence on these states, since the choices in the flight plan can, for example, influence consumption, but the system has no direct control over these states, which here too it undergoes).

Transition from one state to another is often involuntary, and will therefore result, for example, in a change in property for one or more elements in the system (availability/unavailability for example).

EXAMPLE.– *The system can move from a state of good performance to one (or more) failure states. Each of them will be characterized by the integrity or failure properties of the system elements involved.*

The formalization of states identified is the same as that retained for the modes. Transitions are characterized by the changes at the root of the transition to the subsequent state (such as the change of an availability property). Generally, unlike with modes, a change of state is not triggered by a functional element. A set of states and the transitions that govern them will be described in what we will call a "states machine" (see note 1).

EXAMPLE.– *The failure of a system component – electrical or IT breakdown, rupture of a cable or hose, etc. – will only be manifested in the model by a change in the property associated with this component.*

Note that a states' machine does not contain modes and vice versa: states and modes are defined separately from one another and potentially cohabit, but always in separate machines.

To characterize the system when it is in a given mode or state, we will define the notion of *configuration*: a configuration identifies a set of model elements, of all types (for example functions, components, exchanges, etc.), globally involved in use of the configuration, at a given instant. A configuration can be attached to one or more modes and/or states.

A configuration intended to describe the expectation of a mode will tend to be (though not exclusively) function dominant (capabilities, functions, exchanges, functional chains and scenarios, etc.) to express the expected functional content – or if it is easier to express, the functional content not present in this mode.

EXAMPLE.– *The configuration associated with the Train departure mode will mention in particular the road traffic control and detection and train departure functions, functions for operating the departure procedure, and command functions for appropriate train and road traffic signals and devices. It will not on the other hand mention anything that manages trains arriving.*

A configuration intended to describe a state may be structural dominant (hosting physical components, physical links, indeed behavioral components hosted on the former, etc.), but could also include functional aspects, depending on the nature of the states considered (for example attack or failure scenarios, from a security viewpoint).

EXAMPLE.– *The configuration associated with a state of system failure will, for example, express those components unavailable because of the breakdown.*

During a transatlantic flight, the loss of a VHF or UHF data link (due to its limited scope) above the ocean will be communicated by passing from a state of good reception to a state of communication loss, to which will be attached a configuration that makes the physical links associated with use of this link unavailable. It will be able to lead to a change in communication mode, this time, the new mode replacing the UHV/VHF means by satellite communications for example.

In both cases, each model element's contribution to the configuration will be characterized by properties associated with the element in the configuration.

EXAMPLE.– *For example, a component will be qualified as being in a good state of operation, partially failing, in breakdown; a function could be qualified by its nominal or limited performances, etc.*

For a given mode or state, it is sometimes necessary to define several configurations, whose rules of cohabitation should be clearly defined: for example, we can choose to define configurations that list the elements to be included in the mode or state, and other configurations listing elements to be excluded. By default, we will consider that the resulting global configuration, characterizing the mode or state, is the union of all the configurations mentioned, by inclusion or exclusion.

Moreover, a single configuration can be used in several modes or states.

Different types of modes, and different types of states, can cohabit at a given instant for a single element.

EXAMPLE.– *Thus, the traffic control system can simultaneously be:*

– *in operational mode (with a real circulation of trains and road vehicles) or instead in training mode, and in this case not connected to signaling and control devices (each mode is exclusive of the other);*

– *and at the same time in a mode paired with the station information system, or instead in autonomous mode if this is unavailable;*

– *in the train departure, or train arrival, or road traffic, or emergency stop mode.*

At the same time, it can be, always simultaneously:

– *in a complete or partial configuration state due to maintenance (crossing prevention devices for example);*

– *and in a state where some of its components may be in breakdown.*

Therefore, the model will be able to include for a single element, several modes machines and several states machines, which will cohabit and be active simultaneously.

It is therefore necessary to define the combination of these states and modes to be able to study their consequences. For this, we will use the notion of *a situation of superposition*. A situation is defined as a logical combination of modes and states (for example (mode1 AND state1) OR (mode2 AND (state2 OR state3)), which would express the superposition of modes and states likely to occur at a given instant.

EXAMPLE.– *Operational mode AND (autonomous mode OR paired mode) AND (train departure OR train arrival) AND complete configuration state AND good working order state.*

A scenario can mention the transition from one situation of superposition to another, in the same way as it will mention changes of states and modes in the course of time.

***

States and modes engineering will rely on these different concepts and their links, to confront them and verify that the system's expectations are really met in all situations; if not, the architecture should be revised to minimize deviations in behavior.

Finally, supervision engineering will define the functions required of it, and especially each component's contribution, the associated exchanges and interfaces, and the dynamic behavior associated with each change of state and mode.

The following sections detail this approach. The different concepts mentioned are an integral part of the Arcadia model described above, and are linked to other elements of this model. The formalization mentioned in the following is therefore a necessary complement to modeling, and the analyses indicated rely entirely on the model, through manual use or assisted by an appropriate tool.

14.3. Articulation between states and modes in Arcadia perspectives

As we have seen in Chapter 4 (section 4.2), the definition of states and modes is one of the views that form and support Arcadia's functional analysis, in all its uses. There are, therefore, states and modes machines in each perspective and each level of engineering. However, a correct approach is needed to ensure coherence of the whole between the different perspectives of an engineering level, and between engineering levels. This section introduces the nature of state and modes in each perspective, and their articulation between perspectives. Section 14.3.1 will detail the conditions for defining them in a perspective.

14.3.1. *States and modes in operational analysis*

In operational analysis, states and modes most often describe either general situations that the organization considered confronts (usually rather states such as routine conditions, states of crisis, a situation where there is a lack of resources, for example), or the stages of a mission, or of the organization's normal functioning (usually rather modes, such as an airplane's or space launcher's stages of flight).

They can be common to all the analysis' operational entities, or to one of them in particular. Operational processes differ depending on these states and modes, and the scenarios bear a trace of them, mentioning the modes or states and situations involved.

14.3.2. States and modes in system needs analysis

The principle states and modes defined here are those describing the expectation on the system, as desired by the customer; they are most often perceived and employed by the final users. In particular, they capture the different modes and conditions of use required of the system in different situations, and feared situations, with the minimal behavior required when facing these situations.

These system states and modes should be coherent with those defined in operational analysis if these involve the system; consequently, a traceability will be maintained between each system mode or state and its homologs in operational analysis to which it contributes. On the contrary, nothing demands that each operational mode or state have an equivalent in system analysis.

However, if a system mode contributes to one or more operational modes, for example, it would be desirable to check that the associated configurations are fully compatible with one another, i.e. the traceability links between system modes are fully coherent with the traceability links between the system functions of the associated configurations and the corresponding activities in operational analysis.

Each actor can also carry states and modes, often issuing from operational analysis.

These actor states and modes can impact the functioning expected of the system.

EXAMPLE.– *Seen from the traffic control system, the external actor station information system may be in an available state, or for example be undergoing maintenance. Passing into this second state, which causes its link with the system to rupture, can lead to a change in the system's state (since communication is no longer possible), and the switch to Autonomous mode, providing a more limited service.*

There, too, it must be possible to carry out coherence verification. In particular, it can be useful to include, in situations of superposition, the states and modes of actors linked to the system and likely to influence it. Functional verification will consist especially of verifying the feasibility and continuity of the scenarios and functional chains associated with the required capabilities, between system and actors, in the different situations of superposition defined.

14.3.3. States and modes in logical architecture

The same approach should be considered and applied as in system needs analysis: the coherence and traceability of states and modes in logical architecture with regard to system needs analysis states and modes (and coherence of the content of associated configurations), taking account of the actors' states and modes.

However, the system states and modes respond this time to design choices or constraints. New modes and states reflecting the choices of solutions can appear, which cannot be linked to those of need analysis.

Moreover, articulation between system states and modes and those of components, within the logical architecture, should be ensured. This is described in the generic approach to definition in section 14.5.2.

14.3.4. States and modes in physical architecture

The same approach as in logical architecture is applied here, too, especially coherence and traceability with states and modes in logical architecture.

However, it is applied to the system, but also to each logical architecture component and to the physical architecture components linked to it: modes and states, as well as the content of their associated configurations, should be coherent with traceability links (between functions, between components, between exchanges triggering transitions, etc.) between both architecture perspectives.

Moreover, the appearance of hosting physical components, providing resources for implementing or executing behavioral components most often adds an additional dimension, linked in particular to these components' possible failure conditions. The articulation between modes and states then becomes particularly crucial, as the general approach in the following describes.

14.3.5. States and modes between engineering levels

In conformity with the general principles of articulation between levels of engineering described in Chapter 13, the definition of the expectation for each subsystem is created in coengineering in the system's physical architecture. The definition of the states and modes of each subsystem or component is part of it; it is described in section 14.5.2.

The states and modes thus defined and allocated to the subsystem in system physical architecture will therefore be those that will define their own (sub)-system needs analysis.

14.4. Approach to defining states and modes and the system supervision

The general approach to engineering states and modes shown here is generic, it is applied to each level of engineering and in the different Arcadia perspectives (OA, SA, LA, PA); of course, the aspect involving components only applies in the perspectives concerned (LA, PA).

This approach can be summarized in a few steps:

– definition of expected behaviors;

– analysis of superpositions of states and modes;

– adaptation of the architecture to superpositions.

This approach will be followed by designing the associated supervision.

The generic approach is shown below (and illustrated for the system itself); the different ways to apply it to the system, to actors, subsystems and components depending on the perspective considered are specified in section 14.3.

14.4.1. Definition of expected behaviors

14.4.1.1. Modes

The first stage of this definition of states and modes consists of the behavior expected to face the different situations the system will encounter: the principle modes of operation, and the capabilities, functions... required in these modes; but also the system's conditions for evolving in its environment, and the different states of the environment, independent of its own choices and functions, with which it is likely to be confronted. This approach is carried out jointly with the functional analysis described earlier in this book.

First, we identify the different types of modes required simultaneously: for example, use in an operational or training situation; operational use or maintenance, autonomous mode or piloted by an operator or an external system, etc.

For each type of mode, we then define the list of required modes, and the possible and desired transitions from one to the other, formalized in as many (simultaneous) modes machines as there are types of modes required.

The content of each mode is then specified by one or more unitary configurations describing the expected functional and non-functional content (in first place, required capabilities and functions, functional chains or scenarios it should be possible to play out in this mode, performances and other associated properties, etc.) or indeed expected structural aspects (components, interfaces, exchanges, physical links, etc.), when in operational use of the system, in nominal conditions. A single configuration can be shared by several modes.

The conditions for the transition and triggering of passage from one mode to another within each machine are then defined, relying also on functional aspects (performing functional exchanges, running functions, etc.).

14.4.1.2. States

The different simultaneous state machines that can impact the system's content and performance will be defined in a similar way (especially states of the presence or absence of components, good operation or failure of components or physical links, of degradation of the resources or capabilities offered, etc.).

As above, we will also describe the unitary configurations associated with these states, describing the predictable structural content (components, interfaces, exchanges, physical links and associated properties – the availability of each component for example) or indeed functional and non-functional content (associated functions, functional chains, performances or integrity, etc.).

14.4.1.3. Situations of superposition and global expected configurations

Once the behavior expected of the system is defined, it is necessary to confront it with the situations that can influence it, or indeed call it into question, in the course of the system life and use. This consists first of describing (for example for each first-level mission or capability), the probable situations that the system will encounter corresponding to specific contexts: each critical or essential "life stage" and each "context of interest or use" for example.

Each situation will identify the modes required for the system to provide the service expected in each situation, and their superposition (the logical combination of the modes and states considered), as well as the states likely to be produced in this situation, especially feared states (attacks, failures or breakdowns, external disturbances, etc.). It is therefore a situation of superposition of current modes and states, i.e. all active simultaneously at a given instant.

It is often useful to time order or situate these situations of superposition in time to express a general evolution; this can be captured in the scenarios.

***

It is also necessary, independently of the modes and states to be considered in each situation, also to define an objective, a "global configuration of interest" or "expected configuration" (at least from a functional point of view) in this situation, to be able to verify that the design underway fully conforms to it. This configuration will, for example, include scenarios it is desirable to be able to run, or expected capabilities that should absolutely be preserved (Figure 14.2).

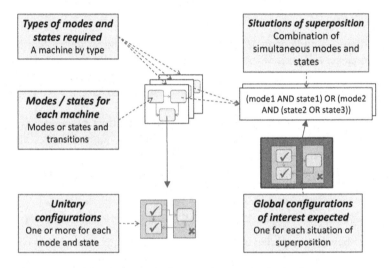

Figure 14.2. *Definition of expected behaviors*

14.4.2. *Analysis of superpositions of modes and states*

14.4.2.1. *Resulting configuration observed for each mode situation*

Until now, nothing has made it possible to verify that the configurations associated with each mode of a given situation are coherent with one another. Each situation of superposition of several modes causes constraints resulting from configurations associated with each mode, which should combine with one another, but may be incomplete or contradictory (for example a function can be required in one mode and eliminated in another, or a functional chain can become incomplete if the functions it uses are not available in this mode, etc.).

To verify it, the following stage of the approach therefore consists of building the "global calculated configuration", or also "observed configuration", as the superposition of the envisaged modes imposes. This configuration is calculated by combining unitary configurations of the modes superposed in the situation. Combination rules should be defined there as well, starting by default from a union of all the constraints belonging to each mode (Figure 14.3).

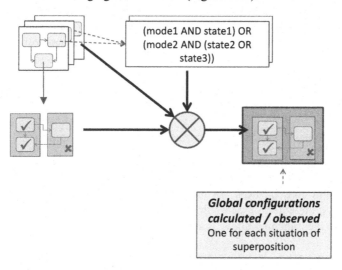

Figure 14.3. *Resulting configuration observed for each mode situation*

We must then verify the internal coherence of this resulting, global calculated configuration (in structural, functional and non-functional aspects). In cases of incoherence, this means revisiting the unitary configurations and/or the modes machines.

14.4.2.2. *Confrontation with the global expected configuration*

Once the stage above has finished, the coherence and content of the resulting global calculated configuration for each situation have been established, but still, do they satisfy the capabilities expected of the system in its entirety, in this situation?

For each situation of superposition, it is in fact possible to compare the global resulting calculated configuration, and the global configuration of interest expected, (elements present only in the configuration expected, or partially present in the configuration observed, etc.) (Figure 14.4). In case of incoherence, it is then necessary to revisit the unitary configurations and/or modes machines defined above.

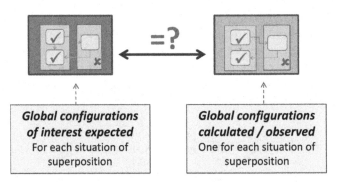

Figure 14.4. *Confrontation between global expected and calculated configurations*

14.4.2.3. *Analyzing configurations caused by states and modes*

States and their configurations could be processed as modes in the approach as it has been presented earlier. However, taking account of the fact that their trigger conditions and consequences are most often not of the same nature as those of modes, it is preferable to process them separately, a second time, as although their proximity to the principles above is substantial, the operation is different.

For each situation, it is thus necessary anyway to confront the content of the global calculated configurations associated with states, on the one hand, and that associated with modes, on the other hand.

For example, if structural elements (e.g. hosting physical components) are not available in the state considered, it is necessary to propagate this unavailability (for example to the behavioral components allocated to these physical components, then to the functions carried out by the latter, associated functional chains, scenarios and capabilities using them, etc., which will no longer be available). The non-functional properties borne by these elements should also be confronted (resources, performances, status of availability, etc.).

We see that it is no longer a question of combining unitary configurations of modes, but of propagating to configurations of modes the constraints issuing from configurations of states.

This analysis also leads to a resultant global, calculated configuration for each combination of states and modes carried by a situation, which may not include some of the initial elements, or characterize each by resulting properties such as its real availability, the performances or resources it may have, etc. (Figure 14.5).

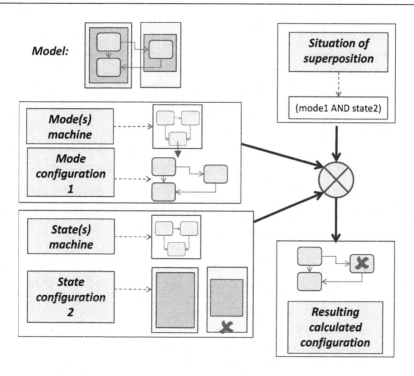

Figure 14.5. *Analysis of superpositions of modes and states*

14.4.2.4. Second confrontation with the global expected configuration

As mentioned, for each situation of superposition, it is then necessary to compare the global resulting calculated configuration – this time on the basis of the situation's modes and also its states – with the global configuration of interest expected (elements present only in the expected configuration, or partially present in the observed configuration, etc.).

If should be verified if the loss of unavailable capabilities remains acceptable taking account of the predicted operational mission and use.

14.4.3. Adapting architecture to superpositions

If the differences between the expected behaviors and the result of the analysis above are not acceptable, then a compromise solution should be sought that is acceptable, by revising the architecture to try to restore its capabilities.

EXAMPLE.– *This may, for example, involve*:

– *functional change or reallocation (to move critical functions to a less vulnerable component, or functional priorities, favoring the most important);*

– *defining degraded modes triggering a dynamic reconfiguration of resources, and the moving of behavioral components onto the hosting physical components that remain available;*

– *introducing active or passive redundancies between several processing chains with the same functions, and monitoring coherence between these chains;*

– *or also improving configurations linked to states, by replacing components with other, more reliable ones.*

***

All this work on revising the architecture necessarily results in the need to revisit, modify or complete system modes and states, the transitions between them, and of course associated configurations consolidated by the approach discussed earlier.

Finally, as a last resort, it may be necessary to renegotiate the expected need and functional or non-functional content, by relying on traceability links and analyzing the impact starting from operational analysis and system needs analysis.

14.5. Designing supervision associated with system and components states and modes

14.5.1. *Supervision functions and behavior*

The first stage of building supervision aims to define the different functions that will contribute to it. It should be noted that, taking account of its high dependency on the component architecture studied previously, this definition will most often be finalized after the principle definition of these components.

We can start by defining the function(s) responsible for orchestrating the system's global supervision:

– governing the startup and shutdown of the system;

– piloting its global changes of mode and reconfigurations;

– monitoring its status of operation;

– detecting situations requiring a change of mode;

– and carrying out the change of mode.

This orchestration function should be allocated to the component[3] best placed in the system to do this (central location and extended communication capability, dependability, protection against attacks, etc.).

This orchestration function for supervision will provide commands for modes changes and reconfigurations to homologous functions carried by the different components, which are themselves supervised. These commands will also be completed by those that should trigger functional effects of the mode change.

The supervision function will moreover receive information about the status of the system and its components, resulting from other functions in charge of detecting changes of state (functions also to be defined), which will be allocated as close as possible to the sources of states changes (for example detecting a component that has broken down, an actor who is not responding, a change in the environment, etc.). Examination of the conditions of states changes is a favored opening for this definition and allocation. Of course, this should be carried out for each states machine identified previously.

This supervision function should also receive all the information likely to trigger a change of mode that appear in the conditions for transition from one mode to another. There too, this should be carried out for each modes machine identified previously.

Of course, additional work on defining the functional chains involved, interfaces of the supervision and scenarios specifying the dynamic behavior expected of the supervision (including changes of mode and states or situations) should be carried out, as described in the general approach to designing the architecture. In particular, we will describe scenarios for taking account of predictable (or feared) change of the system's states and its environment, implementing associated degraded modes and reconfiguration.

14.5.2. Articulation between system and components supervision

As we have just seen, the design of functions contributing to supervision is as close as possible to the architecture and components at work. The allocation of these functions – supervision and management of modes and states machines, monitoring of operation states, command of changes of mode and their effects – on the components involved occurs in conjunction with the functional definition. It means

---

3 The hypothesis considered here is that of a supervision centralized in a component responsible for this function. Other decentralized or distributed possibilities exist, of course, but this is the simplest to tackle here.

first identifying components responsible for piloting the supervision and reconfigurations, then allocating the required functions to them, and defining the paths to route commands and status information in the architecture.

Next, the impact of the supervision on each component of the architecture is considered. Some components are not impacted at all. For the others, two cases can be considered.

In a case where the components are only "reactive" faced with the system supervision, they configure their behavior when they receive a command following a change of system mode. In this case, to facilitate the description of their expected behavior, we can define, for each machine defined at system level, a modes or states machine dedicated to the component, but issuing from the machine at system level. Configurations restricted to the component's perimeter are also defined, from those described at system level. The conditions for transition between modes are the commands sent by the system supervision.

However, in some cases, a component (which we will label "pro-active") can necessitate description of its own behavior, determined especially either by its state or its internal operation, or by external information or events with which it is the system's point of contact. This is also particularly important in the case of autonomous systems or components, or in the case of a degraded operation, when it must be reconfigured separately to the rest of the system for example. Either this proactive behavior is described by states machines separate from the previous ones, and in this case, they cohabit – it must only be ensured that their configurations are coherent and compatible when a situation superposes them. Or the behavior is in one way or another linked to the system behavior. In this case, a specific states machine should be built, which will mix or combine modes or states that should manage the component from the viewpoint of the system supervision, and those its internal (proactive) behavior requires.

In all cases, it is important to maintain the traceability of component modes and states with the corresponding system modes and states, as well as between configurations.

Note that nothing requires here that the system modes or states are strictly represented by as many component modes; it is only necessary to verify that each command for transition to a system mode will indeed lead to the configuration change required by the system machine, and that each configuration associated with a state or mode internal to the component really conforms to the system's expectations as described by the last supervision command received (i.e. by the associated system mode and configuration).

EXAMPLE.– *It is, for example, possible that a system mode is conveyed by a component's or subsystem's state: thus, if a smartphone enters energy-saving mode, the components (applications, especially) can pass involuntarily and in an unpredicted manner into a limited-resource state (communications, processing resources, etc.) – unless the smartphone and its operating system engineering team have foreseen an explicit notification for applications – which would then in this case pass to a mode this time degraded, but chosen and designed in consequence.*

It is also desirable to verify that the coherence between the system modes and states, and those of the components that include some modes or states management; this is especially necessary when existing components are reused to build a system.

To this effect, for each situation previously defined for the system – so consisting of a combination of system states and modes – we will define the situation(s) in which each component (at least, the most important ones) is likely to be found – a combination of component modes and states supposed to take account of the previous situation, so in principle they are triggered following a request from the system supervision. The confrontation of resulting configurations will make it possible to detect potential incoherences and to modify components' modes and states machines in consequence.

14.5.3. Analysis and verification of the conditions for system reconfigurations

Sources of system reconfigurations are multiple: a change of system mode, an automatic reaction to a change of state or an action planned by the supervision to pass to a degraded mode following a change of state imposing it, for example (see Chapter 14, section 14.4.3).

In these situations, besides verifying the content of each starting and ending situation described previously, it is necessary to define the stages leading to the configuration and states desired, and to verify their feasibility, from the viewpoint of the supervision. In fact, it may be that a change of state – indeed of mode – leads to the unavailability of resources that allow reconfiguration commands to be rerouted, or also that perform part of this reconfiguration.

The stages that make it possible to pass from an initial situation to another desired situation, may be expressed by scenarios describing the successive functional stages, but it may also be useful to define intermediate modes between the starting and ending modes, which will cause the configurations of the system and its components to evolve little by little. These changes of mode will also be captured in the former scenarios, and will be subject to the same design approach described in the previous sections.

It is to be noted, however, that within this approach, particular attention should be paid to the feasibility of carrying out supervision, as the unavailability of components, interfaces, functions, exchanges, etc. can make it inoperative, even if the starting and ending configurations satisfy operational need. It should be ensured in particular that:

– sources of transitions between modes (and between states) are fully available (that the components hosting them are fully active, with adequate resources);

– means to route information associated with each supervision function are also available; this applies in particular to chains detecting changes of state due to breakdowns, etc.;

– resources for performing each supervision function are also available (for each component involved);

– means to route supervision commands are available;

– and the functions and components that should act in consequence to carry out the reconfiguration are completely able to do this.

14.6. Using the model for startup and shutdown procedures

Without pretending to tackle here the subject of designing the startup and shutdown procedures of a system, it is still possible to give indications of the way in which the model and its analysis can contribute to defining conditions for starting the system and its components, for example.

Most complex systems have startup and shutdown procedures that are themselves complex; these procedures are generally described by a succession of functions that the system and its operators should carry out (a set of scenarios is enough to illustrate them), governed by "state machines" (similar to modes and states machines above): these "state machines" characterize the different stages of these procedures (each stage being a "state" in the machine), their content (functions, etc.), the conditions for sequencing them and for passing from one to another. These "state machines" are generally defined for each system component; all these machines are most often supervised by a central supervision component (see above).

One of the major difficulties with this type of definition is designing and verifying the order in which the initialization should be carried out. Indeed, many of the constraints that influence the order of initialization are present in the system model. We cite, for example:

– the functional dependencies that give rise to an order of operation between certain functions: for example, data or material suppliers and actions carried out by external actors, should be active or operated before the consumers. The model captures them through the dataflow and exchanges between functions;

– non-functional dependencies, such as safety rules (not starting an energy supply without first having secured the system and actors), potential priorities (first starting critical chains). These are present in the model through enrichments for each viewpoint: feared events, criticality, etc.;

– technical dependencies (for example electronic power supply, IT servers, pressure pumps, electricity sources, etc.). They are often expressed in the model by hosting physical components that supply behavioral components with their resources and place constraints on them;

– performances (time for power raise, for filling a reservoir, speed of communications internal or external to the system). They are also most often captured through properties associated with elements of the model (functional chains, scenarios, etc.).

The simple fact of confronting startup or shutdown procedures with these different constraints is often already enough to identify errors or inadequacies in these procedures, and it can be left at that.

A subsequent capability, which is very ambitious and far beyond the state of the art, would consist of building, from the preceding elements, the graph of constraints applicable to these procedures, then making it possible to define the order of precedence required between functions, components and state changes, potential needs for synchronization or "meeting" between initialization functions, and events and data that trigger transitions.

14.7. Summary

The notion of system supervision considered here covers several aspects: management of the system's and its components' modes and states; monitoring correct operation of the system and detecting potential failures; dynamic reconfigurations to operate during operation, especially for failure recovery; starting up and shutting down the system and its components.

Orchestration of supervision is governed by system states and modes and their transitions, which determine the configurations of the system or a component in given conditions. These states and modes complete and detail the functional description in each perspective, from the OA to the PA.

States and modes engineering uses confrontation between behaviors expected in the different situations the system will meet (behaviors described in functional analysis), and conditions for the availability of the elements that carry them out (described in the structural part of the architecture, components, resources, physical links, etc.).

Contribution to Product Line Engineering

15.1. Context and position of the problem

Among the business practices likely to profoundly impact the engineering and definition of system architectures, the product policy definition is now making its impact as one of the most efficient levers for action; in fact, it favors a shared core between the business' different products and projects, identifies and minimizes the differences between them and favors construction of a new product based on existing components, within a global vision called a product line. However, efficient implementation of this product policy in engineering (to which we will limit ourselves here) means rising to several challenges.

One of the first peculiarities of the product policy to be taken into account is the multiplicity and diversity of the actors involved, with different concerns (marketing, architects, engineering, development and production, business, etc.). In addition, these concerns apply to the vast majority of engineering artifacts (requirements, architecture models, software and hardware production elements, test campaigns, etc.) and beyond (user manuals, logistics, business catalogues, etc.). This gives rise to a great diversity of expectations and contributions. Each actor on the product line has a different, non-correlated viewpoint, responding to different concerns in different approaches: marketing focuses on the market, business on the content of offers to customers, engineering on elements reusable from one project to another and the product's global coherence.

A second source of complexity is linked to the number of elementary differences and therefore of possible versions of the product to answer different customer needs. These sources of variability result from different actors and their contributions to the product definition, and can amount to more than several hundred or indeed several thousand possible choices. This can lead to a "combinatorial explosion" of possible combinations or product versions to be considered. To this quantitative dimension is added, moreover, a qualitative complexity in building due to dependencies that appear between the elementary choices possible (incompatibility, prerequisites, etc.); thus, their validity and the capability of verifying their content become very problematic, as well as their use.

Finally, the definition of this variability in the product gives rise (most often implicitly and informally) to requirements on the product architecture and definition, which are often ignored, although they would require a feasibility verification of these choices and of their multiple combinations, which creates risks and leads to a surplus of iterations, both in the product definition and in each of its variants.

***

The state of the art in industry distinguishes engineering of the product line itself (we also speak of domain engineering), and the engineering of a given product, destined for a customer or market. The first therefore defines the possible variation domain for the product line, with the possible and desired variants; the second chooses from among these options those required for the desired product, while potentially adding characteristics belonging to the product.

Formalization of these elements of product line definition mainly uses the principle of a so-called "feature model" (FM) to capture all the possible variants for a given product line. This model is generally defined in the form of a tree of which each node (we call it a variation point) expresses the possibility of choosing from among several possible variants (its daughter branches in the tree) for a single element (or set of elements). More details are given in Chapter 22 (section 22.1).

The process of using this product line for a given customer or market is called derivation: it consists of choosing, for each node of the tree, one or more of its sub-branches (options, alternatives, etc.) with a view to satisfying customer demand. The result of this derivation is called a product configuration. Current technologies make it possible to identify the variants possible in different engineering artifacts (requirements, engineering models (EMs), test campaigns, etc.) and to generate for each configuration the body of artifacts corresponding to the choices made during the derivation: only those requirements, model parts, test campaigns, etc., that correspond to these choices will be integrated into this corpus.

However, this practice, although entirely to be recommended, quickly meets its limits when it is employed alone:

– the process of defining and verifying the FM correlates little with other activities and constraints of the engineering mentioned hitherto;

– this FM often becomes very voluminous, and thus, difficult to manage, with nodes that lists the elements forming the need and solution rather than define real variants;

– the complexity resulting from this size and the internal dependencies between variation points makes the derivation very complex, as the user is guided only by the model's "tree" structure, which is not enough to guide choices, detect incompatibilities, etc.;

– it is difficult to separate the customer need from the solution's constraints and contingencies, hence the difficulty in fully identifying what can satisfy this need, and which should be subject to customer choices;

– nothing in this process guarantees that the product line architecture and its reusable components are adapted to the variabilities identified;

– there is also no guarantee that the product architecture generated by a configuration is valid, and that it fulfills the services expected by the customer.

NOTE.– *Incorrectly, but for the sake of simplicity, outside the context of the feature or EM, a possible localized choice may be called an option in current parlance (so including the variant and variation point).*

15.2. General approach to product line engineering

15.2.1. *Principles of the approach*

To find a solution to the sources of complexity encountered here above, Arcadia suggests basing the approach to building the product line – especially the FM – on the principles and perspectives of the engineering approach, and jointly carrying out the two approaches in a unified manner.

Arcadia guides and optimizes development of the FM from start to finish by segmenting it by perspective, in the same way as the EM (the Engineering Model, support model for the method as defined above), and by developing the two models simultaneously, to find a global optimum for the product definition, to secure the definition of product variabilities and configurations as well as the architecture, while minimizing efforts in modeling and verification.

In operational analysis, product users' operational need feeds and guides market analysis for marketing, and an initial segmentation of this market, with an FM more specially dedicated to marketing:

– in system needs analysis, the capabilities and services expected of the product form a basis for defining a second FM that supports the offer portfolio and customer options, for business;

– in logical and physical architecture, the consequences of these variabilities and the adaptations required of the product line architecture are analyzed and also constrain construction of this architecture, especially in multiple viewpoint analysis; this leads to a more technical FM with more architectural choices and constraints, and which identifies the concrete elements contributing to building the product line (reusable components for example);

– finally, the two models (engineering and feature models) are linked to one another and are complementary, the perimeter of the EM concerned with a variant is defined by link(s) to the FM variation point. It should be noted that beyond the EM, this applies more generally to different engineering artifacts, such as requirements, test campaigns and results, flaws and change requests databases, configurations, etc.

The previous approach is applied to building the product line itself (called domain engineering). For each particular customer or market, a dedicated engineering (called project engineering) is built, as a complement to the domain engineering, from the elements that domain has developed. This project engineering is described later in Chapter 15 (section 15.3.4) as well as deriving a configuration for a given customer or product using a subtractive approach (Chapter 15, section 15.4).

15.2.2. Drivers and key activities in the approach

More precisely, through the perspectives above, the approach uses a number of structuring activities, involving, on the one hand, the FM:

– separating the kinds of variabilities, with each role (marketing, business, architects…) focusing more on one kind, with its own dedicated FM;

– creating an FM for each perspective of the product above (so operational, system needs, logical or physical architecture variabilities), and no longer a single "catch-all", destined for the roles involved (above);

– identifying elements of variability for each FM, depending on those defined at the previous level, while maintaining traceability and justification links with them (e.g. commercial options for the customer built and justified from marketing segmentation, defined product variants associated with commercial options, etc.);

– deducing the variabilities and options for this, which will form the global FM consolidated in this way;

and, on the other hand, joint development of both engineering and feature models:

– differentiating and separating the EM describing the elements contributing to the product line – called a domain model – and the models belonging to each project, final product or customer – called project models;

– using the EM's perspectives as a basis for constructing and justifying each of the previous FMs;

– identifying elements of the EM (capabilities, functional aspects and chains, scenarios, available components, etc.) that may be optional or generic by nature, favoring high-level elements, expressing need and expected uses (capabilities, functional chains, scenarios, etc.);

– from this, deducing variabilities and options that will form the associated FM, on the basis of those elements of the EM that are considered variable, rather than building them *a priori* independently of the product architecture;

– defining the desired architecture options and configurations by automatically building an (engineering) architecture model for each desired product configuration (project model);

– verifying the validity of each architecture thus produced, through a multiple viewpoint analysis of the model, detecting incoherencies (e.g. an optional component useful for another, non-selected option).

15.2.3. *Benefits of the approach*

The benefits of this joint definition of the FM and the EM are multiple:

– building the FM is easier; its justification by the need and solution is assured. This also provides an approach to verifying the FM, using its coherence with the EM;

– the description of the architecture in the EM reduces the size and complexity of the FM: the whole description of the architecture occurs only in the EM, and the variants are expressed on higher level elements in the EM (capabilities, functional chains, subsystems, etc.), by grouping basic variabilities thanks to the structure of the architecture and the EM;

– use of the FM is guided by the EM to build the configurations more easily: rather than very detailed variation points on the product's elementary components, we will instead choose the main capabilities expected by the customer, and the variability details will be supported by the EM (via capability/functions/component links, etc.). Dependencies between variants and variation points will largely be expressed already by architecture constraints in the EM, without any need to plot them in the FM;

– dependencies between variations points are minimized, as they most often result from constraints expressed by the EM (e.g. joint market expectations, functional coherence of commercial options, or technical and architectural dependency between components forming options); since they are at present built from elements of this model, their coherence is guaranteed by this building process;

– the combination of options is reduced as the architecture constrains these and eliminates unrealistic combinations;

– most of the selection criteria are explicit in the EM (required capabilities, expected functions, the type of customer targeted, technical and architectural constraints imposed, etc.);

– joint construction of the FM and the EM makes it possible to take account as early as possible the constraints linked to the product line (mutualization of shared parts, segregation of variabilities, identification of dependencies between variation points or variants, etc.) and integrate them into the architecture definition;

– finally, the feasibility of each configuration or choice of options in the FM is verified, thanks to the fact that an EM can be generated automatically from each configuration, and subject to a multiple viewpoint analysis that will detect potential incoherences in it.

***

The following sections first describe the approach to building the product line, then current derivation variants for a given product.

The general Arcadia approach presented above is quite clearly applied here; therefore, in the following we will only mention the specifics linked to product line engineering.

EXAMPLE.– *The example that illustrates this approach is a product line engineering for a road vehicle. This example of course claims to do nothing more than to aid understanding of the concepts presented; the reader is therefore asked to forgive its lack of realism or indeed pertinence.*

15.3. Joint construction of architecture and product variability

This section describes in a more linear way the global approach to building a product line *a priori* and the integration of this product line constraint into the engineering as early as possible.

It focuses on activities belonging to the product line approach for each of the Arcadia perspectives, taking account of the specifics of this perspective. However, the guiding drivers and principle activities mentioned above apply to each stage, although they are only mentioned in this description.

15.3.1. *Market analysis in operational analysis*

15.3.1.1. *Market and stakeholder segmentation*

The first stage of the product line approach is to characterize the target market, and to segment it according to the expectations of potential customers and other stakeholders involved: to do this, operational entities and actors are principally used, to capture the segmentation of different potential customers and users, and missions and operational capabilities, to characterize their objectives and expectations, respectively.

EXAMPLE.– *For the road vehicle product line considered, an initial segmentation between users can identify, in the form of operational entities, with which some required missions and operational capabilities are associated:-*

– families (operational entity): whose main aim is to have a safe and pleasant journey for all passengers (mission), and who therefore want to drive safely and rest comfortably (operational capabilities);

– amateur racing club member (operational entity): whose aim is to participate in amateur competitions (mission), who also wants to drive safely, but above all to have maximum driving performances (operational capabilities);

– companies (operational entity): whose aim is to transport materials onto construction sites (mission), and wish to have a safe journey in doing so, but above all need to carry heavy loads, sometimes off-roads (operational capabilities).

15.3.1.2. Stakeholder expectations

Each customer's or user's expectations are specified by operational activities, and scenarios or operational processes involving these activities, to provide the expected capabilities. These expectations may already be formed into groupings (of operational activities in particular) representative of users' global expectations.

Moreover, an initial analysis of a needs community or specificity can already be carried out on this basis: some customers can share the same capabilities or activities for example, or, on the contrary, have their own different needs. Links between operational entities and capabilities, activities, etc., will therefore be established to convey this initial allocation of shared or specific needs.

EXAMPLE.– *Several expectations involving the vehicle may be identified from the capabilities required above – expressed here by grouping operational activities:*

– ensure safe driving, especially by ensuring short-distance breaking, and assisting vehicle parking (activities);

– ensure traveler comfort, accommodating the whole family, carrying all their luggage, with comfortable sitting, and helping with unfamiliar routes;

– minimize travel cost;

– enable sports driving, so accelerating fast, having a high peak speed, being able to turn at high speed, etc.;

– carrying heavy and potentially voluminous loads;

– driving off-roads, so being able to climb steep hillsides for example, still while carrying heavy loads, etc.

Ensuring safe driving is without doubt a need common to all users. On the contrary, it can be assumed that sporting performances mainly interest amateur racing club members, and carrying heavy and voluminous loads above all interests companies, the corresponding activities will therefore be allocated selectively or collectively to actors in consequence.

15.3.1.3. *Characterizing stakeholder expectations*

An initial characterization of the elements formed up to this point can already be made, with a view to guiding definitions of the product line's operational variabilities.

Each operational entity, capability, scenario, activity... can be characterized according to its value or importance to the end user, its criticality, its frequency of use, expected quality of service, etc.

The conditions for association, dependency, exclusion, must also be sought and formalized, in the shape of constraints linking several elements of operational analysis.

EXAMPLE.– *Some characteristics and conditions for association or exclusion can be applied (or not!) to the domain of vehicles considered:*

– ensuring safe driving is an imperative and a differentiator imposed on all segments of the market and customers;

– the activity of sports driving is most often accompanied by an expectation for comfort amenities;

– traveling off-road can be accommodated with fewer comfort amenities;

– sports driving rarely requires economy in the cost of the journey.

When a need for sports driving and the ability to travel off-road are both required, then sports driving should be preferred. This association is moreover the prerogative of high-range versions in general.

In the model, this characterization is expressed by specific constraints, or attributes, applied here to groupings of the previous activities.

15.3.1.4. *Prioritizing stakeholders expectations*

This addition to characterization makes it possible to evaluate the importance of each of the previous elements for each type of customer or user depending on their own expectations, by defining which characteristics are indispensable, expected and desirable for each clientele, so prioritizing criteria for choice. The resulting constraints are associated with the preceding operational modeling elements (capabilities, activities, entities, etc.).

EXAMPLE.– *For a family, safety, and the ability to transport all its members and their baggage are indispensable and the first criterion for making a choice. Comfort and the ability to minimize travel cost are expected, but assistance, or sports driving, are merely desirable.*

For an amateur racing club member, the capacity for sports driving is indispensable, comfort is expected and assistance with unfamiliar routes is desirable.

Table 15.1 illustrates indispensable (must have), expected and desirable (nice to have) aspects.

Operational entities	Characterization	Operational activities (or grouping)
Family	Indispensable	Ensuring safe driving, carry several luggage, accommodating the whole family
	Expected	Travelling comfortably, minimize travel cost
	Desirable	Travel to unknown places, parking assistance, enabling sports driving (as an option ?)
Amateur racing club member	Indispensable	Driving fast, braking at short distance, accelerating quickly, having a high top speed, being able to turn at high speed
	Expected	Having comfortable sitting
	Desirable	Being assisted on unfamiliar routes
Company	Indispensable	Carrying heavy loads
	Expected	Travelling off-roads, minimize travel costs, climb steep hillsides
	Desirable	Having comfortable sitting, being assisted on unfamiliar routes

Table 15.1. *Prioritizing stakeholders expectations*

15.3.1.5. Defining operational variabilities

At present, it is possible to build an operational FM whose development is based on using the analysis above, and is justified by it.

The variability tree can be initialized, in its early stages, from the market segmentation made previously, or the main capabilities identified at the outset. The characterization made during the previous stages will also be a potential entry into the tree, additional nodes identifying indispensable, desirable characteristics, as possible variation points.

Then, on the basis of the characterization of elements of operational analysis, those that are generic and should form part of the core common to all segments of the market and stakeholders are identified, but *a priori* only in the EM. It is in fact preferable to avoid uselessly overburdening the FM with the architecture's or need's description elements, which are best described in the EM, and linked to the rest of it.

The elements of the EM that have been characterized as specific to such or such a segment are then subject to the definition of variants, alternatives, options, etc. This makes it possible to complete the tree of operational variabilities, of which each node will moreover reference the element(s) of operational analysis considered, to link the two models.

In this process, we will seek to use the most all-encompassing elements of operational analysis possible: grouping of activities, or operational capability for example, and not elementary activities. This simplifies the FM, and several elementary options can be synthesized by a single variant applying on a high-level element, which is also generally more significant for uses and customer expectations. Moreover, this also limits the need to introduce dependencies between variants or variation points; these dependencies often being present already in the form of encompassing or grouping elements in the EM.

The operational FM and operational analysis of the EM are therefore connected by links which both describe the content expected of each variation point and variant and form a justification and "user manual" for the FM.

EXAMPLE.– *The principle operational variation points to consider for the road vehicle are, for example:*

– *conditions for comfort;*

– *means for sports driving;*

– *economy of use;*

– *capabilities for off-road driving;*

– *the number of passengers;*

– *the transport capacity.*

This defines the principle nodes structuring the operational FM of the vehicle.

Then, it will be possible to refine the tree by, for example, considering navigation aids, for instance the degree of comfort in the seating, as options that may or may not be offered depending on the cases. The simplified model is presented Table 15.2.

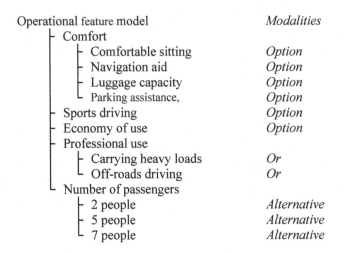

Operational feature model	Modalities
⊢ Comfort	
⊢ Comfortable sitting	Option
⊢ Navigation aid	Option
⊢ Luggage capacity	Option
⊢ Parking assistance,	Option
⊢ Sports driving	Option
⊢ Economy of use	Option
⊢ Professional use	
⊢ Carrying heavy loads	Or
⊢ Off-roads driving	Or
⊢ Number of passengers	
⊢ 2 people	Alternative
⊢ 5 people	Alternative
⊢ 7 people	Alternative

Table 15.2. *Operational feature model (partial)*

It is in fact much simpler, for example, to consider a single variation point for sports driving, rather than having to define four separate ones, such as acceleration performances, top speed and turning speed, breaking power. This also expresses the fact that not treating these variation points together, as a whole, would compromise the sports driving capability, which is less apparent if we limit ourselves to listing elementary variation points in an FM developed alone.

Moreover, if braking at short distance is considered indispensable regardless of use, then it should not appear in the FM.

15.3.1.6. Defining standard reference configurations

From this level, it is possible to define standard reference configurations, which will structure both the marketing configurations and the product offer configurations. Each configuration will include common expectations of general interest, and choices from among the available variants of the FM, justified by the analysis carried out previously.

This definition uses market segmentation to design offers adapted to each segment and relies on characterization made previously to build associated reference configurations. One could, for example, imagine building, for each market segment, an initial entry-range configuration formed of elements considered indispensable in each segment, then add options up to the higher range.

It should be noted that a reference configuration can include unresolved nodes, i.e. variation points conserving multiple variants, to take account of uncertainties in the market, potential changes, for example. It will therefore be necessary, in forming a final configuration for a given customer, for example, to be able to start with a standard, chosen configuration, and to define only the nodes that are not yet resolved by it. Management of feature and configuration models should offer this capability.

EXAMPLE.– *Some operational reference configurations for our vehicle could, for example, be:*

– an offer intended for families based on capabilities for safe driving and comfort, a high number of passengers; various additional options could involve parking assistance and assistance on unknown routes;

– an offer destined for an amateur racing club member, favoring performance capabilities, with options for the level of comfort;

– an offer targeting companies, choosing carriage of heavy loads, with, as an option, off-road driving capabilities.

A simplified description is presented in Table 15.3.

Operational feature model	Family offer	Sports offer	Business offer
├ Comfort			
│ ├ Comfortable sitting	Basic	Basic	*Option*
│ ├ Navigation assistance	*Option*	Basic	*Option*
│ ├ Luggage capacity	Basic	Non	Basic
│ └ Parking assistance,	*Option*	*Option*	*Option*
├ Sports driving	~~No~~	Basic	~~No~~
├ Economy of use	*Option*	~~No~~	*Option*
├ Professional use			
│ ├ Carrying loads	~~No~~	~~No~~	Basic
│ └ Off-roads driving	~~No~~	~~No~~	*Option*
└ Number of passengers			
│ ├ 2 people	~~No~~	Basic	Basic
│ ├ 5 people	Basic	*Alternative*	~~No~~
│ └ 7 people	*Option*	~~No~~	~~No~~

Table 15.3. *Operational reference configurations (partial)*

15.3.1.7. Verifying coherence between FM and EM

Verification of coherence between the FM and the EM occurs at two levels: the variability tree with regard to the complete model, and for each reference configuration.

It will be verified especially, for example, that:

– selecting a variant leads to a coherent state of the model (no activity missing from the required capabilities, no operational process or scenario incomplete, etc.), including prerequisite relationships between variants;

– not selecting a variant maintains the model in a coherent state, both for the part common to all variants, and for the other variants and variation points defined (especially for alternatives to this, and the exclusion relationships resulting from this variant or variation point);

– combinations of variants do not lead to incoherences (for example two contradictory scenarios, or operational processes interfering when involving an activity);

– each configuration's architecture conforms to the expected rule book, and to the requirements that define its need (to do this, one could use multiple viewpoint analysis of the EM).

15.3.2. Defining customer options in system needs analysis

15.3.2.1. Defining services required for each operational variant

Over the course of system needs analysis, the capabilities and functions (or services) that will be asked of the system to meet users' operational needs are identified, chosen and traced in relation to elements of operational analysis.

EXAMPLE.– *An example of the service functions expected of our vehicle (intentionally caricatured, to draw out that these services are exclusively for specification purposes, as opposed to solution functions) is presented in Table 15.4 and, in Figure 15.1, in front of the operational activities to which they contribute.*

Operational activity	System functions (services)
Accelerate fast	Deliver high performance
Break in short distance	Ensure efficient braking
Carry heavy loads	Adapt to various loads; support heavy loads; maintain the vehicle horizontal; ensure efficient braking; deliver high performance
Carry several luggage	Adapt to various loads; preserve room for luggage; maintain the vehicle horizontal; ensure efficient braking
Climb steep hillsides	Allow high ground clearance; deliver high performance
Drive fast	Allow low ground clearance; deliver high performance
Drive fast in turns	Absorb irregularities of the road; deliver high performance; keep vehicle on curve in turns; maintain driver body during turn; maintain the vehicle horizontal
Drive off-roads	Allow high ground clearance; ensure good grip on ground
Minimize travel cost	Allow low ground clearance; reduce fuel consumption
Park easily	Detect short distance obstacles
Rest comfortably	Absorb irregularities of the road; maintain driver body during turns; maintain the vehicle horizontal; offer comfortable sitting
Transport the whole family	Adapt to various loads; allow five or seven seats configurations
Travel along unfamiliar routes	Provide itinerary guidance

Table 15.4. *Operational activities and system needs functions that contribute to them*

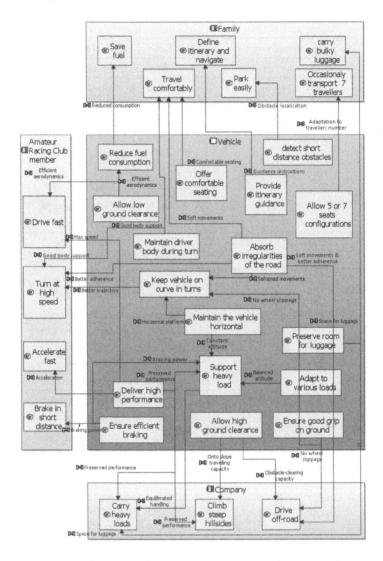

Figure 15.1. *Functional analysis of system needs (partial)*

By following these traceability links from the operational elements on which the variation points lie, the variabilities identified in operational analysis can be propagated, not to form system analysis variabilities, but to guide their definition. One can therefore obtain the "footprint" of each operational variant in the service functions expected of the system (which can be materialized by dedicated groupings for this purpose).

The functional breakdown constrained by the variabilities should in principle be coherent with that resulting from operational analysis: separate functions, coherence and continuity of functional chains, etc. This can sometimes lead to the modification of the content of system capabilities, the breakdown of functions, of their exchanges, of functional chains, or to give rise to new chains or scenarios for example, so as to separate the variants, and especially the alternatives.

EXAMPLE.– *For each of the variation points and variants identified in the operational FM, the functions potentially concerned may be "automatically" listed by following the links between modeling elements: variation points in the FM → capabilities or operational activities → system needs functions. The functions thus identified (presented in the Table 15.5 below) are candidates for variability at the system level; they should consequently be analyzed, for example, to verify that two references to the same function in two operational variants indeed require the same content (otherwise it would be necessary to break the function down into two functions): as an example, the needs for power for sports driving and professional uses are not necessarily of the same nature (power and torque in one case, torque alone in the other).*

Operational feature model	System functions involved
├ Comfort	Absorb irregularities of the road; provide itinerary guidance; maintain driver body during turns; maintain the vehicle horizontal; offer comfortable sitting
├ Sports driving	Deliver high performance; maintain the vehicle horizontal; allow low ground clearance; keep vehicle on curve during turns; absorb irregularities of the road; maintain driver body during turns
├ Economy of use	Allow low ground clearance; reduce fuel consumption
├ Professional use	Adapt to various loads; support heavy loads; maintain the vehicle horizontal; ensure efficient braking; Deliver high performance; allow high ground clearance; ensure good grip on ground
└ ...	

Table 15.5. *Identifying possible variabilities in system functions based on operational variabilities*

15.3.2.2. Characterizing expected functional services

Beyond their contribution to sources of operational variability above, system capabilities and identified functions may be characterized according to their level of necessity or attractiveness for the end user, their criticality, frequency of use, expected quality of service, as well as their feasibility or complexity, etc.

EXAMPLE.– *For our vehicle, it may be interesting to start from expectations of the main types of customer identified in operational analysis, and to characterize the functions expected of the system this time, after operational activities.*

Operational entities	Characterization	Required system functions
Family	Indispensable	Ensure efficient braking; preserve room for luggage; allow five or seven seats configurations
	Expected	Absorb irregularities of the road; offer comfortable sitting; reduce fuel consumption
	Desirable	Provide itinerary guidance; detect short distance obstacles
		Sports driving
Amateur racing club member	Indispensable	Deliver high performance; ensure efficient braking; allow low ground clearance; absorb irregularities of the road; keep vehicle on curve during turns; maintain the vehicle horizontal
	Expected	Maintain driver body during turn; offer comfortable sitting
	Desirable	Be assisted on unknown routes; detect short distance obstacles
		Ensure good grip on ground during sports driving
Company	Indispensable	Adapt to various loads; support heavy loads; maintain the vehicle horizontal; ensure efficient braking; carry heavy loads
	Expected	Allow high ground clearance; deliver high performance; *ensure good grip on ground on any terrain*
	Desirable	Provide itinerary guidance; detect short distance obstacles; offer comfortable sitting

Table 15.6. *Prioritization of stakeholder expectations of the system*

EXAMPLE.– *In Table 15.6, we see that expectations can appear at this stage, such as the possibility of offering sports driving capabilities to a family clientele, which could result in enhancing the operational analysis subsequently and will influence the FM of the system need below. Similarly, an "ensure good grip on ground" function has been identified, which at this stage may be desirable for sports driving as well as for driving off-road; but it requires different means and design depending on its use, as we will see in defining the solution architecture.*

A type of characterization important at this stage involves financial and economic aspects: each element above should be dimensioned, as much as possible, according to criteria such as its market price, whether it is offered by competitors, its estimated cost, the possible margin above this cost... Initial orientations involving individual variability may be posed.

As during operational analysis, it means evaluating the importance of each of the services likely to be rendered for each type of customer or user, by listing the characteristics of each as indispensable, expected or desirable.

EXAMPLE.– *Analysis of required functions may be followed to define and justify the possible conditions for their individual variability, as presented in Table 15.7.*

Required system functions	Characterization	Justification
Offer comfortable sitting	Option	Not indispensable, making it possible to justify and create various versions up to high range
Maintain driver body position during turns	Option	
Provide itinerary guidance	Option	
Detect short distance obstacles	Option	
Reduce fuel consumption	Incompatible (alternative) options	Reduced consumption assumes limited power
Deliver high performance		Probable high cost
Adapt to various loads; support heavy loads	Single/joint option	No need identified justifying their separation, always associated in professional use
Allow five or seven seat configurations	Alternatives exclusive of one another	The two ground clearances are incompatible; moreover, their uses (sport vs. company) are different and are incompatible with seven seat configurations
Allow low ground clearance		
Allow high ground clearance		
Keep vehicle on curve during turns; maintain the vehicle horizontal	Several options, increasing performances	Probable high cost, so split offer moreover, this specificity is detrimental to comfort, and so optional
Ensure good grip on ground on any terrain	Option	Probable high cost

Table 15.7. *Characterization of some system need functions*

The resulting constraints are associated with the functional modeling elements above: functions, of course, and also capabilities, functional chains or scenarios, but also non-functional elements such as the level of security, expected performances, etc. It will always be attempted to apply these to the most encompassing elements, which may also lead to these needing to be changed or enhanced.

EXAMPLE.– *Individual options may be defined individually on each of the functions above, but there are dependencies between them.*

For example, road-holding performances during turns simultaneously requires the functions "absorb irregularities of the road; deliver high performance; keep vehicle on curve during turns; maintain the vehicle horizontal"; this is precisely what the functional chain "drive fast in turns", illustrated by Figure 15.2, describes. Therefore, a single option will be placed on this functional chain, instead of there being different options on each of the functions it involves.

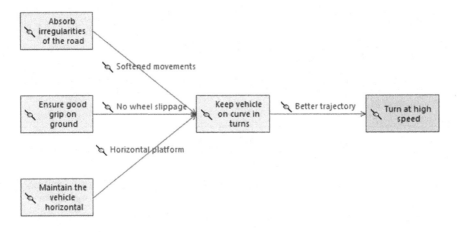

Figure 15.2. *Functional chain "drive fast in turns"*

Similarly, there will be a single option on the functional chain "transport heavy loads", rather than on the functions it uses: "adapt to various loads; support heavy loads; maintain the vehicle horizontal; ensure efficient braking".

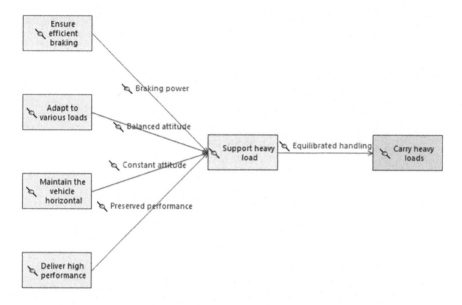

Figure 15.3. *Functional chain "carry heavy loads"*

15.3.2.3. *Defining variabilities on the expected functional services*

The FM on the functional need is built from the characterization above: it first identifies the services required by all customers, those which may be optional, then the different possible variants of offers on these services, and the nature of the associated variation points (option, alternative, etc.).

There too, it will be attempted to develop the initial levels of this model from the most encompassing elements of system analysis possible: grouping of functions, system capability or functional chain for example, and not basic functions, always with the aim of simplifying the FM. The generic, specific, optional, alternative character for each of them is defined in the FM.

The links between the FM of the system needs and elements of the EM subject to these variabilities are put in place; conditions of association, dependency or exclusion between variabilities are also formalized.

Engineering and FMs of the system needs should also be linked to operational analysis level models, by traceability links, or indeed links expressing, especially, market constraints and marketing positioning constraints, etc., which may orient the definition of system configurations.

EXAMPLE.– *The characterizations above lead, for example, to the definition of individual options, which may be structured.*

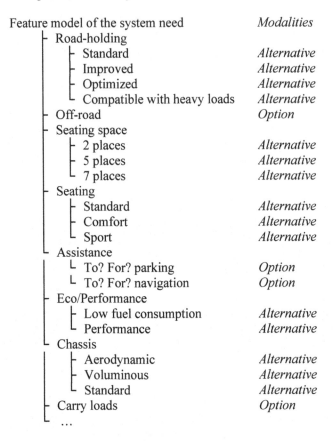

Feature model of the system need	Modalities
├ Road-holding	
├ Standard	*Alternative*
├ Improved	*Alternative*
├ Optimized	*Alternative*
└ Compatible with heavy loads	*Alternative*
├ Off-road	*Option*
├ Seating space	
├ 2 places	*Alternative*
├ 5 places	*Alternative*
└ 7 places	*Alternative*
├ Seating	
├ Standard	*Alternative*
├ Comfort	*Alternative*
└ Sport	*Alternative*
└ Assistance	
└ To? For? parking	*Option*
└ To? For? navigation	*Option*
├ Eco/Performance	
├ Low fuel consumption	*Alternative*
└ Performance	*Alternative*
└ Chassis	
├ Aerodynamic	*Alternative*
├ Voluminous	*Alternative*
└ Standard	*Alternative*
├ Carry loads	*Option*
└ …	

Table 15.8. *Feature model of the system needs (partial)*

15.3.2.4. *Defining customer reference configurations*

The definition of standard customer reference configurations at system needs level corresponds directly to formation of the customer offer "catalogue": one or more "ranges" or "versions" of predefined products are therefore formed, for each of which will be chosen some variants responding both to market and user expectations as captured previously, but also to commercial constraints. A range, a product, therefore potentially forms a configuration or set of configurations.

From the variabilities defined and their characterization, each range is therefore formed of a set of common system capabilities (indeed functions, etc.), and of chosen alternatives or options, fixed in advance, to form a complete proposition coherent with a given customer type.

It should, however, be noted that a reference configuration can include unresolved nodes, i.e. variation points retaining multiple variants, which leave it to the final customer (or business) to finalize their own configuration, in a general framework fixed by the reference configuration, when its own configuration is created, as already mentioned above for operational analysis.

Each configuration should be analyzed and verified, indeed completed according to the different viewpoints that can influence it (functional coherence, safety, security, performance, etc.), as well as from an economic viewpoint: the cost estimate, the possible margin (which may be subject to viewpoint analysis) are relevant in particular to drawing the contours of each configuration.

EXAMPLE.– *The different versions of our vehicle could be defined first depending on the market and its customers in a conventional way:*

– *coupé favoring sports driving;*

– *SUV offering a hybrid solution;*

– *van for professional use;*

– *saloon car;*

– *potentially MPV for large families.*

Feature model of the system need	Coupé	SUV	Saloon	Van
├ Road-holding				
│ ├ Standard	No	Basic	Basic	Basic
│ ├ Improved	Basic	*Alternative*	*Alternative*	*Alternative*
│ ├ Optimized	*Alternative*	No	No	No
│ └ For heavy loads	No	*Alternative*	No	Basic
├ Off-road	No	*Option*	No	*Option*
├ Seating space				
│ ├ 2 places	Basic	No	No	Basic
│ ├ 5 places	No	Basic	Basic	No
│ └ 7 places	No	No	*Alternative*	No

⊢ Seating				
│ ⊢ Standard	~~No~~	Basic	~~No~~	Basic
│ ⊢ Comfort	Basic	*Alternative*	Basic	*Alternative*
│ └ Sport	*Alternative*	*Alternative*	~~No~~	~~No~~
└ Assistance				
│ └ To? For? parking	Basic	*Option*	*Option*	*Option*
│ └ To? For? navigation	Basic	*Option*	*Option*	*Option*
⊢ Eco/Performance				
│ ⊢ Low fuel consumption	~~No~~	*Option*	*Option*	~~No~~
│ └ Performance	Basic	*Option*	*Option*	*Option*
└ Chassis				
│ ⊢ Aerodynamic	Basic	~~No~~	~~No~~	~~No~~
│ ⊢ Voluminous	~~No~~	~~No~~	~~No~~	Basic
│ └ Standard	~~No~~	Basic	Basic	~~Non~~
⊢ Carry loads	~~No~~	*Option*	~~No~~	Basic
└ ...				

Table 15.9. *Reference system needs configurations (partial)*

It can sometimes be beneficial to define partial configurations with an initial level of selections that should be grouped, and then to choose them, or not, as a single whole in each configuration. This makes it possible to orient and simplify choices, and makes it possible to restrict the degrees of liberty in these choices as far as the final configuration for a customer.

It is therefore important that in managing FMs and configurations, it can be possible to define partial, "re-usable" configurations, and that the configuration definition that follows (standard, customer configurations) may be able to select what is necessary from among these partial configurations, in the same way as for the variation points of the FM themselves, or reference configurations.

EXAMPLE.– *The characterizations above can lead, for example, to defining options grouped in partial configurations (here called "packs"), which express both functional or structural constraints (the sport pack for example), or business choices, to differentiate and limit the complexity and number of the different versions in the customer catalogue (Table 15.10).*

Feature model of the system need	Sport pack	Sport+ pack	Comfort pack	Superior pack
⊢ Road-holding				
⊢ Improved	X			
⊢ Optimized		X		
⊢ Seating spaces				
∟ 7 places				X
⊢ Seating				
⊢ Comfort			X	X
∟ Sport				
∟ Assistance				
∟ with parking			X	X
∟ with navigation				X
⊢ Eco/Performance				
∟ Power		X		
∟ ...				

Table 15.10. *Grouping options into partial configurations*

Reference configurations will therefore choose those that will form their ranges from among these packs (Table 15.11).

Feature model of the system need	Versions of the Coupé		
	"Essential" Version	"Racing" Version	"Premium" Version
⊢ Sport Pack	X		
⊢ Sport+ Pack		X	X
⊢ Comfort Pack		X	
⊢ Superior Pack			X
∟ ...			

Table 15.11. *Building reference configurations using partial configurations*

15.3.2.5. *Verifying coherence between feature and engineering models*

Verification of coherence between FM and EM happens on two levels: the full feature tree versus the complete product model and for each reference configuration. This occurs in the conditions described above in operational analysis.

In reference to operational analysis, the coherence of feature trees and EMs between the two levels will also be verified.

For example,

– variabilities in system analysis should be coherent with operational variabilities (which are manifested at least in traceability and justification links between the elements subject to variability in both perspectives);

– the variabilities placed on elements of system analysis should be coherent with those placed on the elements of operational analysis to which they are linked (correspondence and traceability of variabilities for capabilities, functional chains etc.).

15.3.3. Designing a logical and physical architecture compatible with the product policy

The approach shown is the same, in its outlines, for logical architecture as for physical architecture, and it is therefore only described once here. Moreover, it is similar to the need analysis above and the reader is asked to refer to it.

15.3.3.1. Defining the chosen behavior for each system need variant

Building the architecture consists, as we have seen, of designing both a global behavior of the product responding to a need defined at the outset (in the form of a functional analysis), and a structure of components each ensuring a part of this behavior, which is allocated to this component.

Traceability links are established between the functions, capabilities, functional chains, etc., of the system needs analysis and their equivalents describing the behavior in logical and physical architecture. They make it possible, in particular, to identify for each variant of the need, the functional content (its "footprint", in the form of grouping functional elements of the logical or physical architecture) in the behavior that the solution must meet.

EXAMPLE.– *The example of the vehicle studied previously will be, for this architecture perspective and for the sake of simplicity, focused on the mechanical and technical platform (motor, chassis, transmission, etc.), omitting aspects of comfort (seating, volume, etc.) and the body.*

An extract of the logical functions corresponding to the vehicle's performances is shown below (Table 15.12). It can be seen that a single logical function may be useful for several of the functions expected of the system, as is the case for the suspension or braking functions.

System functions (services)	Logical solution functions
Deliver high performance	Deliver power & torque; rigidify chassis; select ignition map; prevent wheel skid during acceleration
Ensure efficient braking	Wheel braking Control dynamic stability through individual wheel braking
Maintain the vehicle horizontal	Control dynamic attitude through individual suspension hardness
Keep vehicle on curve during turns	Same as "maintain the vehicle horizontal" + Harden/soften the dampers Increase/reduce dampers travel distance Engage 4-wheel drive Prevent wheel blocking when braking Prevent wheel skid during acceleration Control dynamic stability through individual wheel braking
Adapt to various loads	Harden/soften the dampers Increase/reduce dampers travel distance
Absorb irregularities of the road	Harden/soften the dampers Increase/reduce dampers travel distance
Allow high/low ground clearance	Harden/soften the dampers Increase/reduce dampers travel distance
Other functions as examples	Optimize engine consumption Drive the rear wheels Drive the front wheels Disengage/engage clutch Engage selected gear on gearbox Lock the differential Dampen chassis movement versus wheel Automatically park the car Select driving mode Detect short distance obstacles Provide itinerary guidance Find lower cost itinerary Tightly adjust seat to dedicated driver Allow seat recline and cushion height adjustment; Adapt to passenger corpulence Allow adding/removing extra seats Preserve room for luggage Ease luggage loading Allow entering a steep slope Optimize aerodynamics

Table 15.12. *System needs functions and the logical functions that meet them (extract)*

Moreover, it should also be noted that some potential alternatives in system needs analysis, such as road-holding or performance need, are carried not only by functional differences, but also by "non-functional" properties, such as dampers' travel distance, the value of power and torque delivered,... variabilities should therefore be applicable to this type of engineering artifact too, in the same way as the non-formalized requirements that are also often a vector of them.

Finally, large, very structuring options, such as off-road capability or sports driving, require a global study of the adaption of architecture to their specificities. This will lead, for example, to defining specific functional chains (associated with these capabilities), and functions dedicated to each, which will carry the corresponding specificities, including non-functional ones. Thus, there will be two "drive the rear wheels" functions, one carrying expectations of 4 × 4 driving off-road, the other, those for 4 × 4 racing. It is on these chains (or the overarching capabilities) that associated variants will be carried, via links with the FMs variation points.

Important work in this stage of building the architecture is the search for the largest possible shared core between all the product configurations envisaged. This is key to the product policy's efficiency and profitability and should not be ignored. The approach relies on the functional and structural relationship between different needs, alternatives, existing re-usable components, etc., to maximize commonalities at all these levels.

It is also from this moment that the use of predefined re-usable components (or "building blocks") is considered: in this case, these components are described with their functional description, and it remains to determine if all or part of the global designed behavior can be created with the aid of the functional content available from the chosen components. In this case, this functional content will replace the that which was initially designed, and traceability and justification links with the needs analysis will be established.

EXAMPLE.– *For example, some of the functions involving the suspensions identified above could come from a common platform generic to many types of vehicles; this is practiced frequently by car makers. In this case, the functions mentioned in logical architecture would result from a model of this platform reused in each model of a product (just like the associated components are reused).*

15.3.3.2. Characterizing behaviors required for the solution

For each capability, or set of functions thus identified and corresponding to one or more need variants, it is therefore necessary to define behavioral commonalities and specificities that will characterize each option or alternative. To integrate the variability constraints, it will therefore be useful, for each logical function, to verify if its definition is really in line with the different variants resulting from the system needs analysis.

EXAMPLE.– *Thus, functions involving damping, being involved with off-road and sport or comfort variants, should either be adapted to each, or themselves give rise to variants, depending on the design possibilities available.*

Different solution possibilities are revealed with the aim of increasing customer satisfaction or expected properties, in line with the characterization resulting from system analysis: increase in performances, in functionalities, in user safety and economic considerations mentioned above...

EXAMPLE.– *Analysis of the previous logical functions and associated functional chains leads to the characterization presented in Table 15.13.*

Logical functions	Characterization	Justification
Traction		
Select ignition map Optimize engine consumption	Alternative ignition profiles: economy and racing	Consumption and performances are mutually exclusive
Deliver power and torque	Engine alternatives: economy, high torque, torque and power	Needs in delivering power differ with different uses
Braking		
Wheel braking	Braking power alternatives	Demanding but costly needs in sports driving
Prevent wheel skid during acceleration	Option	Above all, performance need
Control dynamic stability through individual wheel braking	Option	Improve road-holding and braking, but the cost justifies an option
Transmission		
Drive the front wheels	Basic for family versions	Forward traction is the easiest to drive
Drive the rear wheels	Basic for high-range sports versions, if the additional cost of design is acceptable	Efficiency and pleasure are greater in sports driving
Engage/disengage clutch Engage selected gear on gearbox	Basic, economy mechanical gearbox Options: off-road gearbox, standard automatic gearbox, automatic sport gearbox	Automatic gearbox, dedicated gearbox reporting needs for sport and off-road + rapid speed changing in sport

Drive the front/rear wheels	Two alternative options: 4-wheel drive, sport or off-road	Different design required
Differential blocker	Option, only on off-road	Increases traction but expensive and heavy
Suspension		
Dampen movements relating to wheels and chassis Harden/soften the dampers	Alternative options: comfort dampers, non-adjustable or adjustable dampers	Adjustable damper systems are very expensive; damping is decisive for road-holding and use
Increase/reduce dampers travel distance Harden/soften the dampers	Option for adjustable ground clearance and damping	Possible for high ranges if damper control is available
Control dynamic attitude through individual suspension hardness	Option	Expensive, but greatly improves road-holding when turning

Table 15.13. *Characterization of some logical functions*

It will be noted that already at this stage, different options or alternatives depend on the available solutions and the state of the art (alternatives for suspension for example). In addition, potential dependencies between different options have already appeared, for example between ground clearance/adjustable damping and dynamic attitude control.

This analysis also draws out new possible variants – or on the contrary the impossibility of some variants hitherto envisaged – linked to the technologies used, existing reusable components, or new ideas for design, innovations, etc.

Reusable components can also bring their own variabilities to be integrated in this case with those of the system.

15.3.3.3. Defining variabilities on the solution's behavior

The FM of the solution architecture is built from the previous characterization of the functional analysis describing the solution's chosen behavior by formalizing the different possible solution variants and the nature of the associated variation points (option, alternative, etc.). The conditions for association, dependency and exclusion of different options and variants are also formalized.

EXAMPLE.– *From the analysis and characterization of logical functions carried out previously, one can define and structure our vehicle's FM, for example in the following way, here according to technical rather than architectural criteria (Table 15.14).*

Solution feature model	Modes	Constraints
├ Engine		
│ ├ Power		
│ │ ├ 150 CV (economy)	*alternative*	*c*
│ │ ├ 150 CV (torque)	*alternative*	
│ │ └ 200 CV (torque +power)	*alternative*	*a,b,f*
│ ├ Ignition		
│ │ ├ Economy	*alternative*	
│ │ ├ Performance	*alternative*	
│ │ └ Switchable	*alternative*	
├ Braking		
│ ├ Brakes		
│ │ ├ Standard discs	*alternative*	
│ │ ├ Ventilated discs	*alternative*	*f*
│ │ └ Double ventilated discs	*alternative*	*f*
│ ├ Anti-skid	*Option*	
│ ├ Dynamic stability control	*Option*	
├ Transmission		
│ ├ 4 wheel-drive		
│ │ ├ 2 wheel-drive	*alternative*	
│ │ │ ├ Front wheels	*alternative*	
│ │ │ └ Rear wheels	*alternative*	*a*
│ │ └ 4 wheel-drive	*alternative*	
│ │ ├ 4x4 sport	*alternative*	*b*
│ │ ├ 4x4 off-road	*alternative*	*c,d,e*
│ │ └ Differential blocking	*Option*	
│ ├ Gearbox		
│ │ ├ Mechanical gearbox	*alternative*	
│ │ ├ Standard automatic gearbox	*alternative*	
│ │ ├ off-road mechanical gearbox	*alternative*	*a,c,d*
│ │ └ Automatic sport gearbox	*alternative*	*a,b*
├ Suspension		
│ ├ Dampers		

		├ Standard	*alternative*	
		├ Comfort	*alternative*	
		├ Off-road	*alternative*	
		├ Sport	*alternative*	
		└ Adjustable sport	*alternative*	e
	├ Adjustable ground clearance and damping		*option*	e
	└ Dynamic suspension control		*option*	e
└ ...				

Constraints (extract)			
	a	Rear wheel drive only with max power and sport gearbox	
	b	4x4 sport only with max power and sport gearbox	
	c	Off-road 4x4 excludes insufficient torque	
	d	Off-road 4x4 requires an adapted gearbox	
	e	Adjustable ground clearance and dynamic control require adjustable dampers	
	f	A powerful engine requires powerful braking	
And also...		Suspensions/power/4x4/heavy load/braking, etc. links	

Table 15.14. *Solution feature model (partial)*

Here too, the first levels of this model shall favor the most overarching variants possible, and a structuring favoring understanding and use of the FM.

EXAMPLE.– *Thus, grouping the option for differential blocking under the 4-wheel drive variation point above is chosen, rather than creating a dependency between two variation points belonging to different branches, since the blocking need only be available in the case of four-wheel drive.*

It might also be preferred, instead of the very technical orientation of the FM above, to group variation points addressing the same types of need, especially from operational and system needs FMs, which of course reduces the number of possible variants and variation points, but also simplifies the choices and can also take account of dependencies between basic variants without having to make links between variation points. An example is presented in Table 15.14.

Solution feature model	Modes	Constraints
├ Road-holding		
│ ├ Standard	*alternative*	
│ │ ├ Standard dampers		
│ │ └ 2 wheel-drive (front)		
│ ├ Improved	*alternative*	
│ │ ├ Sport dampers		
│ │ ├ 2 wheel-drive (rear)		
│ │ └ Dynamic stability control		
│ └ Optimized	*alternative*	
│ ├ Adjustable sport dampers		
│ ├ 4 wheel-drive sport		
│ ├ Dynamic stability control		
│ └ Dynamic stability control for suspensions		
└ ...		

Table 15.15. *Example of an alternative solution feature model (partial)*

The links between the solution FM and the system needs FM are formed to verify coherence between them and enable navigation during later impact analyses. It is also possible to use other links, between system needs analysis and logical architecture in the EM, and to verify coherence between these two types of link.

Similarly, links between the solution FM and the EM are also put in place, at the functional level initially, and always seeking to favor groupings of functions, system capabilities, functional chains, etc. These links rely on characterizations carried out on functional elements, and on the definition of the FM that results from them. The simplest is often to build them progressively along the path presented thus far, for example by creating a variation point when creation of a functional element is desired, and linking them to one another.

EXAMPLE.– *The link between the FM and the EM (functional part) is easy to establish by comparing Tables 15.13 and 15.15.*

15.3.3.4. *Adapting architecture components to the variability*

The components that form the system's structure are built, as we have seen, to conciliate a number of functional and non-functional constraints, to determine for which part of the functional analysis above each of them will be responsible.

EXAMPLE.– *The architecture of the vehicle considered, at logical level, could, for example, include subsystem components such as:*

– *the engine;*

– *the transmission (sub-)system;*

– *the chassis and suspension system;*

– *the braking system;*

– *the vetronics suite;*

– *the body;*

– *seats and passenger compartments, etc.*

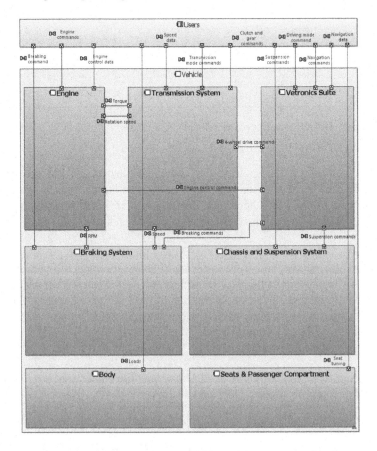

Figure 15.4. *The vehicle's logical architecture components (before applying product line constraints)*

The corresponding function allocation (from the logical functions already introduced previously) is shown in Figure 15.5.

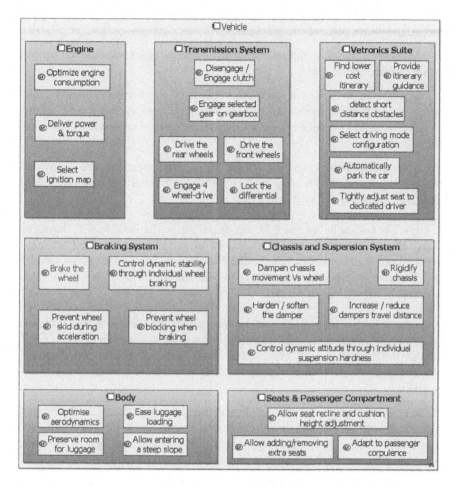

Figure 15.5. *Function allocation on the vehicle's logical architecture (before applying product line constraints)*

One of the viewpoints to reconcile is adequacy to constraints and variability choices developed hitherto, and for now carried essentially by this functional description. Definition of the contour and content of components should be subject to certain rules or recommendations, which will influence its definition (without however being absolute, as other more important viewpoints can lead to them being called into question). As an example, some rules can be cited that constrain the component's perimeter depending on the variability characterization of the functions it hosts:

– a component should not mix functions characterized as generic and of general interest, and others particular to one variant;

– functions associated with independent variants or options should not be united in a single component;

– functions associated with different variants of an alternative should each be carried by a distinct component. The connections and exchanges of all these components should be defined, especially for the generic components with which they interact;

– as far as possible, variability should be accommodated at each component's boundaries, which avoids having to place variabilities inside the component, which would then cause variability in its design.

Applying variability to the EM can therefore on its own lead to component breakdowns to separate independent options or alternatives, or to the creation of "overarching" components to "encapsulate" the variety of alternatives to consider in a single shared interface for example, or to redundancies of definitions able to adapt to several configurations of options.

EXAMPLE.– *Following this revision of the architecture in the light of constraints imposed by the product line, the vehicle's architecture is shown in Figure 15.6. The constraints associated with the product line have led to the modification of components in the following way (some links with the FM are mentioned as an example).*

The engine component is divided into three components: the engine block (in two or three variants depending on the power and torque – a single block that can be optimized for two different torques cannot be separated into two at this level), ignition control, monitoring and control of fuel consumption.

The transmission (sub-)system separates the front axle transmission, two variants for rear axle transmission (off-road and sport), four gearbox variants and an optional 4-wheel drive command. The off-road option applies to two components simultaneously: rear off-road transmission and the 4-wheel drive command.

The chassis and the suspension system is divided into five components: chassis (with comfort or sport variants), suspension (with three variants, comfort, sport and adjustable sport), damper adjustment (optional), dynamic stability control (optional) and ground clearance adjustment (optional).

The braking system includes discs (standard, ventilated and double ventilated disc variants), anti-skid (as an option), dynamic trajectory control (as an option) and an anti-wheel blocking that, being indispensable, does not appear in the FM. It can be noted by analyzing the architecture, that both dynamic controls, for stability and trajectory, could be correlated with one another, and so offer a new option, which would come to enhance the FM and offer based on architectural considerations ....

The embedded electronics, or vetronics, here groups a GPS navigator (optional), parking assistance, (option with two variants: sonar or camera), a driving mode selector (eco, sports, 4 × 4, etc.) as an option, automatic seat adjustment as an option, and automatic parking, also as an option.

Note that architecture analysis will highlight a dependency not necessarily visible in the FM alone: the fact that the video screen is needed for the rear-view camera and GPS, which could orient the options or configurations. Similarly, automatic parking requires distance information to operate; therefore, it should be associated with the sonar parking assistance variant, and not the camera variant.

The body will have various types (coupé, SUV, saloon, minivan).

The seating and passenger compartment will have options for type (comfort, sport), number, electric adjustment (which there too carries a dependency with a vetronic component).

Once the right compromise is found between the component breakdown constraints, the features should be reviewed. Generally, the architecture reduces the field of possible options and configurations and adapts to them in an iterative process.

In fact, it can happen that variability hypotheses need to be reviewed due to contradictions with the result of the architecture's design: groupings imposed by other viewpoints can render some options useless or impossible, or they create technical or architectural dependencies between them.

In some cases, in fact, the architecture itself creates dependencies between distinct variation points, for example when the resources of one are shared with another, or one provides input needed for another to function properly. This leads groupings of options to form a single option, the deletion of options or variants, etc., which, we note, can often end in reducing the number of variation points or their dependencies, and in simplifying their expression.

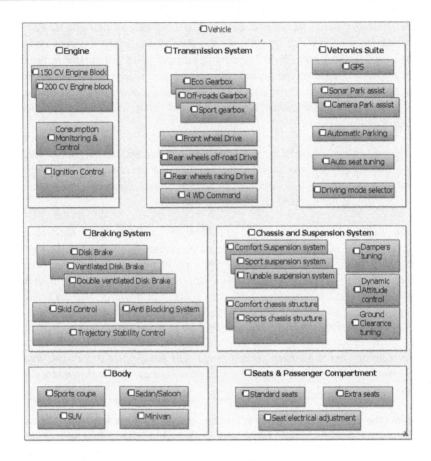

Figure 15.6. *New breakdown of the vehicle's logical architecture (after applying product line constraints)*

Generally, a large number of dependencies required between options can highlight architecture constraints that the FM reflects badly. It is therefore wise to ask if the breakdown into options should not be reviewed to correspond more directly to these architecture constraints. This restructuring of variabilities is even more useful as it is often accompanied not only by the disappearance of complex constraints and dependencies between variation points, but also by a reduction in the number of these variation points.

EXAMPLE.– *Some examples of optimization are illustrated below.*

The ignition variation point involves two components: ignition control, on the one hand, and monitoring and control of consumption, on the other hand; but it is applied to each of them, by configuration (for example ignition maps and control strategy specific to each case, downloadable or selectable from among many) and not via component interchangeability.

Adjustable ground clearance and dampers are possible only with the option adjustable sports dampers, like dynamic control, which was hitherto expressed by a constraint (written e) in the FM. But in the EM, there is very probably at least one capability and one functional chain that illustrate these two functions and highlight this dependency between functions and so between the components that operate them (Figure 15.7). It might therefore be more sensible for the FM to evolve into two options associated with these capabilities rather than with technical components, which would also remove the associated constraint.

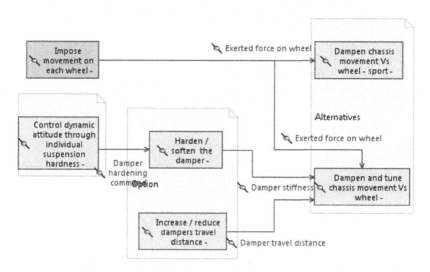

Figure 15.7. *Functional chain: suspension for a sports driving capability highlighting dependencies between basic options*

More radically, taking account of the multiple architecture constraints highlighted in the previous FM (constraints a to f, above), a more drastic restructuring of it is possible, as shown in Table 15.16 (if one focuses on these mechanical platform elements alone). It relies not on basic variabilities per function or component, but on those sets of elements showing the most constraints and dependencies between them: here, it will be those associated with off-road and sport capabilities in particular, subject to numerous constraints and dependencies.

The number of leaf variation points is a little more reduced, but above all there are far fewer dependencies to be taken into account, and the FM provides more guidance in selecting options and alternatives. Of course, the number and nature of possible configurations is more limited, but they are much simpler to use, including the definition of reference configurations.

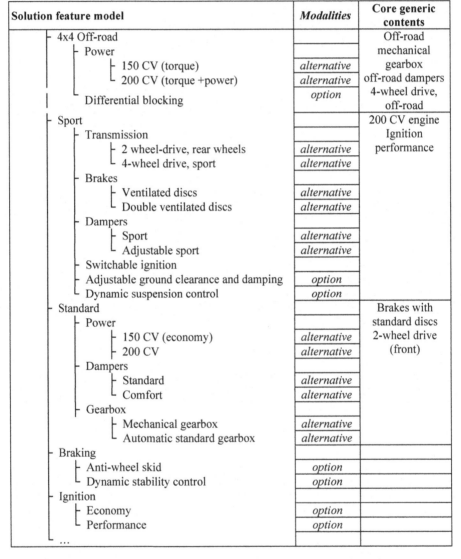

Solution feature model	*Modalities*	Core generic contents
⊢ 4x4 Off-road		Off-road
⊢ Power		mechanical
⊢ 150 CV (torque)	*alternative*	gearbox
⌐ 200 CV (torque +power)	*alternative*	off-road dampers
	option	4-wheel drive,
⌐ Differential blocking		off-road
⊢ Sport		200 CV engine
⊢ Transmission		Ignition
⊢ 2 wheel-drive, rear wheels	*alternative*	performance
⌐ 4-wheel drive, sport	*alternative*	
⊢ Brakes		
⊢ Ventilated discs	*alternative*	
⌐ Double ventilated discs	*alternative*	
⊢ Dampers		
⊢ Sport	*alternative*	
⌐ Adjustable sport	*alternative*	
⊢ Switchable ignition		
⊢ Adjustable ground clearance and damping	*option*	
⌐ Dynamic suspension control	*option*	
⊢ Standard		Brakes with
⊢ Power		standard discs
⊢ 150 CV (economy)	*alternative*	2-wheel drive
⊢ 200 CV	*alternative*	(front)
⊢ Dampers		
⊢ Standard	*alternative*	
⌐ Comfort	*alternative*	
⊢ Gearbox		
⊢ Mechanical gearbox	*alternative*	
⌐ Automatic standard gearbox	*alternative*	
⊢ Braking		
⊢ Anti-wheel skid	*option*	
⌐ Dynamic stability control	*option*	
⊢ Ignition		
⊢ Economy	*option*	
⌐ Performance	*option*	
⌐ ...		

Table 15.16. *Another example of an alternative solution feature model (partial)*

Then, the characterization of each model element in relation to the variabilities it should carry should be extended or "propagated" from functional elements to components (logical, behavioral) and the elements of structural architecture that host them (hosting physical components, physical links, etc.), and the links between the two models of engineering and variability completed and updated.

Finally, if an architecture has been stabilized enough for this (especially when predefined re-usable components are used), it may be interesting to move (rather than extend) the characterization of functions to components, for example to simplify managing them. The links between the solution FM and the EM are then modified, moved or completed, this time at the structural component level.

15.3.3.5. Defining reference configurations for a product building

Standard reference configurations formalize the creation of different "ranges" or "versions" of the product and its architecture that respond to the customer offer "catalogue" defined at the outset.

Each range is built from the variabilities defined and their characterization by choosing the desired options and alternatives. The development process can start from configurations formed in system needs analysis, and by following traceability links with the previous perspective, especially that of need. The minimal variation points to be considered in creating a product building configuration are obtained that way, and other choices are generally added to these, taken from variabilities particular to architecture and design; some choices can remain open and unresolved at this stage.

Here as well, each configuration should be analyzed and verified, or indeed completed according to the different viewpoints that can influence it (functional coherence, security, safety, performances, etc.), but also the economic viewpoint: cost estimate and the possible margin (which might be the subject of analysis viewpoints) are particularly relevant in drawing each configuration's contours.

EXAMPLE.– *The reference configurations are defined here from the last FM formed above, because it simplifies the choices to be made for each of them.*

As an example, two "catalogue" configurations are defined for each type of vehicle identified during the previous stages: coupé (basic and sports versions), SUV (basic and off-road versions) and saloon (basic and luxury versions). The definition is restricted here to the mechanical platform, as for the previous FM.

	Coupé		SUV		Saloon	
	Basic	**Racing**	**Basic**	**TT**	**Basic**	**Luxury**
Solution feature model	Alt^tive =alternative, No =not available					
├ 4x4 Off-road	No	No	*Option*	Basic	No	No
│ ├ Power						
│ │ ├ 150 CV (torque)	-	-	*Alt^tive*	Basic	-	-
│ │ └ 200 CV	-	-	No	*Alt^tive*	-	-
│ └ Differential blocking			*Option*	Basic		
├ Sport	Basic	Basic	No	No	No	*Option*
│ ├ Transmission						No
│ │ ├ Rear wheels	Basic	Basic	-	-	-	
│ │ └ 4 wheel-drive sport		*Alt^tive*	-	-	-	
│ ├ Brakes						
│ │ ├ Ventilated discs	Basic	No	-	-	-	*Alt^tive*
│ │ └ Ventilated discs	*Alt^tive*	Basic	-	-	-	No
│ ├ Dampers						
│ │ ├ Sport	Basic	Basic	-	-	-	*Alt^tive*
│ │ └ Adjustable sport	*Alt^tive*	*Alt^tive*	-	-	-	No
│ ├ Switchable ignition	*Alt^tive*	Basic	-	-	-	*Option*
│ ├ Adjust. ground clearance /damp.	No	*Option*	-	-	-	No
│ └ Dyn. Suspension control	No	*Option*	-	-	-	No
├ Standard	No	No				
│ ├ Power						
│ │ ├ 150 CV (eco)	-	-	Basic	-	Basic	No
│ │ ├ 200 CV	-	-	*Alt^tive*	-	*Alt^tive*	Basic
│ ├ Dampers						
│ │ ├ Standard	-	-	Basic	-	Basic	No

| | └ Comfort	-		Alt^{tive}	-	Alt^{tive}	Basic
| └ Gearbox		-	-			
| ├ Mechanical gearbox	-	-	Basic		Basic	Basic
| └ Automatic std gearbox	-	-	Option		Alt^{tive}	Alt^{tive}
├ Braking					-	
| ├ Anti-wheel-skid	Basic	Basic	~~No~~	Basic	~~No~~	Basic
| ├ Dynam.stability control	Alt^{tive}	Basic	~~No~~	Option	~~No~~	Option
├ Ignition					-	
| ├ Economy	-	-	~~No~~	~~No~~	Option	Basic
| └ Performance	-	-	~~No~~	Option	~~No~~	Option
└ ...						

NB: for the basic SUV, the off-road option is not compatible with the automatic gearbox (etc.)

Table 15.17. *Solution reference configurations (partial)*

15.3.3.6. Verification of coherence between feature and engineering models

Verification of coherence between the FM and EM occurs on two levels: the variability tree in relation to the complete model and for each reference configuration. This takes place in the conditions described in operational analysis and system needs analysis previously.

15.3.4. *Deriving a configuration for a given customer or product using a subtractive approach*

Until now, the approach does not fundamentally affect the way in which the EM describing the product line architecture is structured, how the different variants and options cohabit or not in this model, or how the model describing each customer product is formed.

The approach often thought to be most natural consists of describing in the same model the set of variants, as and when they appear; there is therefore a product line model (called a domain model) that contains all the possible variants; to satisfy a given customer need, a model dedicated to this project will be created (a so-called project model), obtained by "filtering", i.e. selection/removal of elements of the domain model, according to the corresponding configurations defined in the FM. This operation is called configuration derivation.

It is therefore called a subtractive approach, or 150% approach, the domain model containing more elements than a project model (Figure 15.8).

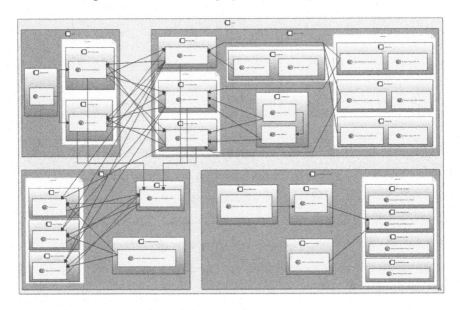

Figure 15.8. *Extract of the 150% model, mechanical part*
(in yellow, the alternatives cohabiting in the model)

A variant of the subtractive approach is the parametric approach, which expresses several variants of a component, only by "configuring" it, i.e. modifying its behavior or use by choosing appropriate values for predefined parameters (a software, for example can be configured in novice or expert mode, a mechanical system can have stops adapting to its environment or uses, etc.). These parameters can be chosen during the product's design, its installation or indeed its use. The method used differs depending on the implementation contexts and technologies: one can imagine a static parameterization in the form of attributes characterizing the component from the system model; for complex components justifying it, this can be through defining the component's different modes of functioning during its implementation, this then being configured in one or more particular modes dedicated to each project using them depending on its expected behavior.

The advantage of the subtractive approach is that each variant is integrated by construction in the domain model, and that the derivation process is simple, and above all guided by the initial 150% model. On the other side, the domain model is complex to form and use (in case of superposition of variants in particular, for example, if two alternatives for components or their interfaces should cohabit, and are connected to a single third component).

***

When a new need appears for a new customer in a dedicated project framework, the approach in principle is the following:

– an operational analysis and system needs analysis are carried out for this new need. So far as possible, during discussions with the customer, one tries to make their need converge with that of the product line as defined in the domain model;

– these analyses are confronted with the product line's operational analysis and the system needs analysis (of the domain model), to define the deviations between the existing product line and the new customer's needs;

– for the needs thus identified as covered by the product line, a customer configuration selecting the variants appropriate to their need is derived from the FM. A project EM is obtained, which serves as basis for continuing its engineering. Initial needs analyses of the domain and project are then merged to form a reference analysis of the project (Figure 15.9 below);

– then, needs not covered by the product line are taken into account by the evolution of the project EM, in particular the complements specific to it. The opportunities to reuse these specific complements for the product line are eventually studied (see section 15.4);

– where deviations are too great, then the system needs analysis belonging to the project should be retained, and only the architecture section resulting from the domain model will be reused, which will be linked by the usual traceability and justification links to the project needs analysis.

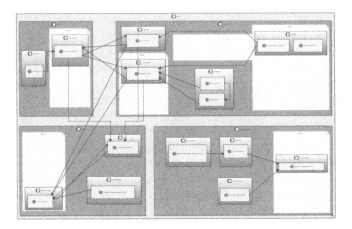

Figure 15.9. *High-range sport configuration, mechanical part*
(in yellow, the alternatives from which an element is chosen)

Of course, in reality, cycles are not so separate or so one directional; it often happens that they mix, that a project model become a domain reference model, that they evolve in parallel, etc. Similarly, it often happens that a subtractive approach is completed by reusing building blocks (below).

15.4. Additive or compositional engineering by building blocks

15.4.1. *Engineering using reusable components, building blocks*

Another approach for implementing a product line consists of defining reusable components (also called "building blocks"), in advance of any given project, and then building the solution required for each customer or project, by assembling reusable components (hence the term "build for reuse"). The domain model therefore contains descriptions of building blocks and their rules of assembly, and for a given need, blocks responding to this need will be chosen and assembled.

It is then called an additive approach, or 80% approach (or 50% approach), the domain model being a subset of a project model.

The advantage of the additive approach is the simplicity of the domain model, which can even be multiple and distributed in several organizations; moreover, if the components are well chosen, very stable over time and fully cover the general need, the approach can be very profitable and simpler to operate than the subtractive approach. On the other side, the derivation process is more complex, often guided little by the domain model itself, beyond rules for local assembly between components communicating with one another. It is also difficult to envisage all the possible configurations and validate them. Finally, there is rarely in this case a global and unified vision of operational and system needs, which impoverishes the previous needs analysis and presents risks in customer needs adequacy.

15.4.2. Building a base of reusable components

This approach aims to build components specifically with a view to their reuse in a large number of projects (it is often called "building for reuse").

The choice to reuse components can be opportunistic, benefiting from a particular project in which some components are identified as of more general interest. In this case, it involves extracting from the project model a description of the component but also of its environment, which makes reuse easy. This component's dependencies on its environment will be verified, especially by analyzing the model, which could lead to its content and perimeter being reviewed, the addition of elements from other neighbor components or its external interfaces; its non-functional properties should also be considered and capitalized on, such as its resource consumption, its criticality and certification levels, etc.

The choice to reuse components can also be deliberate and proactive, constructing an engineering dedicated to these re-usable components, with an adapted approach. In this case, it is generally desirable to include the constraints of the first user projects in the component's definition; it thus means conducting a "multicustomer" engineering (the user projects are customers for component engineering), which is similar to building a product line: comparing operational and functional needs, seeking to maximize shared elements, defining a behavior that satisfies these different needs and federating them. Either projects are similar enough to one another for the projects to have a shared solution, or it will be necessary to think of a product line approach applied to the component.

***

In both cases, it is recommended to build at least one model dedicated to the component's own engineering, and one model intended for its integration in a system model including this component in its architecture.

The component's EM – and more generally the associated engineering data – will include at least:

– the operational and system needs to which this component responds;

– the component's environment: the components with which it communicates, associated protocols and scenarios, hosting component if necessary;

– the component's logical and physical architecture, including non-functional dimensions: required resources, performances, security or certification level, possible settings and parameterization, etc.

– the body of requirements associated with the component, test campaigns and proofs, associated documentation, supporting justification files (reliability, security, etc.), possible user manual, etc. (see also Chapter 9).

The component's integration model is a sort of "caricature", a simplified version of it, with a less fine (coarser grain) level of detail, as it is intended to be inserted into the overarching system model, at a level just sufficient to make it possible to make decisions on the system engineering. This model can be restricted to the physical or logical architecture for example, but can also provide elements of operational or needs analysis, to which must be added other engineering artifacts useful at the system level (requirements, tests, possible FM of the component, etc.).

As far as possible, if a number of reusable components exist in a single context, it is useful also to have a global domain model, which is similar to that mentioned in a subtractive approach, and which will include an operational analysis and system needs analysis describing the main cases where components are used, and a logical and physical architecture describing the component's conditions and rules of assembly, to enable their global, rather than only unitary and separate reuse.

15.4.3. *Defining a configuration by reusing components in an additive approach*

One of the potential difficulties mentioned for the additive approach using separate components involves verifying customer needs adequacy. To do this, Arcadia suggests relying on the different perspectives illustrating the need and the solution, in the project model:

– operational analysis and system needs analysis capture the customer need to which the project considered should respond;

– the logical architecture formalizes the architecture desired by the architect to meet this need optimally. Comparison of this architecture with models of reusable components makes it possible to identify candidate components for integration in the project;

– the physical architecture, initially, is the place in which the reusable components will be assembled, to form a coherent architecture. This can lead to the development of adaptors between reused components, for example if their interfaces are compatible but not identical. The coherence according to non-functional viewpoints should also be verified;

– this initial physical architecture is then compared with the project's logical architecture, to verify that it responds to it well at least in part. Traceability and justification links formalize this adequacy. Possible evolutions of one or the other are possible, so long as they still conform with the project's needs analysis;

– the physical architecture is at last potentially completed, for all the functional aspects not covered by the reused components. Opportunities for future reuse of new components can be detected on this occasion.

NOTE.– *Where a component is not developed internally, but bought on the market for example, there is a great temptation not to model it, or to do so without functional content, on the pretext that its functioning is not known. It is strongly recommended on the contrary to model components not developed internally, in the same way as the others. In fact, it is vital to have analyzed the component's functioning, interfaces and non-functional characteristics, as soon as it interacts with others and contributes to the global need.*

15.5. Articulating system and subsystem product lines

Without entering again into detail, we simply mention here some specificities of the system/subsystem articulation for a product line based on models.

We first consider the top-down approach, in which the system engineering alone specifies those variabilities to which the subsystem should be subject.

The approach carried out at the system level favors variabilities at a grain greater than or equal to the subsystem component; it is therefore enough to build target configurations by choosing complete components, which in particular simplifies management of the product line, and imposes no constraint of this nature on the subsystem components. These are not subject to any variability constraints and are always used in the same way and with the same content.

If this is not enough, the following stage consists of having recourse to the parametric approach mentioned previously. In this case, the subsystem model receives the required parameters, for example in the form of attributes, or modes of functioning imposed during its operation.

If the variabilities should be applied at a grain finer than the component, then those defined at the system level should also be imposed at the subsystem level. An extract of the system FM, restricted to the subsystem component involved, should therefore be provided for it, at the same time as the subsystem needs model, its requirements and other engineering artifacts. This extract will be linked to elements of the subsystem needs model and to artifacts with the same links as those that exist at the system level.

***

When the subsystem is in existence before the system, especially in the case of an additive approach, and when it has its own variability, there too, several potential cases can be considered.

So far as possible, an approach will be favored in which the subsystem defines some standard configurations adapted to its different uses. In this case, system engineering chooses only, with the help of the subsystem engineering, the right "ready to use" configuration.

If the system's product policy requires the ability to extend variability to the subsystem, because it is desirable to offer several versions of the subsystem or because the dependencies with other subsystems require it for example, then the FM defined for the subsystem should be "sent upwards" and inserted in the system FM. There too, as we have seen for reusable components, the subsystem engineering can send upwards a simplified ("caricature") version of this FM, to mask its complexity and simplify the definition of system configurations.

We note that in an additive approach one may be led to build an FM and/or system level configurations, by composing variabilities of reused components. This therefore assumes composable, potentially hierarchical FMs, etc., coupled by dependency, traceability and justification links, just as EMs.

15.6. Summary

A good product policy aims especially to fully understand the market segmentation, and user expectations in their specificities and variety, and to build an architecture that responds to them by maximizing reusable elements and minimizing specific developments.

Arcadia models contribute efficiently to this objective from the engineering viewpoint. In each of the method's perspectives, activities belonging to product line engineering can be identified: they make it possible to analyze need and its variabilities, help to define an adequate product catalogue, make it possible to structure the product to respond as effectively as possible to these variabilities and also contribute to simplifying its definition and management.

The suggested approach is adapted as much to a top-down definition from the product need and to a subtractive approach (through selection from a complete product definition), as to a bottom-up approach assembling existing reusable components (by composition).

PART 3

Encyclopedia of the Language and Glossary of the Concepts of Arcadia

16

Introduction to Arcadia
Modeling Language

The chapters that follow introduce the principal concepts needed for modeling when applying the Arcadia method, as well as their relationship to each other, in the form of a reference "encyclopedia".

EXAMPLE.– *The reader is also invited to look through the examples given in the earlier parts of this book.*

16.1. The perimeter addressed

The modeling language defined by Arcadia focuses on the domain for applying this method, and therefore the *"in extenso"* functional and structural definition, of system, software and hardware architectures.

Some of the concepts and formalisms chosen may present varying degrees of semantic similarity to various modeling languages (we cite *Architecture Frameworks* such as NAF [NAT 07], the UML software language [OBJ 15a] and its adaptation to system description, SysML [OBJ 15b] and the AADL language for architecture description [FEI 06]). However, the *Arcadia concept definition is self-sufficient, and so it nowhere refers to other definitions in the literature or state of the art.* As a matter of fact, and in particular to make the language easier for system engineers to adopt, but also to mask as well as possible the complexity of the models manipulated and their construction, these concepts retain their own meaning and semantics. This semantics is generally simpler than in the literature, and adapted to

All the figures in this book are available to view in color at: www.iste.co.uk/voirin/arcadia.zip.

the architecture building approach described above. This meaning is moreover agnostic from the viewpoint of the domain in which it is used, to be adaptable to the largest number.

Similarly, the types of diagrams and illustrations used are sometimes similar to those presented by the languages above, but there again, they are simplified or adapted to best meet the language usage domain and simplicity of use by system engineers.

Only some of these concepts may be needed in a given context, depending on many factors, among them:

– the domain and engineering level considered (complex system, equipment, software, electromechanical component, etc.);

– the Arcadia perspective considered (operational analysis, system needs analysis, logical architecture, physical architecture, product building strategy);

– the main engineering challenges to be met (managing interfaces, performance, security, IVV, etc.);

– product complexity and the size of the engineering team;

– the qualification/certification and development assurance level.

Moreover, the level of detail with which the model is described should be conditioned by the return on investment for the modeling effort: as an example, only new or critical parts of the system may be described in much detail, or only those for which an expected verification is needed.

Finally, we note that the concepts presented below are aimed at modeling in general; they do not include specific concepts required by the specialty viewpoints supported by Arcadia (for example, performance, cost, security, etc.); they do not include either concepts belonging to a specific domain or product, although these should be added coherently if there is need.

16.2. The logic behind presenting these concepts

Most of the language's concepts are applied to several Arcadia perspectives. This is why they are presented, initially, independently of any perspective.

Functional description concepts are presented, including those involving states and modes; structural concepts then follow, then the link between the two, and finally concepts involving data and exchange content, and the link with the rest of the model.

Chapter 23 especially describes the structure of an Arcadia model and some additional concepts, and in particular indicates the use of appropriate concepts by each perspective (section 23.3).

16.3. Conventions for representation in figures and diagrams

Two sorts of figure illustrate the concept definitions below.

The illustrative figures represent examples of model elements that conform to the concepts explained (illustrated elements are therefore examples of functions, components, ports, exchanges, etc.).

These figures, however, follow the color code defined for greater convenience along with the method, and also used in the diagrams describing the sample models shown in the first part of this work:

– the functions are green, function ports red or green and operational activities are in orange;

– the operational entities are gray-brown;

– the behavioral components are blue and their ports white;

– the hosting physical components are yellow, as well as their physical ports;

– the states and modes are gray, as well as data, exchange items and interfaces.

The diagrams for describing concepts, which are most formalized, use a conventional representation, in a form often called "metamodel": graphical elements therefore describe generic types (concepts), such as the concepts of Functions, Components, etc., in which the elements in a model will be instances or exemplars: a model element will be ONE function or ONE component, etc.

– Each concept is represented by a rectangle with rounded corners, the name of the concept in the upper part is followed by a horizontal line.

– An arrow represents a relationship link between two concepts, pointing from the source concept to the destination concept; the direction indicates that the source knows the destination (but in principle, not the reverse).

– The relationship identifier is usually a verb; the link directed from the source to the destination reads "'source' 'verb' 'destination'".

For example: "'System Capability' 'is described by' 'Functional Chain'", which means: "any system capability is described by [one or more] functional chains".

– The number of source or destination elements at work in a relationship is indicated by symbols in brackets at each end of the relationship (we speak of cardinalities):

- the absence of any cardinality at an end of the relationship indicates one and only one element of this type at work in each relationship;

- a value indicates the exact number of elements required ([2] signifies exactly two elements);

- an asterisk [*] indicates any number of elements, or none (in which case, there is no relationship);

- two values indicate a range of values: [2..6] signifies from 2 to 6 elements, [1..*] signifies at least one element.

For example, the relationship A → [*] B signifies that an element of type A could be linked to any number of type B elements, or to none; but also that a type B element should be linked to one and only one type A element. The relationship Function [0..1] → [*] Function (relation with the same source and destination concept, named Function) signifies that a function can have any number of (sub-)functions (or none), but also that a function can only have one mother function (or none).

– A filled black lozenge at the end of a relationship signifies that the source is composed of destinations; so if the source is deleted, the destinations will be too.

***

The concepts are colored according to the color code above: functional in green, structural behavioral in blue, structural physical hosting in yellow, structural operational in gray-brown, states and modes in gray, as well as data, exchange and interface items.

Concepts of Functional and Operational Description

17.1. Concepts and relationships of functional description

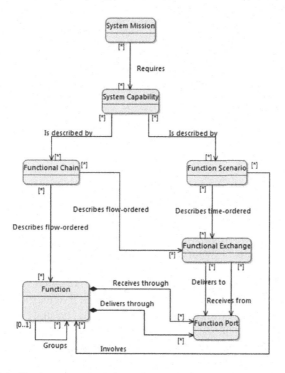

Figure 17.1. *Concepts and relationships involved in functional description*

All the figures in this book are available to view in color at: www.iste.co.uk/voirin/arcadia.zip.

Figures 17.1 and 17.2 represent the principal concepts used and their relationships to one another.

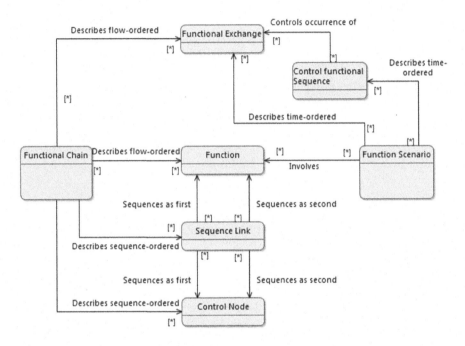

Figure 17.2. *Complementary concepts for describing functional chains and scenarios*

17.2. Function

A function is an action, an operation or a service, performed by the system or one of its components, or also by an actor interacting with the system.

Performing a function generally produces exchange items expected by other functions, and to do this, it requires other items provided by other functions.

Several functions can be grouped into a mother function (they are then called subfunctions, or daughter functions, of this function). Symmetrically, a function can be refined into several functions. This grouping is not a strong structural decomposition relationship; *function grouping only forms a synthetic representation of these, essentially for documentary purposes. Generally, in a finalized model only the leaf functions (without subfunctions) refer to and carry the functional description expected.*

By convention, a function is named with a verb.

17.3. Function port

A function port is a place where the function interacts with other functions of its environment. A function port has an orientation; it can be either an input port or an output port, exclusively.

Each output port specifies that the function is capable of producing particular exchange items, eventually with a particular quality of service attached to the port (performance, precision, supply frequency, data confidentiality level, physical parameters, etc.).

Each input port specifies that the function requires a particular type of exchange item, in the same conditions.

Function ports thus contribute to defining the function "user manual", which should be respected each time it is used. They contribute to making the function definition self-sufficient to make it reusable in several contexts without ambiguity, even if it is still not linked to other functions.

17.4. Functional exchange and exchange category

A functional exchange is a possible interaction between a source function and a destination function, likely to transmit exchange items through their output and input ports, respectively.

A functional exchange is oriented: it links a single output port to a single input port.

A functional exchange expresses only a possible functional dependency relationship between two functions: the source function is likely to provide the exchange items involved, and the destination function is likely to receive them from this source function, and is likely to use them (or not) in a given context.

A functional exchange should represent a real communication or interaction between the functions it links, and should not in any case be confused with a pure sequence link, which would express order of precedence or anteriority in performing the two functions.

The grouping of exchanges (for synthesis or organization) is expressed by the notion of Exchange Category. A category represents a set of exchanges semantically close to each other (in their content, their usages, etc.). The categories may be structured as a tree, and a set of exchanges may be associated with one or more categories and/or subcategories.

17.5. Synthetic representation of functions and functional exchanges

As indicated above, function grouping is only one synthetic representation of functions, essentially for documentary purposes. *At the end of model building, the exchanges should link only the leaf functions, and only the leaf functions should host ports.* On the one hand, this is to avoid leaving any ambiguity or imprecision in the model, as if two mother functions are linked by an exchange, there is nothing to indicate which of their subfunctions should take it into account[1]; on the other hand, it is to avoid redundancies or incoherencies between exchanges that would be defined both on the functions and their subfunctions. This makes it possible to adapt easily to various functional analysis approaches, as mentioned in Chapter 4.

However, it is useful to be able to visualize a more synthetic representation of functions as well as functional exchanges. The function ports and functional exchanges remain allocated only to leaf functions in the model itself; the following rules enable construction of an "automatic" synthesis:

– a synthesis level is defined first by choosing a set of mother (or "ancestor" functions rather than leaf functions;

– if a mother function is represented and not its subfunctions, then these sub-functions' ports and exchanges should be represented as if they were allocated to the mother function;

– to synthesize a set of exchanges belonging to the same category, a single synthetic exchange will replace them whenever they have the same source function and the same destination function at the synthesis level considered. Synthetic input and output ports are also represented.

In Figure 17.3, the functions are in green, the output ports in dark green and the input ports in red. A function placed inside another is this function's subfunction.

---

1 The other possible solution, based on possible delegation links between function ports, in fact makes creating and above all changing the model difficult and expensive: if we move a sub-function we must modify all the links; a direct link between sub-functions is prohibited in principle; etc.

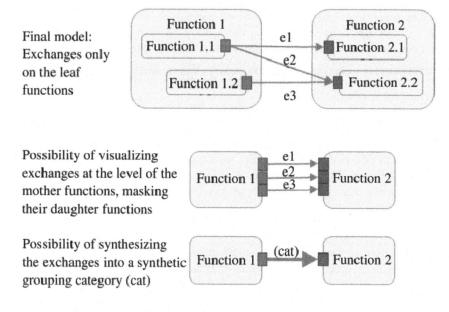

Figure 17.3. *Automatic synthesis of functions and exchanges*

17.6. Dataflow and flow control functions

As we have seen, dataflow describes the functional dependencies between functions by means of functional exchanges connected to the function ports.

When several exchanges arrive at the same input port on a function, this only expresses the fact that exchanges are likely to bring (or not) elements toward the function, in a way that is completely independent and not correlated to each other: this may be in parallel, successively, or only from one of the sources, etc., and each time it involves a new exchange item, different from the previous one *a priori*.

Similarly, when several exchanges leave the same output port on a function, this only conveys the fact that the function is likely to supply the same types of exchange items to several destination functions, there again, in a way that is completely independent and non-correlated *a priori*: no hypothesis is made on broadcasting single exchange item to several destinations, simultaneously or not, etc.

If a function should supply a single type of exchange item, without any distinction between destination functions from its own viewpoint, then it will include a single output port, from which several functional exchanges will leave toward user functions (which does not specify anything about the function that initiates the exchange or its conditions). If it should differentiate between several sendings (either with each having a different quality of service, or to receivers that the function should process differently), then this is manifested by several output ports of the function.

If a function receives a set of exchanges with the same type of exchange item, then by default each associated input exchange will arrive at the same input port of the function. We will choose to define several ports rather than a single one, only if the function should process the inputs differently depending on their source, or if each input requires a different quality of service.

***

There may, however, be cases in which it is necessary to specify the routing conditions more precisely. This is then indicated by flow control functions, which are intermediaries between the source(s) and recipient(s), responsible for controlling the interaction conditions:

– to specify a simultaneous diffusion from a source exchange to several recipients, we define a *Duplicate function* that transmits the same exchange items to all the recipients;

– to specify the simultaneous diffusion of some of the exchange items to each recipient selectively, a *Split function* that routes each part to a separate recipient;

– to specify selection of one among several potential recipients, a *Route function* that transmits (most often subject to conditions) to each destination only some of the exchange items received;

– to specify the combination of items of several exchanges from different sources, a *Gather function* can be a single exchange item combining those received from different sources;

– to specify selection of one source among many, a *Select function* that directs only the elements coming from the selected source (most often subject to conditions).

These flow control functions (Figure 17.4) should only be used if their role is limited to governing the routing of data according to the above-mentioned principles. In the opposite case (in the case of own data processing, modification of exchange items contents, additional outputs, etc.), it is preferable to use a normal function.

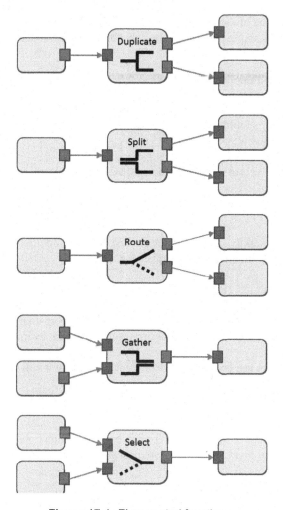

Figure 17.4. *Flow control functions*

One condition (and only one) is associated with each Route or Gather function, to determine the flow to follow; it can be defined especially by a logical combination of Boolean expressions (true or false) based especially on:

– mainly the content of the exchange item transmitted by the incoming exchange (or the input port);

– or an active mode or state;

– or a function attribute.

A different value of the condition is defined for each possible path traversing the control function. A single path should be selected for each value *a priori*.

17.7. System mission

A mission is a high-level goal to which the system should contribute. To be fulfilled, a mission should use a number of system functions, regrouped within one or more system capabilities.

A mission can be broken down into submissions with more limited scope.

17.8. System capability

A system capability is the system's expected ability to supply a service contributing to fulfilling one or more missions.

A system capability represents a system usage context. It is characterized by a set of functional chains and scenarios that it references, and which more precisely describe the conditions for performing the system functions that contribute to it. A capability can also reference a function that contributes to it by itself.

A capability can use one or more other capabilities that it will reference.

17.9. Functional chain

A functional chain is an ordered set of references to functions and the functional exchanges that link them, describing one possible path among all the paths forming the dataflow.

A functional chain is used to describe the system behavior in a particular usage context, to contribute to one or more system capabilities, and especially to specify the non-functional expectations on this path (latency between the chain's start and end, quality of service, criticality level, association with a feared event, etc.).

Each reference to a function or exchange inside the chain can be qualified by an expectation in the context of the chain (the value that an exchange item or a function attribute should take, for example).

If a functional chain should carry data from end to end (latency, etc.), then some interpretation conventions should be defined (only one a single function allowed as the start or end of the chain, for example).

A functional chain can also specify constraints or expectations of precedence or anteriority via oriented sequence links: a sequence link between two functions (between function references, in fact) indicates that the source function should operate before the destination function, at least in the context of this functional chain. A set of functions and sequence links is a sequence.

Control nodes can be defined between the sequence links, to express the parallelism or alternative between several sequences of functions, or, also the iteration or condition of a sequence to be realized.

In Figure 17.5, the green arrows are functional exchanges (attached to function ports), the black dotted arrows are sequence links and the gray boxes are control nodes.

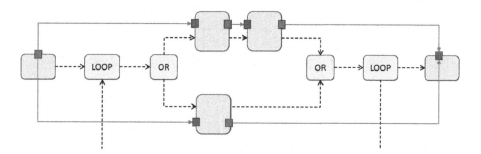

Figure 17.5. *Functional chain with control nodes*

Warning: If two functions are allocated to two different system components, then no hypothesis should be made on the order of precedence between these functions, unless a functional exchange from one to the other carries this constraint. If only a single sequence link is used, nothing will appear in the interface definition between components, based on the functional exchanges, which will not make it possible to concretely ensure the expected precedence.

If a function appears several times in a functional chain, then this should define a different reference to the function for each appearance (except in the case of an explicit loop that properly identifies each appearance's contribution).

***

A functional chain can also be defined by the composition, or assembly, of functional chains. Three types of assembly for two functional chains are possible:

– the two chains are linked by an exchange, existing between a function of one chain and a function of the other. In this case, the composite chain defines two references to two chains in place of references to two functions, and a reference to the chosen exchange between them;

– the two chains are linked by a sequence link, created to link them. In this case, the composite chain defines two references to two chains in place of references to two functions, and the sequence link;

– the two chains are linked by a function common to both (for example a final function of one and an initial function of another). In this case, the composite chain defines, in place of a reference to a function, a single reference that mentions both chains and their common function.

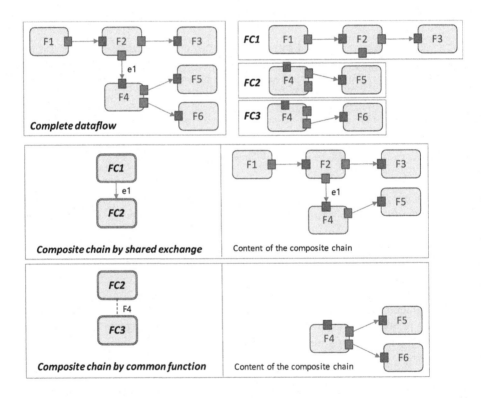

Figure 17.6. *Composite functional chain*

17.10. Function scenario

A function scenario is a time-ordered dynamic flow, on a temporal axis (conventionally vertical from top to bottom), of exchanges between different functions in the context of implementing a capability.

A scenario is formed of a set of references to functions and the functional exchanges that link them, but unlike functional chains, these exchanges (in fact, their references) are ordered in relation to one another on a single temporal axis (Figure 17.7).

Each reference to implementing a function or exchange in the scenario can be qualified by a particular expectation in the context of the scenario (the value that an exchange item or a function attribute should take, for example).

Control sequences can be defined as time-bounded zones (therefore vertical) to express the parallelism or alternative between several sequences of interactions, or also the iteration or condition of a sequence of interactions.

As a functional chain, a scenario describes the system behavior in a usage context to contribute to a system capability.

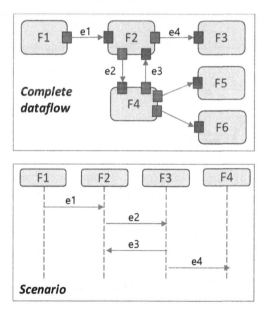

Figure 17.7. *Function scenario*

A scenario can use "subscenarios" defined elsewhere, in the form of a reference inserted between two successive exchanges on the time axis.

17.11. Orchestration

A functional chain or a scenario describes a partial use of the system in a given context (implementing a capability, for example). To specify a complete system usage context at a given instant, we use the notion of orchestration.

An orchestration is an ordering of functional chains or scenarios expressing parallelism conditions between them, and the temporal precedence between some of their elements.

An orchestration is defined by a set of references to functional chains and scenarios, and by precedence links between functions or exchanges belonging to two of them (Figure 17.8).

A precedence link specifies an origin and a destination, each formed of the reference to the chain or chosen scenario, and the reference to the function or exchange. It also potentially specifies a time constraint (minimum or maximum time between the occurrence of two elements).

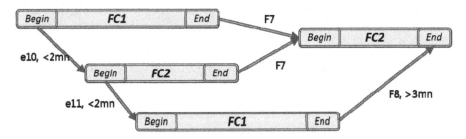

Figure 17.8. *Functional chains or scenarios orchestration*

17.12. Concepts and functional relationships in operational analysis

The operational analysis perspective uses concepts very similar to those of functional analysis described above, albeit a little simplified. The distinction between them has been made to fully mark the difference in nature, justification and lifecycle between the two perspectives.

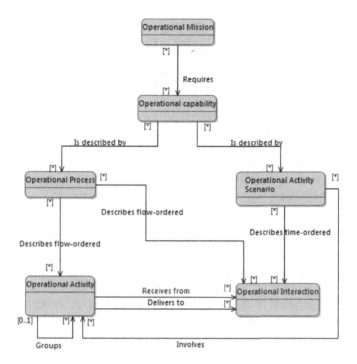

Figure 17.9. *Concepts and relationships involved in the functional parts of operational analysis*

17.13. Operational activity

An operational activity is an action, an operation or a service, realized by an operational entity likely to influence the system definition or usage.

Implementing an operational activity generally produces elements of interactions expected by other activities, and to do this, it requires elements provided by other activities.

Several activities can be grouped into a mother activity (they are then called subactivities or daughter activities of the mother). Likewise, an activity can be refined into several activities.

The notion of operational activity shares most of the properties of the notion of a function, although it tackles a different perspective (operational analysis), with the exception of using ports, which are absent here.

By convention, an activity is named by a verbal form.

17.14. Operational interaction

An operational interaction expresses a possible dependency between two operational activities – the interaction source and destination, in the form of transmitting elements conveyed by the interaction.

An operational interaction is oriented: it links a single source activity to a single destination activity.

The notion of operational interaction shares most of the properties of the notion of functional exchange, although it addresses a different perspective (operational analysis), with the exception of using ports, which are absent here.

17.15. Operational mission

An operational mission is a high-level goal to which one or more operational entities should contribute, and which is likely to influence system definition or usage. To be fulfilled, a mission must use a number of operational activities, regrouped within one or more operational capabilities.

17.16. Operational capability

An operational capability is an ability, expected of one or more operational entities, to provide a service contributing to fulfilling one or more operational missions.

An operational capability represents a context for fulfilling part of a mission. It is characterized by a set of operational processes and scenarios describing more precisely the conditions for performing the operational activities that contribute to it.

17.17. Operational process

An operational process is an ordered set of references to operational activities and the interactions that link them, describing one possible path among all the paths forming the operational analysis dataflow.

An operational process is used to describe a particular context for performing operational activities to contribute to one or more operational capabilities.

The notion of an operational process is similar to that of the notion of functional chain among other aspects characterizing this.

17.18. Operational activity scenario

An operational activity scenario is a time-ordered dynamic flow, on a temporal axis (conventionally vertical from top to bottom), of interactions between different operational activities in the context of implementing a capability.

A scenario is formed of a set of references to operational activities and the interactions that link them, but unlike operational processes, these exchanges (in fact their references) are ordered in relation to one another on a single temporal axis.

The notion of an operational activity scenario is similar to the notion of function scenario among other aspects characterizing this.

Concepts of States and Modes

18.1. Concepts and relationships involved in states and modes

Figure 18.1 represents the principal concepts used and their relationships to one another.

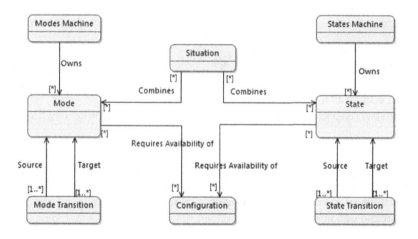

Figure 18.1. *Concepts and relations involved in states and modes*

18.2. Mode

A mode is a behavior expected of the system, a component or also an actor or operational entity, in some chosen conditions.

All the figures in this book are available to view in color at: www.iste.co.uk/voirin/arcadia.zip.

A mode can be broken down into submodes.

It is characterized by at least one or more configurations.

A mode can also specify the imposed occurrence of a function (or activity in OA), or the occurrence of a functional exchange, especially at the moment of entry into this mode, the moment of exit or during the mode without further precision.

18.3. State

A state is a behavior undergone by the system, a component, an actor or an operational entity, in some conditions imposed by the environment.

A state can be broken down into substates.

It is characterized by one or more configurations.

A state can also specify the imposed occurrence of a function (or activity in OA), or the occurrence of a functional exchange, especially at the moment of entry into this state, at the moment of exit or during the state (without other specification).

18.4. Transition

A transition is a change from one mode to another mode or from one state to another state (respectively, called the transition source and transition target).

A transition is characterized by:

– a trigger event that releases the transition, which can principally be a functional exchange (or operational interaction), or the occurrence of a function, but also the specification of a change to the mode or state target of the transition in a scenario (see scenario definition);

– a guard that conditions occurrence of the transition depending on its value. This value is a logical combination of Boolean expressions (true or false) based on the status of the model (attributes of functions or exchanges, values of the data exchanged for example);

– an effect, which can be the occurrence of a function or a functional exchange.

The occurrence of a transition can be represented in a scenario (see scenario).

18.5. Mode/state machine

A mode(s) machine (or respectively, state(s) machine) is a set of modes (or, respectively, states) linked to one another by transitions. Modes and states cannot cohabit in the same machine.

At a given instant, a single mode or state (called a "current" mode or state) is active in each machine.

One or more machines can be associated with the characterization of the system, a component, an actor or an operational entity. In this case, the current modes and states of each machine cohabit at a given instant.

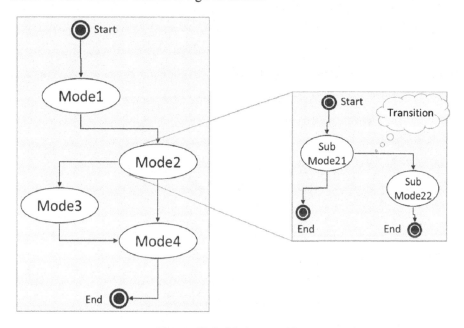

Figure 18.2. *Modes machine*

18.6. Configuration

A configuration is a set of model items that are globally available or unavailable in a given context. A context can here be an active mode or state.

A configuration can be associated with the system, a component, an actor or an operational entity.

18.7. Situation

A situation is a combination of states and modes linked by Boolean operators (of the type AND, OR, NOT), and representing the conditions of superposition of these states and modes simultaneously at a given instant.

The states and modes mentioned in a situation can belong to different elements (the system, several components, actors, etc.).

The occurrence of a situation and the succession of situations in time can be represented in a component scenario (see component scenario); its representation should then be extended to the lifelines of all the elements whose states and modes are involved in the situation.

Concepts of Structural Description

19.1. Concepts and relationships of structural description

Figure 19.1 represents the principal concepts used and their relationships.

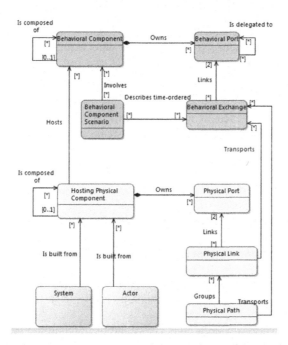

Figure 19.1. *Concepts and relationships involved in structural description*

All the figures in this book are available to view in color at: www.iste.co.uk/voirin/arcadia.zip.

19.2. System

The system is an ordered set of elements functioning as a whole, responding to customer and user demand and needs, and subject to engineering supported by Arcadia.

19.3. Actor

An actor is an entity that is external to the system (human or not), interacting with it, especially via its interfaces.

19.4. Component

A component is a constituent part of the system, contributing to its behavior and/or properties, along with other components and actors external to the system.

A component can be broken down into subcomponents.

To generalize, a component can also be allocated to an actor, to define its interactions and connections with the system or other actors.

19.5. Behavioral component

A behavioral component is a system component, responsible for carrying out some of the functions devolved to the system, by interacting with its other behavioral components and external actors.

19.6. Behavioral port

A behavioral port is a place of interaction for the component to which it is attached to other components or actors in its environment. A behavioral port can be oriented; it can be of three types: input port, output port and bidirectional port.

A behavioral port can have a particular quality of service (performances, precision, supply frequency, data confidentiality level, physical parameters, etc.).

Behavioral component ports thus contribute to defining the component's "user manual", which should be respected each time it is used. They contribute to making the definition of a behavioral component self-sufficient, to be reusable in several contexts without ambiguity, even if the component is still not linked to other components.

A behavioral port belonging to a (father) component should be delegated to a port belonging to one of its (children) subcomponents by a delegation link.

19.7. Behavioral exchange

A behavioral exchange is a possible interaction between a source behavioral component and a destination behavioral component, likely to transmit exchange items via their ports.

A behavioral exchange links a single port of the source component to a single port of the destination component. It is also oriented. This orientation is, however, a convention, most often indicating the direction of dependency between the components, and transmission of principal data involved in the exchange.

If a behavioral component (father) is broken down, it is recommended to place exchanges only on the ports external to this component, and not on those of its subcomponents (children), so as not to oblige components interacting with it to know its content or its internal architecture (encapsulation principle).

The link between the two subcomponents' ports belonging to different father components therefore passes via delegation links between subcomponents' ports and father components' ports, and via the exchange linking these.

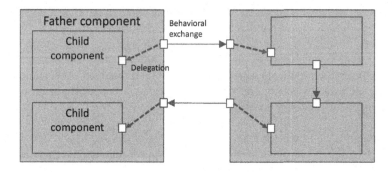

Figure 19.2. *Behavioral components, ports, exchanges and delegation*

The grouping of exchanges for the purposes of synthesis or organization is expressed by the notion of an exchange category, similar to the notion of functional exchanges (see "functional exchanges"). A category represents a set of exchanges that are semantically close (in their content, their usages, etc.). The categories can be structural; a set of exchanges can be associated with one or more categories and/or subcategories.

19.8. Logical component

A logical component is a system component described at a conceptual level (in principle, abstract) in logical architecture.

A logical component has all the properties of a behavioral component, except it is not hosted by a host component.

19.9. Hosting physical component

A hosting physical component is a component hosting a number of behavioral components, providing them with the resources they require to function and to interact with their environment.

A behavioral component is hosted by one and only one hosting physical component.

19.10. Physical port

A physical port is a hosting physical component's point of connection with its environment. A physical port is not oriented.

A hosting physical component's ports thus contribute to defining a component's connectivity, which should be respected each time it is used.

A physical port references the behavioral components' ports hosted by its hosting physical component, which are accessible through it. A behavioral port should be allocated to one and only one physical port, when a behavioral exchange to the component's exterior is connected to it.

The possible link between a father component's physical port and that of one or more of its children components is made by a physical link and not by a delegation link.

19.11. Physical link

A physical link is a means of communication, transport or routing between two hosting physical components, used as a support for behavioral exchanges.

A physical link links two physical ports of two components. It can directly link some subcomponents to one another (via their ports).

A physical link references the behavioral exchanges it transports[1].

The grouping of physical links (for synthesis or organization) is expressed by the notion of a physical link category). A category represents a set of physical links that are semantically similar (in their content, their usages, etc.). The categories can be structured as a tree; a set of physical links can be associated with one or more categories and/or subcategories.

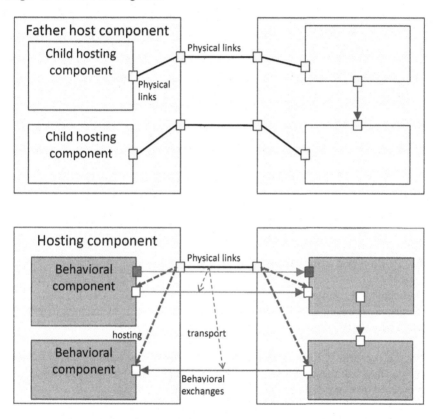

Figure 19.3. *Breakdown of a hosting component and hosting of behavioral components*

---

1 It is sometimes useful, too, to be able to reference a physical link from another, for example to express the notion of nested transport protocols, "tunneling", etc. It would also be conceivable to extend this capability to behavioral exchanges.

19.12. Physical path

A physical path is an ordered set of references to physical links, defining a continuous path likely to route one or more behavioral exchanges between components not linked by a single physical link.

A physical path references the behavioral exchanges it transports.

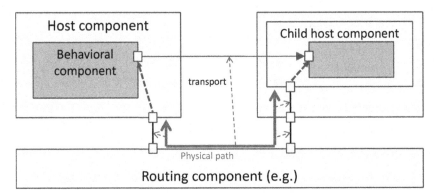

Figure 19.4. *Physical path associated with behavioral exchange*

19.13. Behavioral component scenario

A behavioral component scenario is the time-ordered dynamic flow, on a temporal axis (conventionally vertical from top to bottom), of exchanges between different behavioral components in the context of implementing a capability.

Such a scenario is formed of a set of references to components and behavioral exchanges that link these components. These exchanges (in fact their references) are time-ordered in relation to one another on a single temporal axis.

Each reference to implementing an exchange in the scenario can be qualified by a particular expectation in the scenario context (the value an exchange item should take for example).

Control sequences can be defined as time-bounded zones (therefore vertical) to express the parallelism or alternative between several sequences of interactions, or also the iteration or condition of a sequence of interactions.

Entry into each component's mode or state can be specified on this component's time axis in addition to the exchanges represented.

Similarly, entry into a situation formed of multiple states and modes of different components or elements can be represented at a point on the time axis. Its representation should then be extended to the lifelines of all the elements whose states and modes are at work in the situation.

As a functional chain, a scenario describes the system behavior in a usage context to contribute to a system capability.

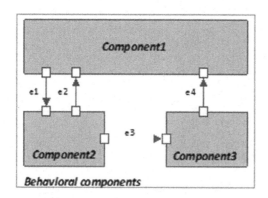

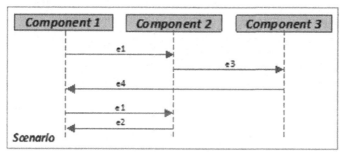

Figure 19.5. *A behavioral component scenario*

A scenario can use "subscenarios" defined elsewhere, in the form of a reference inserted between two successive exchanges on the time axis.

19.14. Structural concepts and relationships in operational analysis

The operational analysis perspective uses concepts very similar to those described previously, albeit a little simplified. The distinction has been made to properly mark the difference in nature, justification and lifecycle between the two perspectives.

In Figure 19.6, the arrow indicates a "is kind of" link.

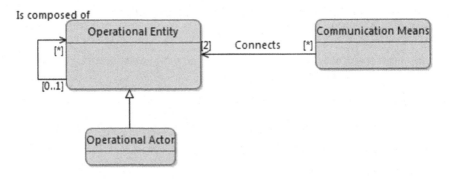

Figure 19.6. *Structural concepts and relationships in operational analysis*

19.15. Operational entity and actor

An operational entity is a real-world entity (a physical element, a group or organization, another system), carrying out operational activities to which the system is likely to contribute, or which can influence the system.

An operational entity can be broken down into subentities or actors.

An operational actor is a type of operational entity, generally human, and cannot be broken down.

19.16. Communication means

A communication means is the support linking two operational entities, and is followed by interactions between these two entities.

19.17. Configuration item

A configuration item is a system part, to be acquired or designed and produced, in as many copies as the physical architecture requires, and for assembly with other items to form each system copy.

The most frequent types of items are, in particular, hardware configuration items (HWCI), computer software configuration items (CI or CSCI), interface configuration items (Interface CI), non-developed configuration items (NDCI) or commercial off-the-shelf configuration items (COTSCI).

Several configuration items can be grouped into a prime item, thus defining the product breakdown structure. The system is most often at the root of the structure thus defined.

Each element of structural physical architecture should be represented by at least one configuration item that references it. If there are several copies in the physical architecture, the corresponding item is indicated only once in the product breakdown structure, but specifies the number of copies required.

Links between Functional and Structural Descriptions

20.1. Concepts and relationships between functional and structural descriptions

GENERAL COMMENT.– In this chapter, the structural part concerned is the behavioral part (behavioral components, ports and exchanges), unless explicitly stated otherwise.

Figures 20.1 and 20.2 represent the principal concepts used and their relationships.

20.2. Performing functions

Any leaf (or terminal, i.e. without subfunction) function should be allocated to one and only one logical or behavioral component, which is responsible for performing it, and which references this function.

To simplify, it is however allowed to allocate a function directly to the system or an actor.

If a behavioral component is broken down (father component), all the functions that it performs should be allocated to its subcomponents (children) and not to the father component itself.

All the figures in this book are available to view in color at: www.iste.co.uk/voirin/arcadia.zip.

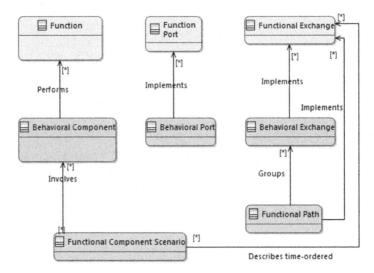

Figure 20.1. *Concepts and relationships between functional and structural descriptions*

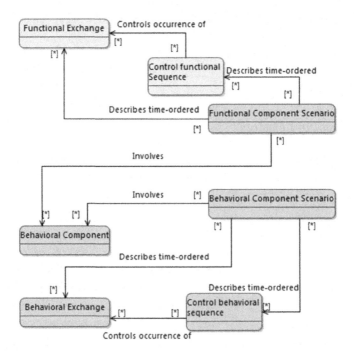

Figure 20.2. *Complementary concepts for describing scenarios*

20.3. Implementing functional ports

Any functional port used by a component that performs the function associated with this port should be allocated to one and only one of this component's behavioral ports, as soon as a functional exchange with the component exterior is connected to this port.

A behavioral port references the functional ports it implements.

20.4. Implementing functional exchanges

A functional exchange between two functions allocated to two behavioral components should be implemented by one and only one behavioral exchange between these two components. The behavioral exchange references all the functional exchanges it implements.

Generally, a behavioral exchange represents a synthesis of several functional exchanges it implements and groups.

The direction of the behavioral exchange is purely conventional, but it should be applied systematically and regularly. The most commonly used convention is that *the behavioral exchange is oriented in the direction of dependency between the source and destination components* (destination being dependent on the source); in cases of data dependence (materials, flow, messages, events, shared data, etc.), which are the majority, the rule is therefore that *the direction of the exchange is from the supplier of principal data exchanges to their user.*

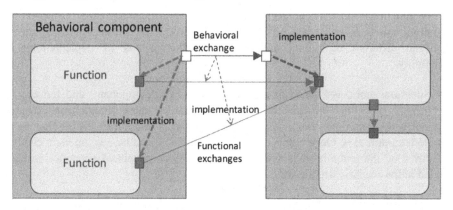

Figure 20.3. *Performing functions by behavioral components*

20.5. Functional path

A functional path is an ordered set of references to behavioral exchanges and delegation links between behavioral ports, defining a continuous path likely to implement one or more functional exchanges between two functions allocated to the path source and destination components.

A functional path references the functional exchanges and delegation links it implements.

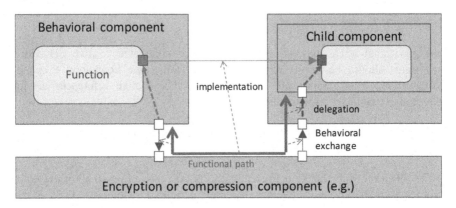

Figure 20.4. *A functional path associated with a functional exchange*

20.6. Functional component scenario

A functional component scenario is the time-ordered dynamic flow, on a temporal axis (conventionally vertical from top to bottom) of functional exchanges between different behavioral components, in the context of implementing a capability.

Such a scenario is formed of a set of references to components and functional exchanges that link the functions implemented by these components. These exchanges (in fact their references) are time ordered in relation to one another on a single temporal axis. Occurrence of a function implemented by a component can be specified on the temporal axis associated with this component. A reference is then added in the scenario description.

Each reference to implementing a function or exchange in the scenario can be qualified by a particular expectation in the scenario context (the value an exchange item or a function attribute should take, for example).

Control sequences can be defined as time-bounded zones (therefore vertical), to express the parallelism or alternative between several sequences of interactions, or also the iteration or condition of a sequence of interactions.

Entry into each component's mode or state can be specified on this component's time axis in addition to the exchanges represented.

Similarly, entry into a situation formed of multiple states and modes of different components or elements can be represented at a point on the time axis. Its representation should then be extended to the lifelines of all the elements whose states and modes are at work in the situation.

As a functional chain, a scenario describes the system behavior in a particular usage context to contribute to a system capability.

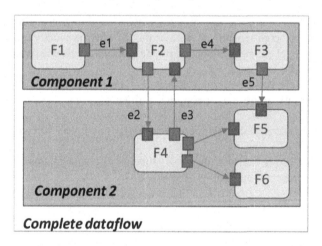

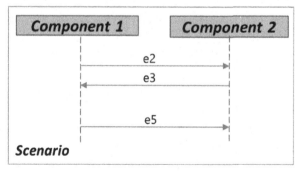

Figure 20.5. *A functional component scenario*

A scenario can use "subscenarios" defined elsewhere, in the form of a reference inserted between two successive exchanges on the time axis.

20.7. Links between dataflow, states and modes, and scenarios or functional chains

The different concepts presented above are all linked to one another to form a global and coherent description of the system behavior. This section recalls the principal of these links.

In particular, a mode(s) or state(s) machine describes the occurrence of a single model element, which may be the system, a component, an actor or an operational entity. Its transitions are commanded by elements of the functional dataflow.

A configuration references any model elements, although most often, this means either functions, or components. A state or mode, when it is active, determines the availability of model elements indicated by the configurations it references.

A situation references several states and/or modes of one or more elements: system, components, actors and operational entities.

A component scenario can mention transition to a new situation on the time axis.

The principal links between dataflow, functional chains, states and modes and scenarios are represented in Figures 20.6 and 20.7.

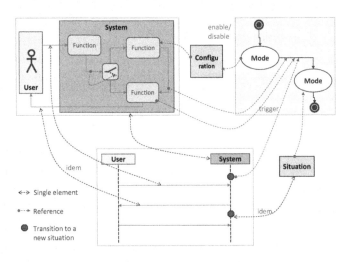

Figure 20.6. *Links between dataflow, states and modes and scenarios (partial)*

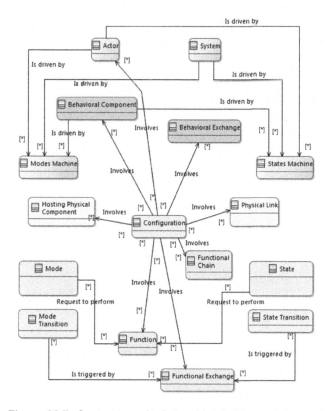

Figure 20.7. *Concepts and relationships between states and modes and functional and structural descriptions (partial)*

20.8. Links between functional and structural descriptions in operational analysis

Any leaf or terminal (i.e. without child subactivity) operational activity should be allocated to one and only one operational entity, which is responsible for performing it, and which references this activity.

An interaction between two operational activities allocated to two operational entities should be implemented by one and only one communication means between these two entities. The communication means references all the interactions it implements.

An operational entity scenario is the time-ordered dynamic flow, on a time axis (conventionally vertical from top to bottom), of interactions between different actors or operational entities, in the context of implementing a capability.

Such a scenario is formed of a set of references to actors or operational entities and operational interactions that link the activities implemented by these entities. These interactions (in fact their references) are time ordered in relation to one another on a single temporal axis. Occurrence of an activity implemented by an entity can be specified on the temporal axis associated with this entity. A reference is then added in the scenario description.

The principal links between these concepts are summarized in Figure 20.8.

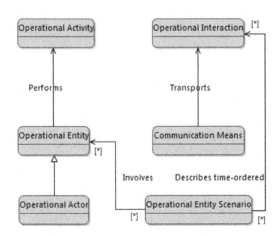

Figure 20.8. *Links between the main functional and structural concepts concerning operational analysis*

20.9. Simplifications in representation

For convenience, a number of simplifications in the representation are possible, especially to represent interactions involving the system in its entirety or actors.

In principle, any function should be allocated to a behavioral component, itself hosted by a hosting component, which can be carried by the system or by an external actor. A simplification could authorize:

– a function allocated directly to the system (only in system needs analysis) or to an actor;

– a behavioral component hosted directly by the system (only in logical architecture) or by an actor;

– a behavioral or physical port carried directly by the system (only in system needs analysis) or an actor.

Representation conforming to relationships between concepts

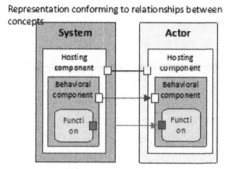

Possible simplified representations

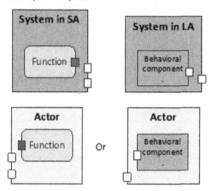

Figure 20.9. *Simplified representation*

21

Data Exchange Concepts and Links with Functional and Structural Concepts

---

21.1. Concepts and relationships involved in data exchanges and their use

GENERAL COMMENT.– In this chapter, the structural part concerned is the behavioral part (behavioral components, ports and exchanges), unless explicitly stated otherwise.

Figure 21.1 represents the principal concepts used and their relationships.

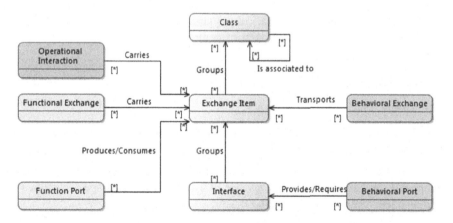

Figure 21.1. *Concepts and relations involved in exchange data and their use*

All the figures in this book are available to view in color at: www.iste.co.uk/voirin/arcadia.zip.

21.2. Exchange item

An exchange item is an ordered set of references to elements routed together, during an interaction or exchange between functions, components and actors.

The items are routed simultaneously, in the same conditions, with the same non-functional properties. These items are called data, and are characterized by the class to which they belong.

An exchange item is defined by:

– a name;

– the list of elements in the exchange item; each element is defined in the exchange item by a name, and the class to which it belongs, and if the exchange is two directional, the direction of transmission (by convention, "in" in the direction of exchange by default, "out" in the opposite direction, or "in/out");

– the description of communication conditions, if needed, for example service, message, event, dataflow, shared data, material flow, physical quantity, etc.

21.3. Data model, class

A piece of data[1] is an element produced or used by functions or components, and routed by one or more exchanges between them.

A piece of data is an exemplar, or instance, of a class (or type) of data that describes the composition and properties common to all similar data used by the system.

A class is defined by:

– a name;

– a list of named properties (or attributes) that characterize each piece of data in the class in its own way;

– potential relationships with other classes; these relationships can be at least composition relationships ("*is composed of*"), relationships of specialization ("*is kind of*"), use relationships ("*uses*").

---

1 The term 'data' should be taken in its most general sense. A piece of data can represent a signal or an image, information, but also the physical state of a fluid (pressure, temperature, volume, viscosity…), a physical quantity (force, torque, velocity, temperature, light…) etc.

A datamodel is a set of data classes and relationships between classes. By extension, we will include in the datamodel the definition of exchange items and interfaces that use these data.

21.4. Allocating exchange items to functional ports and exchanges

One exchange item at least should be allocated to each functional port on a function to characterize the content that the function can produce or which it needs.

This exchange item can be shared by several ports, and notably *should* be by the two ports at the ends of a functional exchange.

If a port carries several exchange items, then we need to specify, on each of the functional exchanges connected to it, the item(s) actually routed, which should be coherent with those of the ports connected by the exchange. Moreover, for convenience, it is possible to start by allocating an item to an exchange, before propagating it to the ports connected to it.

It is recommended to define only a single item on each functional exchange.

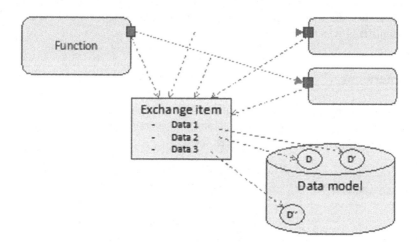

Figure 21.2. *Allocation of exchange items to functional ports and exchanges*

In operational analysis, it is also possible to characterize the content of operational interactions by exchange items.

21.5. Allocating exchange items to behavioral exchanges

In principle, the content of a behavioral exchange is already defined by the exchange items transported by the functional exchanges that it implements. However, it can be useful to specify this content explicitly, for example when the interaction only influences some of the exchange items offered by the interface, or if the physical implementation of functional exchange items is different to their functional representation: this is among others the case if this implementation transforms two functional exchanges (request/response) into a single behavioral service exchange.

21.6. Types and instances of data

As mentioned in the following, the datamodel defines the type of data (their classes). It is the same for exchange items.

The functions and components use real data, which are instances of these classes, each with its own values for the properties defined at class level.

In communications between components, each exchange item routed by a functional or behavioral exchange is an instance of the type defined in the datamodel: the data that it groups are themselves instances of defined types, each being identified by its name in the exchange item.

21.7. Interfaces

An interface is a set of semantically coherent exchange items, allowing two components (and the system and actors), to communicate, according to a communication "contract" shared between them.

Several interfaces can be grouped into a single interface covering them, within which they can cohabit with some exchange items.

21.8. Allocating interfaces to behavioral component ports

One interface at least should be allocated to each behavioral port in a component to characterize the exchange items that the component can produce or which it needs.

The interfaces allocated to the ports of a behavioral component thus also contribute to defining the component "user manual", which should be respected each time it is used. They contribute to making the definition of a behavioral component self-sufficient so that it can be reused in several contexts without ambiguity, even if it is not yet linked to other components.

One interface can be shared by several components, and notably, *should* be, by the two behavioral ports at the ends of a behavioral exchange.

21.9. Links between exchanges, exchange items and interfaces

Normally, function and interface exchange items should be the same. More precisely, all the exchange items mentioned in the functional ports of the functions performed by a component should be referenced by one of the interfaces referenced by the behavioral port that implements these functional ports. It should be same for the items carried by the functional and behavioral exchanges.

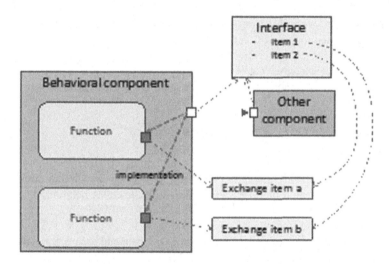

Figure 21.3. *Links between exchange elements involved in the functional and structural description*

If this is not the case, for example if two functional exchanges are implemented by a single behavioral exchange that merges their exchange items, then an implementation link should be defined between the exchange items used by the functional description and those defined by the structural description.

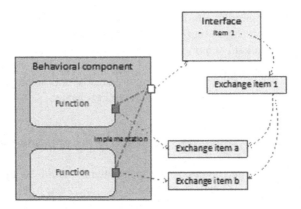

Figure 21.4. *Case of a specific implementation of exchange items*

If a functional exchange carries an exchange item, then this should be coherent with those allocated to the ports connected to it.

If a behavioral exchange carries an exchange item, then this should be coherent with those present in the interfaces associated with the ports connected to it.

21.10. Interaction roles and interface usage

An interaction role expresses the way in which an interface is used by a component, by qualifying allocation of the interface to one of this component's behavioral ports. A role is therefore attached to a link from the behavioral port to the interface.

As a matter of fact, an interface defines only the data and their organization in an interaction between components, but not which of these components is the origin or destination of each exchange. It is the role attribution to the port of the component for this interface, which will make it possible to define the direction of the exchanges for the component. Two strategies are envisaged here.

For example, in producer/consumer type cases, i.e. cases of data-driven dependence, which are frequent (material, flow, messages, events, shared data, etc.), two roles only might be defined:

– the role (*provide*) of supplying the data described by the interface (it is incorrectly called "supplying the interface");

– the role (*require*) of consuming the data described by the interface.

All exchanges involving exchange items of the interface are therefore oriented from the supplier to the consumer (single direction). But this means that an interaction requiring exchanges in both directions should be described by two interfaces and opposite roles (which may seem constraining).

In the more general case, and if it is desirable to avoid these single direction constraints, the following concepts will be defined:

– in an interface, we will define a number of roles that will qualify the different contributions to the interactions likely to use the interface;

– each exchange item in the interface will reference among these roles, the *source* role, and the *destination* roles for any exchange carrying this item;

– for each behavioral port of a component to which this interface is allocated, the link between the port and the interface will reference the role that the component is to play in the interaction.

In these cases, implementation of the interface can carry exchanges in both directions.

21.11. Interaction protocol

An interaction protocol is the dynamic description of implementing one (or several) interface(s) in one interaction between several components.

This implementation requires the components, ports and interfaces involved to be defined, and potentially the functions at work, the functional and behavioral exchanges and their chronology, etc. In addition, this protocol should be definable in such a way that it can be reused and applied to several sets of components during interaction. This therefore involves a modeling "pattern", applicable in a model as many times as needed.

An interaction protocol is described by:

– its name;

– one or several interfaces implemented in the protocol;

– at least two roles defined in the protocol;

– for each role, the functions, functional ports and behavioral ports involved, with the associated interfaces and roles;

– functional and behavioral exchanges routing interface exchange items between the previous ports;

– interactions mode(s) machines: a global machine (attached to the system for example) governing the progress of an interaction, and a machine per role, governing its evolution and its contribution to the interaction;

– component scenarios associated with roles, describing the order in which the previous exchanges occur, including the evolution of their interaction mode machines.

22

Additional Concepts

This chapter merely lists concepts more specific to certain issues, which have however proven valuable, and sometimes vital, in implementing the method in an operational context. However, the limits of this book do not allow for them to be discussed in detail here.

22.1. Concepts for product line engineering

For product line management, see the notions mentioned in Chapter 15 (Contribution to Product Line Engineering), including the following concepts in particular.

22.1.1. *Variant*

A variant is one basic choice alternative among others, forming part of the need definition and/or system solution definition.

Each variant is linked to engineering artifacts, especially to model elements, which characterize it.

22.1.2. *Variation point*

A variation point is a set of variants applying to a single part of the need and/or system solution, in which each forms a different alternative. The choice from among these possible variants can be made according to the different modalities:

– options: each variant may be chosen or not, independently of the others;

– alternatives: one and only one of the variants should be chosen;

– or: one variant at least should be chosen.

These modalities also apply to model elements and other artifacts linked to each variant.

22.1.3. Variability model

A variability model is a graph, for the most part structured as a tree, for describing the different variation points possible for a given product line. Each variation point forms a node in the feature model, whose variants are child nodes. Each branch represents a variant for the variation point from which it arises.

Each node should be characterized as mandatory or optional. Moreover, the modalities presented for a node apply to the whole of any branch that arises from it. Finally, it is possible to specify dependencies – mutual exclusion or a variant being required so as to be able to select another.

22.1.4. Project configuration

A product configuration, for a given project, is a set of basic choices selecting the variant(s) appropriate to the project, for each variation point in the feature model. The set of choices makes it possible to define the content of the product version adapted to the project considered.

22.2. Concepts for the integration, verification and validation approach

22.2.1. Integration version

A system integration version describes an IVV stage, in the form of a required functional version, and an integration configuration that should make it possible to provide the functional version.

22.2.2. Functional version

A functional version of the system is the set of functional model elements (capabilities, scenarios, functional chains, functions, etc.) that are required (or available) in a given integration version.

22.2.3. Component functional contents

A component's functional content is the set of functional items involved in this component (functions, exchanges, contribution to scenarios or functional chains) required in a given functional version of the system.

22.2.4. Integration configuration

An integration configuration is the set of structural elements (behavioral and hosting components, exchanges, physical links, etc.) and their functional content, which are subject to an integration stage.

An integration configuration can include not only the system elements, but also test means, for example.

22.2.5. IVV strategy

The IVV strategy is a time-ordered graph of successive integration versions, which describes, for each integration, verification and validation stage, the functional description expected and the composition of items to be integrated and tested.

22.2.6. Test case

A test case is a reference to a scenario or a functional chain that should contribute to verifying a given system integration version. The test case specifies in particular the running conditions for the scenario or functional chain, as well as the test means required, the expected test results, etc.

22.2.7. Test campaign

A test campaign is a set of test cases needed to verify a given integration version. The campaign can specify in particular the test means required.

22.3. Other concepts not detailed here

This book does not detail additional concepts, such as extensions for specifying test means, support concepts for describing architecture alternatives, grouping elements for diverse synthesis needs, the detail(s) of conditions in state(s) and mode(s) machines and dataflow, etc.

Informal requirements are not explained in detail either, or their links with the model, or identification of model requirements with their own specific characteristics, even if they are an integral part of the approach and modeling in a broad sense.

Finally, of course, each engineering domain and each analysis viewpoint introduces their own concepts, which are too specific to be mentioned here.

23

Building the Global Model

23.1. The structure of an Arcadia model

An Arcadia model exists for each level of engineering and each part of the system considered.

EXAMPLE.– *For the traffic regulation system described in the first part of this book, we could have, for example:*

– a model for the traffic regulation system in its entirety;

– a model for each subsystem, so one for the control system, one for the liftable barrier, one for crossing prevention devices, etc.;

– for the control subsystem, a model for the software, one for the high availability host computer board, etc.

Each model is divided into as many submodels as perspectives:

– Operational Analysis (OA) submodel;

– System Needs Analysis (SA) submodel;

– Logical Architecture (LA) submodel;

– Physical Architecture (PA) submodel;

– Product Breakdown Structure (PBS) description submodel.

Each of these submodels is linked to the previous one by traceability/justification links between model elements. The dependencies are always upward: from the SA to the OA, from the LA to the SA, from the PA to the LA, from the PBS to the PA.

All the figures in this book are available to view in color at: www.iste.co.uk/voirin/arcadia.zip.

In each submodel above, associated with a perspective, the different functional and structural viewpoints are also separated:

– description of the data and interfaces model;

– functional description;

– behavioral structural description;

– structural description of hosting resources.

Each of these descriptions is linked to the previous descriptions of the same submodel by allocation, performance, implementation inks, etc., which will be described next. The dependencies are, there too, always upward: from the functional aspects to the data, from the behavioral to the functional aspects and the data, from the resources to the behavioral aspects.

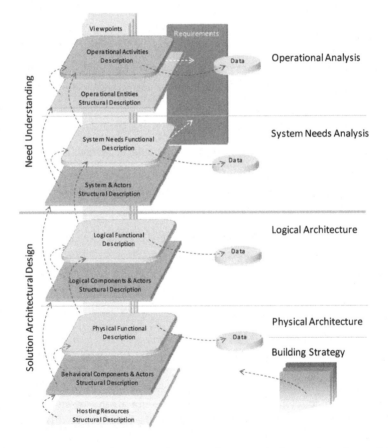

Figure 23.1. *Principal views and perspectives structuring an Arcadia model*

Each type of view above has its own structure:

– each structural description is formed of a "tree" of components (either behavioral/logical in type, or hosting resource type);

– the datamodel has free organization, often formed of one or more graphs of data, exchange items and interfaces graphs;

– each functional description is structured by the missions and capabilities, as Figure 23.2 shows. A mission references several capabilities that it requires to be fulfilled; a capability is illustrated by a number of scenarios and functional chains (which it can share with other capabilities); these scenarios and functional chains define the conditions for performing functions and exchanges from one part of the dataflow, in the context of the capability required by a mission.

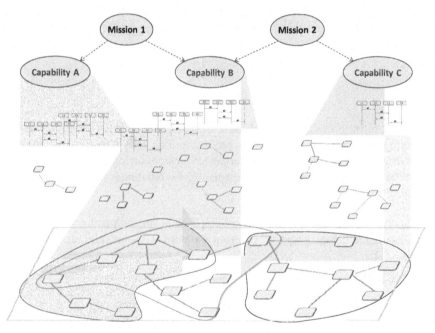

Figure 23.2. *Structure of the functional view in a perspective*

23.2. Model segmentation to support alternatives

The structure of an Arcadia model shown above has been designed to offer initial (limited) possibilities to describe several alternative architectures, without having to redefine the parts of the model common to all these alternatives several times.

It is thus possible, by assembling submodels and descriptions, to build:

– for a single OA, several system need alternatives (with different functions and roles allocated to the system, for example);

– for a single system need, several LAs that respond to it (with various structural breakdowns, for example);

– for a single LA, several PAs (with different technologies, for example);

– for a single functional definition[1], several breakdowns and allocations into components (for comparing performances or security, for example);

– for a single behavioral architecture, several implementations over different resources (to test several uses on a calculator network, for example);

– for a single conceptual datamodel, at a given level (for example LA), several physical implementation datamodels (depending on the projects and technologies, for example);

– etc.

***

To go further, the use of replicable elements (see section 23.6), allied with variability management used in the product policy (see Chapter 15), makes it possible to define any architecture alternatives by minimizing the costs of modeling each due to reusing replicable elements or to references to common, shared elements.

Finally, this structuring also makes it possible, in a situation where existing components are being reused, to confront the need with the solution, as shown in section 15.4.3:

– OA and SA capture the customer need;

– LA formalizes the architecture desired to meet this need;

– PA describes the architecture possible by reusing existing components, which should be compared to the previous architecture.

---

1. This (see Figure 23.3) is in all perspectives (alternatives for allocation to operational entities in OA, to the system and actors in SA and to logical or behavioral components in LA or PA).

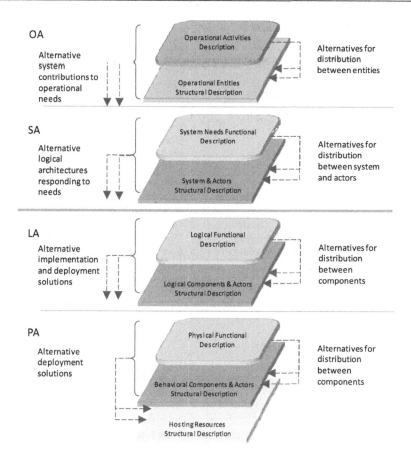

Figure 23.3. *Examples of defining alternatives using model structuring*

23.3. Using language concepts in perspectives

Tables 23.1–23.5 give the distribution of principal concepts shown above in the principal Arcadia perspectives.

A significant part of the concepts shown previously are used in several perspectives. The most important among them are qualified by a name characteristic of the perspective: System Function, Logical Function, Physical Function or also Logical Component and Behavioral Component.

In Tables 23.3–23.5, the concepts added or renamed from one perspective to the next are given in bold.

23.3.1. Operational analysis

Operational Analysis		
Functional concepts		Operational Mission, Operational Capability, Operational Activity, Operational Interaction, Operational Process, Operational Scenario, Modes and States, Transitions, Configuration, Situation
Structural concepts	Behavioral	Operational Entity, Operational Actor, Behavioral Exchange Scenario
	Physical hosting resources	Operational Entity, Operational Actor, Communication Means
Data and interface model		Class, Exchange Item

Table 23.1. *Use of concepts in operational analysis*

23.3.2. System needs analysis

System Needs Analysis		
Functional concepts		System Mission, System Capability, System Function, Functional Port, Functional Exchange, Functional Chain, Function Scenario, Modes and States, Transitions, Configuration, Situation
Structural concepts	Behavioral	Actor, System, Behavioral Port, Behavioral Exchange, Behavioral Exchange Scenario
	Physical hosting resources	Actor, System, Physical Port, Physical Link
Data and interface model		Class, Exchange Item, Interface

Table 23.2. *Use of concepts in system needs analysis*

23.3.3. Logical architecture

Logical Architecture		
Functional concepts		System Mission, System Capability, **Logical** Function, Functional Port, Functional Exchange, Functional Chain, Function Scenario, Modes and States, Transitions, Configuration, Situation
Structural concepts	**Behavioral**	Actor, System, Behavioral Port, Behavioral Exchange, **Logical Component,** Behavioral Exchange Scenario, **Functional Path**
	Physical hosting resources	Actor, System, Physical Port, Physical Link
Data and interface model		Class, Exchange Item, Interface

Table 23.3. *Use of concepts in logical architecture*

23.3.4. Physical architecture

Physical Architecture	
Functional concepts	System Mission, System Capability, **Physical** Function, Functional Port, Functional Exchange, Functional Chain, Function Scenario, Modes and States, Transitions, Configuration, Situation

Structural concepts	Behavioral	Actor, System, Behavioral Port, Behavioral Exchange, **Behavioral** Component, Behavioral Exchange Scenario, Functional Path
	Physical hosting resources	Actor, System, Physical Port, Physical Link, **Hosting Physical Component**, **Physical Path**
Data and interface model		Class, Exchange Item, Interface

Table 23.4. *Use of concepts in physical architecture*

23.3.5. *Product breakdown structure*

Product Breakdown Structure		
Functional concepts		None
Structural concepts	Behavioral	Configuration item
	Physical hosting resources	Configuration item
Data and interface model		None

Table 23.5. *Use of concepts in a product breakdown structure*

23.4. Scope of links in the model

The links between the concepts introduced in the previous chapters are for the most part confined to a single perspective: for example, a link between a logical function and a behavioral component in PA is not authorized.

The only links that form an exception are, on the one hand, links with the textual requirements (outside the perimeter considered here), traceability/justification links (described in a specific section) and the links for using elements of the datamodel.

As a matter of fact, the links for allocating exchange items or interfaces issuing from the ports or exchanges of a perspective can refer to data items or interfaces defined in a previous perspective.

23.5. Traceability between model elements

The model elements of each perspective are linked to those of the previous (or sometimes anterior) perspective by traceability and justification links.

In most cases, these links connect elements of the same nature, as presented in Table 23.6 (which is not exhaustive).

PA		LA		SA		OA
System Mission	→	System Mission	→	System Mission	→	Operational Mission
System Capability	→	System Capability	→	System Capability	→	Operational Capability
Functional Chain	→	Functional Chain	→	Functional Chain	→	Operational Process
Scenario	→	Scenario	→	Scenario	→	Scenario
System, Actor	→	System, Actor	→	System, Actor	→	Operational Entity
Physical Function	→	Logical Function	→	System Function	→	Operational Activity
Behavioral Component	→	Logical Component				
Hosting Physical Component	→	Logical Component				
Class	→	Class	→	Class	→	Class
Exchange Item	→	Exchange Item	→	Exchange Item	→	Exchange Item
Interface	→	Interface	→	Interface	→	

Table 23.6. *Principal traceability links (not exhaustive)*

Moreover, in the PBS, the configuration items can be linked to the behavioral and hosting components of the PA, as well as to physical links and ports.

Links between model elements of a different nature can, nevertheless, be used: for example, an exchange or a physical link between the system and an actor can result in the following perspective in a component responsible for making the connection.

Moreover, traceability links internal to a perspective can sometimes be useful: we can cite links between the exchange items allocated to the ports or the functional and behavioral exchanges that carry them (in case of implementation that differs from the functional vision), between states or modes at system level and at component level, etc.

23.6. Replicable Element Collection and Replica

A Replicable Element Collection (REC) is a set of model elements, identified as being a pattern (a model in the common sense of the term) for building Replicas (RPLs) that maintain conformity with it.

This concept makes it possible to take account of the need to express similarity between model elements. *A priori*, an architect or system engineer, when they build their architecture, reason principally in terms of concrete objects connected to one another. To return to the terminology used in sections 21.3 and 21.6, they manipulate instances rather than types.

It can, however, be necessary to formalize the fact that several model elements are of the same type, and to prevent one of them from being modified by mistake. This need appears in all types of domains and model elements: functional chains subject to redundancy for safety reasons, generic similar components of a network, processing boards duplicated in the architecture, roles allocated dynamically to several actors or components, etc.

We should therefore be able to:

– specify at a given instant of the modeling process that a set of model elements should be replicated as a whole;

– form a type from this whole – called a REC;

– transform the source elements into an instance of this type called RPL;

– create other RPLs or instances at will, from the REC;

– maintain different RPLs synchronized with the REC, and propagate potential evolutions from one to another (updating RPLs on evolution of the REC, propagating the chosen evolutions of an RPL, etc.);

– choose to create, not distinct RPLs, but simply references, for some model elements that are shared and not duplicated, and for which it is desirable to guarantee single usage (elements of the datamodel, exchange items or interfaces for example).

This mechanism is different from that encountered in software engineering, called Types/Instances, especially because we start by creating the RPLs, and one is then put forward as an example of the REC to be formed. Or also because a REC can be any set of elements, potentially straddling several perspectives, and because the mode of building RPLs is more complex than a simple instantiation (creation), with complex connections, the notion of roles, etc.

The detail and justification of the notion of replicable elements largely exceeds the framework of this book.

Conclusion and Perspectives

Lessons drawn from developing and using Arcadia

It has taken 10 years of significant investment by Thales, before the cultural change brought about by model-based system engineering can finally be considered a reality in the varied domains of activity that use it today in its different units on a global level [BON 15].

The principal catalyst has been a massive and continuous funding effort, both to define the Arcadia model and to develop the reference tool to apply the method (Capella). In parallel, a real organizational effort has institutionalized optimization and adoption of the method by engineers, as well as provision of training and support for organizations using the method. It has contributed greatly to highly motivated engineers capitalizing on this expertise, often playing key roles at their own level: system engineers, "modeling champions", support teams, operational managers, etc. The conviction increases each day that model-based system engineering is one of the few ways to face the growing complexity of systems to be designed.

***

As a result of this feedback, the organization's major convictions have been clearly reinforced and can be summarized in a few salient points.

The method is of vital importance and should be seen in a natural way by users: the right approach seems to be to concentrate first on the intellectual approach to solving engineering problems; the method should then come to aid this approach; to sustain it, secure it, assist with it and automate it, and to make it compatible with the complexity to be faced.

A major challenge in adopting these new practices is reducing engineers' difficulty in understanding the concepts involved and their representations. To do this, a specific modeling language, adapted to the exact needs of architects and engineering stakeholders, and as similar as possible to the notions that they use naturally, is vital.

In addition, to be really usable in operational conditions, these languages (and support tools) must imperatively adapt to real-life situations such as large-scale modeling, the ability to maintain models, functional engineering, non-functional constraints and, most especially, agile, evolutive team modeling.

And finally, the entire organization should be structured and federated around implementing these new practices, which should be considered as a key to competitiveness and a major vector for transforming engineering and for product quality.

Perspectives and future work

In parallel with use of Arcadia and Capella and the increasing maturity of the organizations that use them, various research and innovation initiatives aim to extend the method and support tools to some engineering concerns, with short-term or more advanced aims. Some major themes are discussed in the following, in a list that is in no way limiting, and which is limited to aspects involving the method more than the tools :

– integration into disciplines and specialisms: a complete engineering and articulation approach involved especially in:

- security (including confidentiality, non-vulnerability, cyber-security, etc.);

- the safety of goods and people and performance safety;

- human factors;

- logistics (especially reliability, availability, maintainability, testability);

- integrability, simulation conditions and system tests;

- processing or learning algorithms, etc.

– interoperability with business processes and data: production, product lifecycle management, deployment, use and logistical support;

– articulation with work on orientating and exploring spaces for the problem and the solution, prior to implementing the architecture;

– articulation with development, especially software or firmware;

– connection with methods for formal verification; pairing with multiparadigm simulation formalisms (dataflows, discreet events, state(s) machines, etc.);

– integration with multiphysical modeling and simulation;

– support for the progressive concept development and evaluation of architecture alternatives.

For a community of contributors and users

The deployment of engineering systems based on models in large organizations and complex projects is a complex and expensive effort, rarely mentioned in literature. This is why we felt that a detailed presentation of the method and above all the conditions for its success, would be useful.

At present, as the Arcadia method and its reference tool Capella are available in the public domain (as well as the Capella code, which is open and freely accessible), we hope that this approach is adopted in other industrial contexts in order to extend it, enrich it and take it further still for the benefit of what we hope is a growing community.

Appendix

Introduction to Capella: The Benchmark Modeling Tool for Arcadia

The public originally targeted by Arcadia (and which still forms the majority of its users today) was formed mainly of system or specialty engineers with varied experience and skills, and not familiar with modeling; as discussed in the chapter tracing Arcadia's history (section 1.2.4 Chapter 1), the first experiments with the method by these operational users, carried out using commercial off-the-shelf modeling, were considered unsatisfactory when used in real situations, on large-scale projects, requiring a collective development of models.

This is what led to the definition and development of a tool specifically designed to meet the expectations expressed as well as the feedback accumulated. This tool, today freely available in the public domain and in open source, is named Capella. This appendix quickly introduces some of Capella's particularities; further details and the tool itself can be accessed via download, on the Capella reference site [POL 17a]. We also note that all the example modeling diagrams and models shown in this work have been created with this tool.

***

Capella is an original solution in the world of modeling environments. In default of being able to present all this tool's capabilities, we have focused on some that are particularly appreciated by users, among them, and first and foremost, the close link between the method and the tool; but also the availability of multiple productivity tools resulting from users' operational requirements and developed with users; technical methods making it possible to master design complexity; and also the fact that it is an open source solution.

All the figures in this book are available to view in color at: www.iste.co.uk/voirin/arcadia.zip.

A.1. The close link between the method and the tool

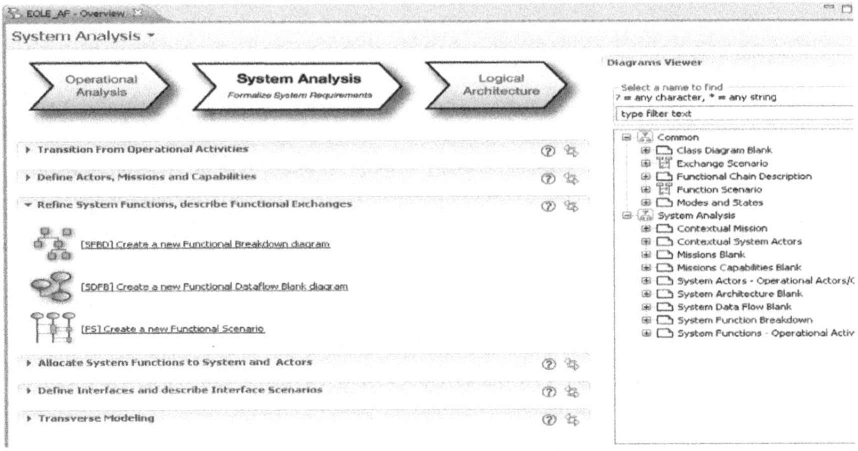

Figure A.1. *Guide to integrated modeling*

Its close link with the Arcadia method is one of the key aspects of Capella. In addition to having its concepts directly aligned with those of Arcadia, three functionalities facilitate and support implementation of the method in Capella models:

– the model structure for each project exactly follows that of Arcadia, and in particular supports the perspectives promoted by the method;

– as a modeling language, Capella implements that of Arcadia, and the illustrative aspect of the elements in all the diagrams is aligned with Arcadia's conventions. For example, green is for functional analysis, blue is for structural elements and yellow for hosting resources;

– a guide to integrated and customizable modeling introduces the perspectives and their content, the types of modeling activities required to form these perspectives and the types of illustrative figures available to do this, as Figure A.1 illustrates;

– in addition, this guide is a means for "methodological" exploration of the model, for a "guided tour" through the model, and is a key interaction interface for navigating the Capella models and diagrams for which it provides an index. This "explorer" is clearly an excellent aid for novices, eliminating the problem of the intimidating "blank page". But beyond this, it is a powerful tool for navigating within Capella models.

A.2. Productivity tools for modeling

A system model respects the rules of construction. It is a graph, where elements are interconnected in multiple ways. Productivity tools help final users to create their models more effectively, by relying on this graph and taking account of existing model elements to initialize others.

An initial, simple example is that of the interfaces between components, which is one of Arcadia's main objectives. In the method, the functions are linked to one another with the functional exchanges expressing dependencies (data, energy, etc.). These dependencies are specified with formal descriptions (generally using class diagrams). As the functions are attributed to components, it is simple to deduce the content of the interfaces between the components depending on the dependencies between their attributed functions. Capella provides specialist generation algorithms, rules for validation and associated, rapid corrections.

To cite another example, to create a functional scenario or a chain, the tool will only suggest those functional exchanges possible in this context, and not all the functional exchanges present in the model. This contextualization greatly simplifies modeling.

Tools for productivity or automation not only accelerate modeling activities from day to day, but also improve the coherence and exactitude of models by reducing human errors. Other Capella productivity tools include automated and iterative model transitions from one Arcadia perspective to another, harmonization of layout between diagrams, etc.

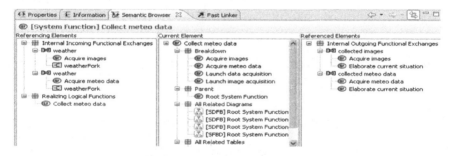

Figure A.2. *Semantic navigator*

Another key characteristic is the instant query capability offered by the "semantic navigator" (Figure A.2). This zone of the user interface provides all the relationships of any object selected in a diagram (on the left, the model elements that reference it, on the right, those that it references, in the center its filiation relationships, the diagrams in which it appears, etc.). A user can query one of the key linked elements instantaneously, navigate to it and to the other diagrams in which it appears.

A.3. Mastering complexity

An important condition for deploying model-based system engineering is the ability to confront systems' growing complexity. It is vital for a modeling tool to provide a concrete aide to mastering this complexity.

This starts by reducing accidental complexity. By simplifying the underlying modeling concepts (in comparison with SysML, for example), Capella reduces the learning curves and improves model readability.

Although this is necessary, it is not however enough, and it is essential to offer mechanisms to concretely make it easier to visualize and navigate models. The most illustrative example is the way in which Capella manages functional analysis with illustrative, calculated simplifications improving readability, understanding and analysis. In particular, Capella implements all the mechanisms for synthesizing and simplifying representation explained in Chapter 4 (section 4.3).

Moreover, to make it possible to master large-scale models, Capella offers diverse modeling aids: verification of the coherence and completeness of the model by semantic rules resulting from the Arcadia method and language; impact analysis where model elements are added, removed or modified; comparison and merging of different models or versions; automatic generation of contextual diagrams; automatic refreshing or control of diagrams; etc.

Different tools also support automatic transitions between system and subsystem models, the definition and management of libraries of reusable components or elements, automatization of some recurrent modeling motifs, etc.

A.4. Free and open source access, extensibility

As such, Capella includes capabilities for extensibility or adaptation to a particular context: it is possible to extend or enrich existing concepts using properties dedicated to a particular need; to create and add new concepts, and new rules for model analysis and verification; to create new diagrams and representations; to include all these elements, and algorithms for analyzing and using the model, to complete viewpoints in the form of plug-ins. And if necessary, to modify profoundly the source code and therefore the tool's functionalities thanks to its place in open source.

Capella was developed as a copyrighted tool by Thales for around 6 years, before it became open source (free software use and access to its source code) in 2014. The ecosystem around Capella is increasing significantly; large industrial organizations are adopting the Arcadia method. The link with other engineering or specialty tools is a direct result of this open source strategy enabling open innovation around Capella.

Open source does not, however, necessarily mean "free" for an organization wishing to the adopt the method and tool; although access to the tool is open and free, support for deployment and coaching are often needed to increase the chances of success. However, open source means "open": final user organizations can join the Capella industrial consortium, and so contribute to its development and indeed influence its "roadmap".

This opening is the greatest guarantee of durability and freedom to customize, use and enrich the tool depending on the needs of each user organization. Free access to the tool and its source code ensures that organizations can fashion Capella's future and take control of their modeling environment in real terms.

Bibliography

Language, formalities, approaches to engineering

[DEL 00] DE LA BRETESCHE BERTRAND, *La méthode APTE: Analyse de la valeur, analyse fonctionnelle*, Pétrelle, Paris, 2000.

[FEI 06] FEILER P.H., LEWIS B.A., VESTAL S., "The SAE architecture analysis; design language (AADL) a standard for engineering performance critical systems", *Computer Aided Control System Design, 2006 IEEE International Conference on Control Applications, 2006 IEEE International Symposium on Intelligent Control*, pp. 1206–1211, Munich, Germany, October 2006.

[KRU 98] KRUCHTEN P., *The Rational Unified Process: An Introduction*, Addison-Wesley, Boston, 1998.

[NAT 07] NATO, *NATO Architecture Framework Version 3*, ANNEX 3 TO AC/322(SC/1-WG/1)N(2007)0004, 2007.

[OBJ 15a] OBJECT MANAGEMENT GROUP, *OMG Unified Modeling Language™ (OMG UML) Version 2.5*, Object Management Group, 2015.

[OBJ 15b] OBJECT MANAGEMENT GROUP, *Systems Modeling Language™ (SysML®), Version 1.4*, Object Management Group, 2015.

[OLV 14] OLVER A.M., RYAN M.J.. "On a useful taxonomy of phases, modes, and states in systems engineering", *Systems Engineering/Test and Evaluation Conference*, Adelaide, Australia, 2014.

[ROS 77] ROSS D.T., "Structured Analysis (SA): a language for communicating ideas", *IEEE Transactions on Software Engineering*, vol. SE-3, no. 1, 1977.

[WAS 11] WASSON C. S., "System phases, modes, and states: solutions to controversial issues" *INCOSE International Symposium*, Denver, USA, 2011.

Publications concerning the preliminary works at Arcadia

[EXE 04] EXERTIER D., NORMAND V., "MDSysE: a model-driven systems engineering approach at THALES", *INCOSE Mid-Atlantic Regional Conference,* Arlington, USA, 2004.

[NOR 05] NORMAND V., D. EXERTIER D., "Model-driven systems engineering: SysML & the MDSysE approach at THALES", *Model Driven Engineering for Distributed, Real-time and Embedded Systems,* Hermes Science Publishing, London, 2005.

Publications on Arcadia

[ARN 13] ARNOULD V., VOIRIN J.-L.,"Toward integrated multi-level engineering – Thales and DCNS advanced practices", *Maritime & Air Systems & Technologies,* Gdansk, Poland, 2013.

[BON 14] BONNET S., LESTIDEAU F., VOIRIN J.-L., "Arcadia and Capella on the field: real-world MBSE use cases", *MBSE Symposium,* Canberra, Australia, October 27, 2014.

[BON 15] BONNET S., VOIRIN J.-L, NORMAND V. *et al.,* "Implementing the MBSE cultural change: organization, coaching and lessons learned", *INCOSE Symposium,* Seattle, USA, June 2015.

[BON 16] BONNET S., VOIRIN J.-L., EXERTIER D. *et al.,* "Not (strictly) relying on SysML for an MBSE solution: the Arcadia/Capella rationale" *IEEE Systems Conference,* Orlando, USA, November, 2016.

[BON 17] BONNET S., VOIRIN J.-L., NORMAND V. *et al.,* "Modeling system modes, states, configurations with Arcadia and Capella: method and tool perspectives", *INCOSE Symposium,* Adelaide, Australia, 2017.

[ROQ 18] ROQUES P., *Systems Architecture Modeling with the Arcadia Method: A Practical Guide to CAPELLA,* ISTE Press Ltd, London and Elsevier Ltd, Oxford, 2018.

[VOI 08] VOIRIN J.-L., "Method & tools for constrained system architecting", *INCOSE Symposium,* Utrecht, The Netherlands, 2008.

[VOI 10a] VOIRIN J.-L., "Method and tools to secure and support collaborative architecting of constrained systems", *27th Congress of the International Council of the Aeronautical Science (ICAS),* Nice, France, 2010.

[VOI 10b] VOIRIN J.-L., "Model-driven architecture building for constrained systems", *Complex Systems Design & Management Conference,* Paris, France, 2010.

[VOI 12] VOIRIN J.-L., "Modelling languages for functional analysis put to the test of real life", *Complex Systems Design & Management Conference,* Paris, France, 2012.

[VOI 13a] VOIRIN J.-L., BONNET S., "ARCADIA: model-based collaboration for system, software and hardware engineering", *Complex Systems Design & Management Conference,* Paris, France, 2013.

[VOI 13b] VOIRIN J.-L., "La modélisation chez Thales: un support majeur à la collaboration des acteurs dans l'ingénierie des grands systèmes", *Congrès Ingénierie des grands programmes et systèmes complexes*, Arcachon, France, 2013.

[VOI 14] VOIRIN J.-L., "Feedbacks on system engineering – ARCADIA, a model-based method for architecture-centric engineering", *MDD4DRES ENSTA Summer School*, Aber Wrac'h, France, 2014.

[VOI 15a] VOIRIN J.-L., BONNET S., NORMAND V. *et al.*, "Model-driven IVV management with Arcadia and Capella", *Complex Systems Design & Management Conference*, Paris, France, 2015.

[VOI 15b] VOIRIN J.-L., BONNET S., NORMAND V. *et al.*, "From initial investigations up to large-scale rollout of an MBSE method and its supporting workbench: the Thales experience", *INCOSE Symposium*, Seattle, USA, 2015.

[VOI 16] VOIRIN J.-L., BONNET S., NORMAND V. *et al.*, "Simplifying (and enriching) SysML to perform functional analysis and model instances", *INCOSE Symposium*, Edinburgh, UK, 2016.

Hyperlinks for information about Arcadia and Capella

[ARC 15] ARCADIA, download.polarsys.org/capella/publis/An_Introduction_to_Arcadia_20150115.pdf, 2015.

[CLA 15] CLARITY CONSORTIUM, available at http://www.clarity-se.org, 2015.

[POL 17a] CAPELLA, available at https://www.polarsys.org/capella, 2017.

[POL 17b] POLARSYS INDUSTRY WORKING GROUP, available at https://www.polarsys.org, 2017.

Index

Printed in the United States
By Bookmasters